End The

IRS

Before It Ends

U$

End The

IRS

Before It Ends

U$

How to Restore a Low-Tax,
High-Growth, Wealthy America

GROVER NORQUIST

CENTER STREET

NEW YORK · BOSTON · NASHVILLE

Center Street
Hachette Book Group
1290 Avenue of the Americas
New York, NY 10104

www.CenterStreet.com

Printed in the United States of America

The map appearing on page 170 is used with permission of the Coalition for Self-Government in the West.

RRD-C

First edition: April 2015

10 9 8 7 6 5 4 3 2 1

Center Street is a division of Hachette Book Group, Inc.
The Center Street name and logo are trademarks of Hachette Book Group, Inc.

The Hachette Speakers Bureau provides a wide range of authors for speaking events. To find out more, go to www.HachetteSpeakersBureau.com or call (866) 376-6591.

The publisher is not responsible for websites (or their content) that are not owned by the publisher.

Library of Congress Cataloging-in-Publication Data

Norquist, Grover Glenn
    End the IRS before it ends us : how to restore a low tax, high growth, wealthy America / Grover Norquist.
        pages cm
    Summary: " As the recent scandal shows, the IRS is big, bad, and out of control. Grover Norquist analyzes the problems within the agency and presents solutions to rein them in. Norquist has a plan for cutting taxes for working Americans and for the major corporations that are fleeing for foreign shores. As president of Americans for Tax Reform, Grover Norquist is the go-to expert on taxation. Now, Norquist makes the case for a major tax reform, including a possible flat tax. On the current path, America will coast through inertia to ever-growing government and taxation, as entitlements consume more of our national economy. Norquist presents an alternative future where government spending is reformed, and taxes and the IRS radically curtailed. END THE IRS BEFORE IT ENDS US lays out what taxation in America should look like. Norquist offers a solution where America thrives, and Americans keep their hard-earned cash"— Provided by publisher.
    Includes bibliographical references and index.
    ISBN 978-1-4555-8582-3 (hardback) — ISBN 978-1-4555-8581-6 (ebook) — ISBN 978-1-4789-0344-4 (audio download)   1. United States. Internal Revenue Service. 2. Tax administration and procedure—United States   3. Flat-rate income tax—United States.   4. Taxation—United States.   I. Title.
    HJ2381.N67 2015
    336.20973—dc23
                                                                                            2014048930

To my parents, Carol and Warren, kind enough to give birth to me in the United States and instill in me a burning commitment to liberty.

And to my wife, Samah, who in addition to "everything" gave me two powerful reasons to fight to restore and expand our freedoms: our daughters, Grace and Giselle.

Contents

PART IV

Six Paths Leading to Abolishing the IRS:
Big Steps, Little Steps

PART V

Defeating the IRS's Brezhnev Doctrine:
The Strategy for Victory over the IRS

PART VI
Changing the Correlation of Forces

PART I

The Present Mess: Overtaxation, Obamacare, and a Politicized IRS

CHAPTER 1

Our Low-Tax Past and Our Present Tragedy

In 1776, before we were an independent nation, the average tax burden for American colonists was 1 to 2 percent of their annual earnings. The economy was strong. Americans enjoyed one of the highest standards of living in the world.

The assertion by the British king and parliament that they had the right to levy additional taxes on the colonists started a revolution.

We were already paying 1, maybe 2 percent. And they want more? The guns came out. We won.

Today, in 2015, 239 years after the Declaration of Independence, "our" federal government confiscates 18.2 percent of the economy in federal taxes.[1] State and local governments take another 12 percent. The federal government spent $3.5 trillion in 2014, which is 20.4 percent of GDP. State and local governments together spent $2.4 trillion in 2014, which is 14 percent of the national economy.[2] All three levels of government together consumed $5.7 trillion, or 34 percent of the economy.[3]

That is somewhat more than 1 or 2 percent.

Soon we will have to pay still higher taxes to pay down the $17 trillion in federal debt. Of that amount, $5.6 trillion was run up in the years 1783 to 2000. Four trillion dollars was piled up in the eight Bush years, and $7.9 trillion was added in the first six years of

President Obama. And unless the federal government's entitlement programs are reformed, our taxes will one day be increased to pay for the $123.1 trillion in "unfunded liabilities" already written in to law.

It is bad. It is going to get worse.

Income taxes, made possible by the Sixteenth Amendment to the Constitution, are collected by the Internal Revenue Service—first named the Internal Revenue Bureau when it was created in 1862. Today the IRS has 94,516 employees. (The United States Marine Corps has 195,657 active-duty personnel.)

The politicians and bureaucrats who write the tax laws and underlying tax code want to be clear and precise, so the tax laws take up one million words, and the full tax code including regulations has four million words. (The Constitution has a total of 4,543 words. The Bible has 774,746 words.)

Since the income tax is a "voluntary" system, we have the privilege of doing our own taxes. Americans, notwithstanding the Thirteenth Amendment, are forced, under threat of imprisonment, to spend 6.1 billion hours,[4] or 696,347 person-years, filling out our individual and business income taxes. For free. And that number—6.1 billion hours of forced labor to prepare and fill out our taxes—comes from the IRS itself in 2012. Wanna bet it is an understatement?

Oh, yes. Please remember that failure to file your federal income tax return by April 15 in our "voluntary" tax system can get you up to a year in prison for each year you do not file a tax return.

Remember how unacceptable taxation seizing 2 percent of our incomes was?

There has clearly been some backsliding here.

What happened to America? What happened to us? Something very big has changed and for the worse.

Can we recapture our liberty? Can we go back to the freedom we knew when earning a dollar meant ninety-eight cents belonged to us? Today federal, state, and local governments see our earned dollar and leave us—on average—with sixty-seven cents. And that average includes people who pay little in taxes or who receive government checks or net benefits. Your tax burden may be significantly higher than "average."

Our forefathers saw 2 percent possibly swelling to 3 or 4 percent and reached for their guns and fought a bloody war of independence that lasted from the Battle of Lexington and Concord on April 19, 1775, to the British surrender at Yorktown on October 19, 1781. During the Revolution twenty-five thousand Americans died on the battlefield or from injuries.

Those Americans who fought for independence and against the growing power of the British Crown were known as "Sons of Liberty" and "Patriots." Those who supported the king were known as "Friends of Government" or "Loyalists." This struggle and this division within the United States continues today.

This book was written for Americans who look in the mirror and see a "friend of liberty" and who daily find their lives and future diminished by those who—to this day—view themselves first and foremost as "friends of government."

We were free in 1783 when the final peace agreement was signed by Benjamin Franklin, John Jay, and John Adams in Paris.

Are we "free" now? How much more of our lives will the government demand? What will be left to us? How much of our earnings, our savings, our homes, our time? Our lives?

Have we reached a tipping point? Has the government made itself too powerful to challenge when it claims new powers over our lives? Or has the government gone a bridge too far with the TARP bailouts, $800 billion in "stimulus" spending, and $1 trillion in new taxes for Obamacare. Has this tidal wave of spending and debt finally awakened Americans in the same way that the attack on Pearl Harbor on December 7, 1941, did? Japanese Marshal Admiral Yamamoto is said to have noted then, "I fear all we have done is to awaken a sleeping giant and fill him with a terrible resolve."

Are we now resolved? Or resigned?

Today, the political struggle is not simply between liberals and conservatives, or Democrats and Republicans. Today there are citizens who wish to fight to restore limited government. They argue in the political arena against those who welcome the warm embrace of the European welfare state of stasis and control. They struggle against today's Friends of Government, those who profit from and revel in ever-larger government power and higher taxes and spending. But there is a third power, not an umpire but an ally of the Friends of Government. It is the government itself. As in 1776, the patriots fought not just the Loyalists, or Friends of Government, but the might of the British government itself, allied with the Friends of Government.

And the IRS, the Internal Revenue Service, which has in the past been politicized by politicians from FDR to LBJ in petty ways, such as auditing and harassing their political opponents, has now arrayed itself on the battlefield to protect and grow big government.

The usual political scandals in big cities, statehouses, and Washington are petty theft. Earmarks sending cash to a committee chairman's friends. Relatives on the payroll in no-show jobs. Contracts given out as favors rather than to the low-cost bid. But the new and more dangerous corruption is less interested in stealing a bit of cash here or there. They are interested in stealing power from the American people and depositing it inside the government. Later they can steal all the money they want without challenge. This is a corruption more dangerous than we have known in the past.

How big? How unprecedented? How dangerous?

Let me present the case that in 2012, the IRS was the decisive player in electing a president. You may wish to argue it was only one factor. True. But if the IRS had remained neutral, Barack Obama would not have won reelection. The world is changed when the most powerful and fearsome government agency is not deciding simply whether or not you are audited but by whom you are governed.

Return to the early days of 2009. Barack Obama has been elected president. The Democrats have a 261 to 180 majority in the House of Representatives and 57 to 41 in the Senate.

Tax increases and budgets can be passed through "reconciliation," which means they cannot be filibustered and only require fifty-one votes in the Senate. The Democrats even had a sixty-vote filibuster-proof supermajority for six months.

United government in all of 2009 and 2010 under the Democrats meant that if Obama, Reid, and Pelosi could come to an agreement, they could do just about anything. Spending exploded. The second part of TARP, another $350 billion, was given to Obama to hand out as he wished. Another $800 billion was spent on "stimulus" spending. A trillion was added to the budget over the next decade. Obamacare, with the promise of higher taxes and new spending, was coming soon and with certainty.

Then Rick Santelli did his rant on CNBC on February 19, 2009. He called for a Tea Party rally in Chicago. The response was somewhat larger. During the week of April 15, 2009, Americans for Tax Reform estimated there were between six hundred and one thousand rallies with up to a million participants. A wall of opposition to government spending rose up.

In November 2010, Republicans campaigning against government spending, earmarks, and stimulus won a gain of sixty-three House seats to capture the House of Representatives, and gained six seats in the Senate.

Two years later, the economy was weak. Obamacare was increasingly unpopular. And yet the Republicans failed to win the small gain of four seats needed to capture the Senate. They failed to defeat Obama's reelection. Why? What stopped the tidal wave of citizen activism?

The Internal Revenue Service.

A government agency with the ability to spy on your life, to demand to see your every bank account and possession, to fine you and assess interest penalties, and even to send you to prison.

Four scholars, two from the Harvard Kennedy School, one from Stockholm University, and one from the American Enterprise Institute studied the Tea Party rallies of 2009 and the election of 2010. They produced a powerful study entitled "Do Political Protests Matter? Evidence from the Tea Party Movement."[5]

Here is what they found:

The scholars studied 542 rallies with an estimated 440,000 to 810,000 individuals protesting nationwide on Tax Day, April 15, 2009.[6] By contrasting areas where rallies were held and those where they were rained out in whole or part, they could calculate how the attendance at Tea Party rallies affected the actual November 2010 votes. It turns out rallies really do matter. People get energy from learning their neighbors share their views and commitments. They meet new people, link up in person, and through social media they keep in touch, create new organizations and collaborate in campaigns.

The study demonstrates that the rallies led to an estimated additional 25,000 to 46,000 local Tea Party organizers, 170,000 to 310,000 protestors who rallied the next April 15 (in 2010) generated between $840,000 to $1,540,000 in contributions to one particular Tea Party PAC, the Our Country Deserves Better PAC, and drove between 3.2 and 5.8 million additional voters to the polls to vote Republican in 2010 House elections.[7]

I repeat, the Tea Party rallies of early 2009 led to an additional 3.2 to 5.8 million votes for Republican candidates in the November 2010 election.

Think about this. The rallies in 2009 created structures, friendships, and relationships that kept the flame of the Santelli rant alive for two years and won a national election for control of the House of Representatives. (No wonder our friends on the Left like to have mass rallies. They work.)

In November 2010, the GOP won 44,593,666 total votes for the House, compared with 38,854,459 votes for the Democrat House candidates.[8] This study argues that 3.2 to 5.8 million of those

Republican votes flowed from Tea Party rally activism. The Tea Party mattered. Dick Cheney would have said, "big-time." Biden would have noted it was a "big, (something) deal."

This was noticed by the new Republican majority caucus, which quickly voted to ban earmarks. The Democrats, who had pooh-poohed the Tea Party as a fiction of right-wing talk radio's imagination or a manufactured movement consisting of paid mercenaries, were shocked. I received regular calls from the establishment press during the early Tea Party days asking—and they were not joking—if this was all paid for by ExxonMobil. They assumed I had organized all this. Personally.

They knew that most of those union pickets in cities that are so annoying, blocking pedestrian traffic and banging drums, are people paid to show up for a few hours. Left-wing rallies against us at Americans for Tax Reform have been filled with "activists" who, when asked, admitted they were paid hourly to show up. Their grassroots was manufactured. Paid for. Not real. They assumed "ours" was too.

That is, until November 2, 2010, when the Obama presidency was cut short. Never again could he pass any bill he wanted through Congress. Now he could be stopped. Obama and his team were angry and surprised—angry to have been surprised and determined to make sure this NEVER happened again.

Fast-forward to November 2012, when Obama won the presidency 51.1 percent to 47.2 percent. The total Obama vote was 65,195,796—3,582,720 less than in 2008. The total Romney vote was 60,933,500—only 985,177 more than McCain won in 2008 before the Tea Party explosion. Had the Tea Party repeated and built on their activism of 2009 and 2010 in 2011 and 2012, Obama would have lost the election. What happened to the Tea Party boost? It didn't grow from 2010. It appeared to weaken.

The public didn't learn what had caused this drop in Tea Party activism and participation in electoral politics until after the autopsy.

The Tea Party didn't fall down the stairs. It was pushed.

Pushed by the IRS, which, we later learned, was run by folks like Lois Lerner. Lerner was not a tax expert. She was not an accountant. Lerner was—as George Will wrote—a partisan bully. President Barack Obama appointed this political enforcer not to be chairman of the Democrat Party but as leader of the political wing of the IRS. Lerner used her specific and critical area of exempt organizations at the IRS as if she was Obama's reelection campaign manager.

Cleta Mitchell, a former Democrat state legislator from Oklahoma and now a tax and FEC lawyer for many conservative groups around the nation, says she began to smell problems in 2010.

The Tea Party exploded on the scene in April 2009. Obama pretended he didn't watch any of the coverage on television, and Democrat operatives publicly pooh-poohed the movement. In private they were terrified. The Supreme Court ruled on January 21, 2010, in the *Citizens United* case, that organizations which are tax exempt under IRS code 501(c)(4) have the right to endorse candidates and to spend some amount less than half of their annual budget on "express advocacy." This meant that the Tea Party groups that were granted 501(c)(4) status could rather quickly grow into serious statewide political operations to compete with the unions and left-wing groups that had used coerced union dues and government funding for decades. This could change the correlation of forces on the ground...just before the 2010 election and—more important if your name was Barack Obama—the 2012 election.

The IRS got public signals that Democrats in the Senate and Obama in the White House wanted "something done." Senators Chuck Schumer of New York and Carl Levin of Michigan wrote the IRS demanding that they attack the Tea Party. Obama gave whiny speeches about the dangers of "secret money" he imagined flowing to the Tea Party. Obama attacked the Supreme Court decision in his January 2010 State of the Union speech. Obama's underlings and followers heard him clearly: "Who will rid me of this turbulent priest?" We know the Justice Department was demanding that the IRS kneecap the upstart Tea Party movement in its infancy.

On October 19, 2010, my birthday, Lois Lerner gave a speech at Duke University where she publicly admitted the pressure she was under to "do something" in the wake of the *Citizens United* Supreme Court decision. "Everyone is up in arms because they don't like it. The Federal Election Commission can't do anything about it. They want the IRS to fix the problem. The IRS laws are not set up to fix the problem...So everyone is screaming at us right now: Fix it now before the election. Can't you see how much these people are spending?"[9]

*   *   *

Here in public Lois Lerner tells a friendly audience how she is being pressured to stop the Tea Party and how the law won't allow the FEC to do so. She admits the law does not allow the IRS to do so... but still she is under this terrible pressure—not because any law is being broken, she says none are...but because "they" want her to "FIX IT NOW BEFORE THE ELECTION." The IRS leader who oversees nonprofits and political organizations tells her friends she hears the message loud and clear and knows what she has to do, even though—she says at the same time—she has no legal authority to do "what must be done" because of the pending election. Note her focus on the election.

Note two things. Here is the smoking gun. No e-mail was needed. Later Obama and his team would brag that there were no extant e-mails proving Lerner was told what to do. Here Lerner is explaining that, "lost" e-mails aside, she knew what she was being told to do. Heck, the president delivered his marching orders in a State of the Union address. All competent conspiracies are carried out in public.

And second, an IRS boss, Lois Lerner, is talking publicly about sandbagging the next election. What is an IRS official doing talking about an election at all? In Latin American countries they get nervous when generals talk about upcoming elections.

The IRS set up a separate bucket to look at groups with the words

"Tea Party" or "Patriot" in their names. This was not some rogue group of IRS staffers in Cincinnati. Washington ordered "special treatment" for Tea Party groups. This was not some bipartisan excess that targeted "everyone."

What did the autopsy report? On April 7, 2014, the House Committee on Oversight and Government Reform published a report titled "Debunking the Myth That the IRS Targeted Progressives: How the IRS and Congressional Democrats Misled America about Disparate Treatment."[10]

The report relates in its executive summary: "In September 2013 *USA Today* published an independent analysis of a list of about 160 applications in the IRS backlog. This analysis showed that 80 percent of the applications in the backlog were filed by conservative groups, while less than 7 percent were filed by liberal groups..."[11]

A separate assessment from *USA Today* in May 2013 showed that for twenty-seven months, beginning in February 2010, the IRS did not approve a single tax-exempt application filed by a Tea Party group. During that same period the IRS approved "perhaps dozens of applications from similar liberal and progressive groups."

A few new details emerged in a December 2014 report summarizing two years of damning findings from Daryl Issa's House Oversight and Governmnent Affairs Committee. The report noted a shocking e-mail exchange between an IRS agent and Cincinnati-based specialist Hilary Goehausen. The agent wrote, "I'm not sure we can deny them because, technically, I don't know that I can deny them simply for donating to another 501(c)(4)....Any thoughts or feedback would be greatly appreciated." The response that came back from Goehausen was chilling: "I think there may be a number of ways to deny them. Let me talk to Sharon [Light] tomorrow about it and get some ideas from her as well.... This sounds like a bad org.... This org gives me an icky feeling."[12]

Twenty-seven months, two years and three months, the entire period between the elections of 2010 and 2012, the IRS shut down the Tea Party and its allies. The IRS was no umpire. Not the law.

Not a faceless bureaucracy equally slow and inefficient and annoying to every citizen.

Eighteen years earlier, Tonya Harding was afraid she would lose her place at the Olympic skating competition to Nancy Kerrigan. Her ex-husband worked with her bodyguard to hire Shane Stant, who hit Kerrigan in the knee to handicap her in the skating competition. Tonya didn't hit Nancy Kerrigan, Shane Stant did.

In our modern kneecapping, President Obama was Tonya Harding. The American people who had voted strongly in 2010 and threatened the president's chances of winning in 2012 were Nancy Kerrigan. The IRS and Lois Lerner played the role of Mr. Stant.

People sensed something was wrong. Normally, approvals for 501(c)(4) tax-exempt organizations took one or two months. Cleta Mitchell, the renowned Washington, D.C., attorney, put together a memo highlighting how much longer than usual the IRS was taking to approve certain 501(c)(4)s after 2010—conservative 501(c)(4)s that is.

Two House of Representatives committees began demanding answers and information from the IRS. The IRS stalled. It promised it was getting the information. In 2013 the IRS announced Lerner's e-mails were "missing." Later we learned the hard drive was simply scratched and the IRS was told by the tech staff the subpoenaed e-mails could be recovered. However, the IRS then said they had destroyed the hard drives.

Before the 2012 elections, the IRS was targeting nascent Tea Party groups and denying them the ability to legally organize in a way that would facilitate their ability to fund-raise and grow. Then the IRS destroyed the proof of this activity. In the summer of 2014 some e-mails from Lois Lerner to friends whose computers forgot to "crash" were exposed, and Lerner's hatred for the Tea Party— her claim that American conservatives and taxpayer activists were a bigger threat than international terrorists and that conservatives were A**-Holes—certainly proved her bias and lack of fitness for office.

Who else was on the Obama/Lerner enemies list for "special

treatment" at the tender hands of the IRS inquisition? Believe it or not...veterans groups. After all the syrupy comments about respecting our vets, under the table the IRS was sicced on the American Legion. In August 2013, Daily Caller broke the story that the American Legion was under attack by Lois Lerner's gang at the IRS. The IRS was threatening to demand "detailed membership lists" for every Legion post. Why? What was this about? The IRS threatened to pull their nonprofit status and to fine them $1,000 a day.[13]

The Watergate scandal was about Nixon supporters breaking into the office of the DNC. They didn't find anything interesting that would change the election. Later, Nixon faced impeachment and resigned, in part because of the cover-up, which included an eighteen-minute gap in a tape recording of a Nixon phone call.

In the two years running up to the 2012 Obama reelection campaign, the IRS, driven by a political activist with no experience that would recommend her for that job, decided to smash the Tea Party movement by stopping them from organizing.

Had the IRS not intervened in our American political process by tripping up new groups, there might have been dozens or hundreds of groups like those that grew up in the wake of the taxpayer movement in the late 1970s, such as the Howard Jarvis Taxpayers Association of California or Citizens for Limited Taxation in Massachusetts.

Delay and denial of new groups incorporating was only one strategy of intimidation. The names of the donors to one conservative group were released by the IRS to a left-of-center group so they could be harassed. This is illegal. But it happened, and no one was fired.

In response to a lawsuit that involved the very effective religious liberty organization the Beckett Fund, the IRS admitted in 2014 that it had a subgroup by the acronym PARC—the "Political Activities Referral Committee"—which monitored sermons in churches. Read this sentence again and try to convince yourself the IRS has not become a very real threat to liberty in America.

The IRS went after Tea Party groups and asked what they prayed about. They demanded—illegally—their donor lists. Why might the IRS do this? Reread the previous two paragraphs and it becomes clear.

On February 6, 2014, too late to fix the damage done in 2010, 2011, and 2012 but not too late to write history correctly, Catherine Engelbrecht testified before the House Committee on Oversight and Government Reform in its hearing titled "The IRS Targeting Investigation: What Is the Administration Doing?"[14]

Ms. Engelbrecht was a double threat to the White House. She was the founder of King Street Patriots, a Tea Party group, and the chair of True the Vote, a group that trained citizens on how to combat voter fraud.

She was not a political figure. She and her husband ran a small business and she had only recently become concerned and involved in citizen activism. Then she made her mistake. In the era of Barack Obama and Lois Lerner, she filed to establish a 501(c)(3) and 501(c)(4) nonprofit so she could grow her two groups.

She testified to the committee what followed…

"In 2011, my personal and business tax returns were audited by the Internal Revenue Service, each audit going back for a number of years.

"In 2012, my business was subjected to inspection by OSHA on a select occasion when neither my husband nor I were present, and though the agency wrote that it found nothing serious or significant, it still issued fines in excess of $20,000.

"In 2012 and again in 2013 the Bureau of Alcohol, Tobacco, and Firearms conducted comprehensive audits of my place (of) business.

"Beginning in 2010 the FBI contacted my nonprofit organization on six separate occasions—wanting to cull through membership manifests in conjunction with the domestic-terrorism cases. They eventually dropped all matters and have now redacted nearly all my files.

"These events were occurring while the IRS was subjecting me to multiple rounds of abusive inquiries, with requests to provide every Facebook and Twitter entry I'd ever posted, questions about my political aspirations, and demands to know the names of every group I'd ever made presentations to, the content of what I'd said, and where I intended to speak for the coming year.

"Three times Representative Elijah Cummings (D-Md.) sent letters to True the Vote, demanding much of the same information that the IRS had requested. Hours after sending letters, he would appear on cable news and publicly defame me and my organization. Such tactics are unacceptable."[15]

Led by the IRS, this was a full-court press that included OSHA, the FBI, the Bureau of Alcohol, Tobacco, and Firearms, and the ranking Democrat congressman who sits on the very committee that is supposed to be investigating and stopping these abuses.

The AEI study showed that the original Tea Party movement, even in embryonic form, drove up Republican votes by three to five million beyond what would have happened without the Tea Party. Imagine how many rallies were not held, how many get-out-the-vote efforts never happened, how many voters stayed home because the Tea Party groups of 2009 and 2010 were stopped from developing normal structures that the Left has created over the years. Enough to elect a president?

One notes that in all this not a single whistleblower came forward to help the investigation or leak to the *Washington Post* or *New York Times*. Every fact had to be dragged out of the IRS bureaucracy. The depth of the cover-up is interesting. The depth of corruption and willingness to tolerate the politicization of the IRS is truly astounding. Yes, FDR unleashed the IRS on his political rival Andrew Mellon. It was illegal and wrong. But it did not steal the presidency. It was petty and, yes, important. But not determinative.

In other nations when the army decides to take a role in deciding who should be president, it is called a coup. When, in the United States, the IRS makes the same move in 2012, what do we call it?

How did it come to this?

How do we stop it?

CHAPTER 2

How the Business End of the IRS Affects You Every Single Day

The cost of our federal, state, and local governments is staggering.

The numbers, once reported in millions, then billions, and now trillions, are so overwhelming they are mind-numbing. How to get one's head around what it all means?

And it is too devastating to fully comprehend the depressing news that the modern IRS has chosen sides and actively fights against Americans who wish to live in a free society with a limited, neutral, and effective government. It is like watching a murder mystery when toward the end we learn the murderer is the police chief.

What does the power and scope of the IRS mean for most Americans—average Americans who aren't rich or famous or politically active?

A fish would be hard-pressed to explain the concept of water. It is all around them. How can we think about and understand the role the IRS now plays in our lives?

Let's look at our situation through the life of an average American, Joe Taxpayer.

Joe is a guy a lot like you or me—he has a life, a family. Joe also

has a stalker. The Internal Revenue Service. Is this an overstate-
ment? Let's follow Joe through a single day of his life and we will
see that the IRS is an unwated partner in virtually everything Joe
does during the day, from when he wakes up in the morning until
he goes to bed at night.

Joe wakes up bright and early. He's in his house, of course. He
has a mortgage on his house, which means he has to tell the IRS
how much he paid in mortgage interest, property taxes, and private
mortgage insurance. He also has to let the IRS know if he uses the
house for a home office, or if he rents it out to anyone (he'll owe
taxes for that). He has to remember what he paid in property taxes
on the house, too. If and when he ever sells the house, he's going to
have to account for any profit he makes on the sale of the house.

As Joe goes downstairs for breakfast, he sees his two lovely children, Joe Jr. and Josephine. They're his dependents, which means
he has to tell the IRS all about them every year. The IRS needs to
know when they were born, their ages, what their full legal names
are, their Social Security numbers, if they were enrolled in child
care anywhere, and who took care of them.

Joe kisses his wife, Josie, good morning. He has to tell the IRS
about her, too. Joe and Josie are married, which means they have to
file a joint income tax return together in order to get the best tax
benefits. If Joe and Josie ever get divorced, Joe will have to report
the alimony he pays her and report to the IRS who is claiming the
kids as dependents.

After breakfast, Joe takes a shower and gets dressed. As he show-
ers, he wonders what all those taxes and fees at the bottom of his
monthly water bill are all about. As he dresses, he is reminded of the
state sales taxes he paid on everything he touches... He heads out to
his car to go to work. The gas in his car faced the federal gas tax of
$0.184 per gallon, plus state gas taxes. He has to pay an annual car
tax to his county, which he also gets to tell the IRS about.

Joe drives out for his annual meeting with his financial adviser
at the bank. Joe has a bank account there, and Joe must report this

bank account to the IRS because they tax any interest he earns on it. He also has a taxable brokerage account he uses to save for a vacation home someday. That throws off taxable capital gains and dividends every year, even if Joe doesn't sell any stocks or mutual funds.

Joe was hoping to use his state income tax refund to save a little more for the house, but first Joe has to let the IRS know about his state tax refund. They tax it. His capital gains and dividends tax can run as high as 23.8 percent (including the Obamacare surtax) on the federal level alone.

Joe's there to talk with his adviser about his retirement accounts. He has plenty of them, and the IRS gets all sorts of annual reports about them. He has a Roth IRA he started after college. He has a rollover IRA from the jobs he's had over the years. His wife has a nondeductible IRA. He has a SEP-IRA for some self-employed income Joe has made. He has a 401(k) plan at work. If any money goes in or out of these accounts, the IRS has to know about it. This is complicated. But without these accounts his taxes would be higher. Much higher.

That's not all. Joe wants to save for his kids' education. So he has a 529 college savings plan for each of them. He also has a Coverdell Education Savings Account (ESA) in order to pay for precollege expenses. Once they get to college, Joe will have to let the IRS know how much he paid in tuition for them, and then have to choose between a tuition deduction and a tuition credit. Again, all of these get reported to the IRS every year. If his kids take out student loans, the interest will be reported to the IRS.

After his financial-adviser meeting, he has his annual physical. Joe gets health insurance from work, so his employer has to report on his W-2 how much health coverage he got. Joe now has to let the IRS know that he maintained qualifying health insurance coverage throughout the year lest he fall prey to Obamacare's individual mandate. Joe has a Health Savings Account (HSA), which he must annually report activity in to the IRS. He uses his HSA at the doctor, who also gives him a prescription.

Joe takes his prescription to the drugstore. There, he uses his HSA again to fill his order. He also uses his Flexible Spending Account (FSA) from work (the use-it-or-lose-it kind) in order to buy a few other items. Joe has to be careful to use neither his HSA nor his FSA to buy nonprescription, over-the-counter medicines. He used to do that, but it has been prohibited by Obamacare. He also has to be sure to use pretax spending accounts instead of spending out of pocket, since Obamacare made it increasingly difficult for Joe to take an itemized deduction for medical costs.

After leaving the pharmacy, Joe decides he wants to attend the Noontime Mass at St. Matthew's (patron saint of tax collectors—really, no joke). Joe gives generously to St. Matthew's, but he has to remember not to give cash in the collection basket, but a check instead. You see, the IRS wants to make sure that Joe has a receipt from the parish to justify the deduction he claims for charitable contributions. He also has to keep a log of any mileage he accumulates for charitable purposes. Finally, if he gives a noncash donation of $250 or more, he may later be sorry if he fails to get another receipt from the parish.

Joe finally arrives at work. He sees his annual W-2 sitting on his desk. The W-2 tells the IRS a lot of information about Joe. It tells the IRS how much he earned, how much was withheld for federal income, Social Security, Medicare, state, and local taxes, how much his employer paid for his health care coverage, how much he put in his 401(k) plan, how much he put in his HSA, if he had any moving costs reimbursed by his employer, and if he elected to pay for any child care on a pretax basis (for the latter he will need the name of the child-care provider, the provider's address, and the provider's tax ID number). That's quite a lot of information.

At work, Joe has a note from Human Resources asking him to confirm the amount of pretax parking he wants to deduct from his paycheck, and reminding him of the IRS limit on this amount. They also want him to make his annual flex-account elections.

Joe's mom sends him an e-mail asking about whether she has to pay taxes on her Social Security benefit. The answer is "it depends—check with your tax adviser." At least that's what the SSA website told him. In fact, Joe's mom will have to use a complex formula to determine whether none, half, or 85 percent of her benefit is subject to income taxation.

Speaking of his mom, Joe pays a nurse to live with her and take care of her. That makes Joe a household employer, or "nanny tax" payer. He has to withhold 7.65 percent of what he pays the nanny to remit the nanny's half of the payroll tax. He has to issue the nanny a W-2 every January and ship it off to the Social Security Administration. He has to report to his unemployment office every quarter to figure and pay unemployment tax. When he does his 1040, he has to pay both halves of Social Security and Medicare tax for her.

Joe finishes up at work and heads home for dinner. His wife, who is a teacher, has just bought some classroom supply items. She'll have to document that to the IRS if she wants to deduct the cost from her income. She's also thinking about taking a class, but she can't figure out the difference between the tuition and fee deduction and the American Opportunity tax credit. They need new windows in the house, and Joe suggests they look into buying some that might qualify them for a residential energy tax credit.

Joe is ready for bed and perhaps he will now be free of his uninvited life partner, the Taxman. And yet, Joe finds it hard to sleep, tossing and turning with the knowledge that if he makes any mistakes in his tax reporting and filing there are real and serious consequences. Underpay and the government will demand its tax dollars with interest. And penalties can be added to the new bill. Interest just keeps compounding and growing. The IRS has the memory, patience, and understanding of a waterfront loan shark. It views money you keep in your pocket as a loan from them. The penalty for failing to file your taxes is 5 percent on any underpayment for each month you are late. That increases up to a 25 percent penalty.

And a separate "failure to pay" penalty, if you do file but underpay what the IRS feels you owe them, is one-half of 1 percent of your underpaid taxes per month—growing to a total of 25 percent.

And Joe's nightmare—or is it simple stress—deepens as he contemplates the possibility the IRS could enact a lien on his property. The IRS helpfully contacts all your creditors to let them know they are first in line to be paid. That is very helpful to your reputation, credit score, and ability to hold your job. Still, this doesn't really happen to people like him, Joe hopes. Yes, it does, 600,000 times a year.

Maybe one of those late-night paid advertisements is on television as Joe hears, "Wait. It gets worse. Listen." The IRS can and will impose a "levy," which is when the IRS actually seizes your property. Your home. Your boat. The cash value of your life insurance, your retirement accounts, bank accounts. It can get first crack at your paycheck. A nightmare? Perhaps, but a real one because the IRS imposes about two million levies each year.

Joe hasn't forgotten the possibility of being audited by the IRS. He'd sure better keep all his paperwork, receipts, paychecks. Every year there are 1.4 million IRS audits. Much more likely than getting hit by lightning. More painful than a visit to the dentist.

And even then, Joe cannot fall asleep; the thought of jail time floats through his wakefulness. The IRS's Criminal Investigation division has 3,700 employees. And to help out, the IRS will drag you before its own branch of the judicial system called the "Tax Court." Forget those *Perry Mason* reruns, where the defendant has a fighting chance. The Criminal Investigations division has a conviction rate of over 90 percent. The average jail time is two years.

And now it's time to wake up and face a new day. Joe must work hard. The IRS is counting on him. And watching.

CHAPTER 3

The Latest Tax Outrage: The Twenty Taxes in Obamacare

There is an old fable about a king who boasted that his imperial guards could protect his walled city because they had various powers: the ability to see through walls, hear anything, smell anything. Middle Age superheros. The king offered to marry his daughter off to anyone who could fool his guards. One day a young boy pulled a red wagon filled with dirt out of the city through the main gate. The next day he returned and that evening he pulled his red wagon filled with pebbles out the front gate past the vigilant guards. Then each day for a month the boy would leave the city with his red wagon filled with sand or dirt or large rocks or straw.

What the guards missed was that he was stealing red wagons.

In the 2008 campaign, Obama talked about reducing the cost of health insurance. Obama talked about expanding the number of Americans who had insurance. Obama talked about the challenges people who had "preexisting conditions" faced in buying insurance.

But Obamacare was not really about health care. It was about the red wagons. Tax increases.

Inside Obamacare there are at least twenty new or higher taxes. Their cost to Americans was hidden under a pile of rhetoric. The agency enforcing the mandate that you buy government-approved/regulated health insurance is not Health and Human Services. It is the Internal Revenue Service. The IRS. This should have been a clue. Some people did see this coming. That is why every single Republican in the House and Senate voted against final passage of the Affordable Care Act (ACA). They could see past the red wagons.

Obama promised Americans that his ACA legislation would reduce their health insurance costs. He told Americans during his campaign that he would only raise taxes on the "rich." To win the election in 2008, he repeatedly and famously promised, "I can make a firm pledge. Under my plan, no family making less than $250,000 a year will see *any form of tax increase*. Not your income tax, not your payroll tax, not your capital gains taxes, *not any of your taxes*."

But the taxes he imposed to pay for "free" health care hit all Americans and certainly raised the cost of health care for those who already had insurance.

What follows is the list of twenty tax increases hidden inside the Rube Goldberg contraption known as Obamacare. They range from well-known ones, such as the tax penalty for not complying with Obamacare's individual mandate to purchase government-approved health insurance, all the way to obscure ones, such as a tax increase on charitable hospitals.

The tax increases arrive in two basic stages—those that went into effect before President Obama stood for reelection in 2012, and those that came afterward. Not surprisingly, the bulk of the tax hikes came after the election. The delay was designed to hide the true cost to taxpayers of Obamacare.

When fully implemented, Obamacare turns out to be the largest tax hike in US history, yet the establishment press was tricked into talking all day about health care policy. This is how large taxes are strapped to the backs of the American people. Repealing Obamacare not only gets the government out from between you and your doctor but would be a significant tax cut for all taxpayers and a great boon to the economy.

Let's go through all of the tax increases by order of effective date.

Taxes That Took Effect Before President Obama's Reelection Campaign of 2012

There were a few tax increases that took effect in time for voters to see them, but they tended to be well hidden. Some were small and probably not noticed by most people.

In this category are some tax increases you may never have heard mentioned by Obama or the media: a tax increase on charitable hospitals, a tax increase on pharmaceutical companies based on market share, a "black liquor" tax hike on paper by-products, and a tax increase just on Blue Cross/Blue Shield companies. Note that every one of the tax hikes just mentioned increased the cost of health care for Americans. Taxing your insurance, your charitable hospital, and drugs does not make your health insurance less expensive, but more expensive. Five other tax increases that hit Americans before the 2012 election are as follows:

1. **Codification of the "economic substance doctrine."** This provision allows the IRS to disallow completely legal tax deductions and other legal tax-minimizing plans just because the IRS deems that the action lacks "substance" and is merely used to reduce taxes owed. This is both an open-ended tax increase and a power grab by the IRS. Yes, your deduction was legal according to the law. But we unelected bureaucrats in the IRS disagree with the law and will tax you as if the law was written the way we wish it were. Think about this and consider how the IRS attacked the tax status of Tea Party/taxpayer groups they did not like. Perhaps, in the not-too-distant future, the IRS may decide it does not think the charity or church you contribute to has "substance." Crazy? Just what, pray tell, would stop them from doing that?

2. **Tanning tax.** This was the one that made the late-night talk shows, so it's better known than most of the small ones. It imposes a 10 percent excise tax on indoor tanning-salon

sessions. Since most tanning salons are owned by women, this is particularly a tax increase on women-owned small employers. This tax costs taxpayers $300 million each year.[1]

3. **Medicine-cabinet tax.** Prior to the Obamacare law, you could use your pretax health spending cards (Health Savings Accounts, Flexible Spending Accounts, and Health Reimbursement Accounts) to purchase nonprescription, over-the-counter medicines. This ability to buy cold and flu medicines and other nonprescription medicinal products was a popular feature of these pretax accounts. Obamacare took away these purchases as allowed under the law. This is a $600 million tax hike each year.[2]

4. **Heath Savings Account (HSA) early-withdrawal tax hike.** People with a Health Savings Account (HSA) can put pretax dollars away to pay for future health expenditures. Like other pretax savings plans (IRAs, 401(k)s, etc.), there is a penalty for taking out HSA dollars either too early (before retirement) or for something other than health care. For all of these other accounts, the penalty comes in the form of having to pay taxes on the withdrawal, plus an additional 10 percent surtax. Obamacare increased this surtax to 20 percent. The clear intent was to discourage people from saving money in HSAs, which, as the best example of consumer-driven health care, is the antithesis of Obamacare. Obama hoped to raise $300 million in taxes this way.[3]

5. **Employer reporting of health coverage on W-2s.** Obamacare required that employers begin reporting the value of employer-provided health insurance on annual W-2 wage forms. At first glance, this seems innocuous—more information is a good thing, right? However, this is clearly a setup. Before something can be accurately taxed, it must be measured and identified. Congress will find it much easier to tax employer-provided health insurance coverage now that a

dollar figure is right there on your W-2. We can only guess how big this future tax will be.

Tax Increases That Only Took Effect after President Obama Was Safely Reelected

The bulk of the tax increases in Obamacare—and the ones that many more Americans would notice—were set to spring like a rat trap only after the 2012 election. It's here that the real economic damage was done.

1. **Surtax on Savers and Small Business Owners.** The first to consider is a new "surtax" on savers and small business owners. To the extent that you make $200,000 per year or more ($250,000 per year if married, and these numbers are not indexed to inflation), you face this tax. It adds 3.8 percentage points to the tax rate you face on capital gains, dividends, interest, rent, and royalties. That effectively means a top capital gains and dividends tax rate of 23.8 percent, and a top tax rate on other investment activity of 43.4 percent. That's not all. This surtax also applies to wages and self-employment income. Obamacare creates a higher Medicare payroll tax for earners in the income band described above. So instead of paying the usual 2.9 percent Medicare tax on all your wages and self-employment, you would start paying a 3.8 percent Medicare tax on wages and small employer income above $200,000 or so. And remember—these numbers are not indexed to inflation, so they will eventually grow to include everybody. Add another $35 billion each year in higher taxes.[4] Every dollar of the $35 billion in higher taxes adds to the cost of American health care.

2. **Medical Device Tax.** The second major post-2012 tax is the medical device tax, which is in the news a lot. It's a

gross-receipts tax on the sale of all medical devices (pace-makers, prosthetic limbs, wheelchairs, etc.). What that means is that it does not matter whether or not the medical device manufacturer had a large profit or even suffered a business loss—they are still liable for the same 2.3 percent tax on all sales. Suppose you and I each sell $1 million in medical equipment. I have a good year and earn a profit. You have a lot of unanticipated expenses and suffer a loss. It does not matter—we each owe the same 2.3 percent surtax, or $23,500 on our sales. Obama plans to raise $3 billion each year with this tax on medical devices.[5]

3. **High Medical Bills Tax.** The third major post-2012 tax is the income tax increase on people who deduct medical expenses. If you pay income tax and itemize your deductions (instead of taking the standard deduction), you have an opportunity to deduct high out-of-pocket medical expenses. Prior to Obamacare, you had to reduce your bucket of expenses by an amount equal to 7.5 percent of your adjusted gross income (AGI). Obamacare increases this threshold to 10 percent of AGI, widening the net of taxable income. Millions now won't be able to deduct medical expenses at all. Almost everyone who claims this deduction makes less than $100,000 per year. So Obamacare makes it more difficult for those in the middle class to get tax relief for their high medical bills. How much does Obama plan to confiscate from the very sick? Nearly $4 billion each year once it's fully phased in.[6]

4. **Flexible Savings Accounts Tax.** The final major post-2012 tax is a new cap on flex accounts, or FSAs, at work. Prior to the Obamacare law, there was no tax-law limit on how much you could defer into these annual "use-it-or-lose-it" accounts. Obamacare imposes a new FSA cap of $2,500 per year. These accounts are a very common middle-class way to get tax relief for out-of-pocket medical expenses. They are also used for onetime large medical purchases, such as laser

eye surgery or braces. This cap is a tax on middle class families who depend on these accounts to make large medical bills a little easier to swallow. This tax on flexible spending accounts is often called the "special needs kids tax" because these accounts are frequently used by parents to care for children with special needs. The tax take is estimated at $2 billion per year.[7]

5. **The "Cadillac Plan" Tax.** There's one more tax that will come online in 2018. This tax is the so-called Cadillac Plan excise tax. It imposes a 40 percent excise tax on health insurance premiums to the extent that those premiums exceed a certain amount. For example, suppose the law says that a $20,000 plan is the "Cadillac" limit. But your plan costs $24,000 per year, or $4,000 "too much." This tax would impose a 40 percent tax on this $4,000 "overage," for a bill of $1,600. While that is supposed to be paid by insurance companies, that's bunk. Companies don't pay taxes—people do. This tax will simply be passed along to customers—all customers, not just the ones with expensive plans. Obama believes this tax will take a growing amount out of the economy each year, starting at $20 billion and growing from there.[8]

What about the Mandate Taxes?

We still haven't mentioned the most infamous of Obamacare's taxes—the tax penalty for not complying with the individual and employer mandates to purchase "qualifying and affordable" health insurance coverage.

When fully phased in, starting in 2017, the surtax you will pay for not buying the Obamacare plan you're told to buy will be pretty steep. For most Americans, it will come out to 2.5 percent of your adjusted gross income on your tax return. To translate that into English, that's a tax of $2,500 for a family of four earning $100,000 per year. It will cost no less than about $700 for an individual, about $1,400 for a married couple, and about $2,100 for a family.

This surtax will be added right onto your 1040 form like any other surtax. It will either decrease your income tax refund or increase the balance you owe the IRS. The IRS can go after you with the full weight of their authority—the only limitation is that they cannot impose criminal penalties against you for not paying. But interest, civil penalties, etc., are fair game.

The individual mandate's kid sister, the employer mandate, has been (probably unconstitutionally) suspended by the Obama administration. That means when Obama or some future potentate says, "Go," it will snap into place. Who knows? The rule of law has become a tad flexible here. It may depend on what side of the bed Obama or some future president gets out of. Therefore, while it is temporarily in remission, it is worth noting that this mandate—which requires employers with fifty or more workers to buy Obamacare-approved health insurance for employees—is still part of the law. If it ever does come online, failure to provide this coverage will cost employers between $2,000 and $4,000 per employee, each year. That means you are more expensive to your employer. This fee will come in part or wholly out of your salary or future pay increases.

Hiding the Ball on Costs to Taxpayers

Delaying the worst of the Obamacare taxes until President Obama was safely reelected was smart politics. It guaranteed that the voters would not feel them until it was too late. Delay also helped shield the true cost of Obamacare from the public. This is a nice way of saying the law was lied into place by Obama and the Democrat majorities in the House and Senate. How bad is this law? Bad enough its supporters knew they had to lie to sell it.

When Obamacare was passed into law in 2010, the Congressional Budget Office (CBO) provided a ten-year scoring estimate.

CBO has to score what is presented to them, and what was written there was a bill that took several years to go into effect. As a result, many of the years had "$0" as the tax increase, since the hike would not have happened by that year. This artificially reduced the tax score of the bill at the time it was passed. CBO reckoned that in the first ten years of implementation (2010–19), Obamacare would cost taxpayers $525 billion.[9]

Fast-forward several years. In 2012—just two years later—CBO updated their score. This time, they estimated that Obamacare would cost taxpayers $1 trillion over the next decade (2013–22).[10] That's a huge jump in just a couple of years. What happened? Simply put, the second window saw more of the tax increases coming online, and CBO was no longer asked to hide the ball.

What does the true cost look like? If you look at the last year CBO has provided (2022), it shows an annual tax increase due to Obamacare of $163 billion. That means that a fully implemented ten-year score would actually be close to $2 trillion. Conveniently, CBO says it can no longer accurately score the measure.[11] Nancy Pelosi once told us that Congress would have to pass the bill and then we would learn what was in it. Now we learn that even the Congressional Budget Office, run by the Congress that passed Obamacare, cannot tell us how much it will cost. We will have to live under Obamacare and year-by-year we will eventually come to learn what was truly "in it."

PART II

How the Government Grew in a Nation Conceived in Liberty

CHAPTER 4

How Taxes and Tax Revolts Shaped American History

The struggle against taxes created and continues to shape American history.

Before the American Revolution, citizens of the thirteen British colonies lived in a Garden of Eden of low taxation. In 1750, Pehr Kahn, a Swedish botanist, wrote, "There is such an amount of good land yet uncultivated that a newly married man can, without difficulty, get a spot of ground where he may comfortably subsist with this wife and children. The taxes are very low and he need not be under any concern on their account. The liberties he enjoys are so great that he considers himself a prince in his possessions."[1]

Thirty years earlier, in 1720, an Irish immigrant wrote home, "Tell all the poor folk of ye place that God has opened a door for their deliverance...all that a man works for is his own, and there are no revenue hounds to take it from us here: there is no one to take away yer Corn, yer Potatoes."[2]

Many of the original colonies were begun as tax havens. The 1629 Charter of Massachusetts Bay granted settlers a seven-year exemption from customs taxes on all trade to and from Britain and a twenty-one-year exemption from all other taxes. In 1621 the Dutch government granted the Dutch West India Company an eight-year exemption from all trade duties between New Amsterdam/New

York and the mother country. Swedish settlers in Delaware were offered a ten-year tax exemption. Immigrants came to America leaving high tax nations to arrive in low tax colonies.

By 1714, British subjects in Great Britain were paying on a per capita basis ten times as much in taxes as the average "American" in the thirteen colonies.

Low-tax Pennsylvania was founded by William Penn, the father of American religious liberty, who also notably refused the Pennsylvania General Assembly's kind offer to establish an import and export tax for his personal benefit.

Taxation in the colonies consisted of property taxes, poll taxes on men over eighteen, excise taxes, and forced-labor contributions of a few days a month to build roads and assume other "public functions," such as constable, assessor, or "hog reeve" ("an officer charged with the prevention or appraising of damages by stray swine," according to the Oxford English Dictionary).

Massachusetts imposed an embryonic income tax in 1634 in the form of a "faculty" tax. In 1643, Alvin Rabushka writes in *Taxation in Colonial America*, "assessors were appointed to rate inhabitants on their estates and their faculties, which included personal abilities."[3] The faculty tax did not tax what you actually earned but what a tax assessor thought you were capable of earning. Somewhat arbitrary, perhaps, but certainly less paperwork and no need to keep receipts. The good news for seventeenth-century Bay Staters was that the tax was only 1 percent of what we would consider income.

Connecticut, anticipating New York mayor Michael Bloomberg's nanny-state tendencies, imposed sumptuary laws in 1676, which taxed any person who wore silk ribbons, gold or silver lace, or gold or silver buttons.

Still, life was good. Taxes were low.

But that was all threatened by Britain's need for new tax revenue. Her wars and empire had tapped out the mother country.

By 1775, the British government was consuming one-fifth of its people's GDP, while New Englanders were only paying between

1 and 2 percent of their income in taxes. The British were also weighed down with a national debt piled up by years of worldwide warfare, while American local and colonial governments were almost debt-free. Against this backdrop, Americans watched as the British monarchy debated how to raise taxes on the colonists to pay down Britain's war debt and pay for the ten thousand British soldiers barracked in the colonies.

The Sugar Act of 1764, a rewrite of the Plantation Duty of 1673, was designed to raise revenue rather than force the colonies to trade with England alone, and it fell mostly on molasses, sugar, and Madeira wine. The colonies reacted particularly poorly to the imposition of the Stamp Act of 1765, which was an effort to impose a direct tax on the colonies rather than tax imports and exports. Benjamin Franklin and others argued to the British government that while the colonies did not object to tariffs, they did oppose direct domestic "taxation without representation."

The famous British writer Samuel Johnson presented the British case in his book *Taxation No Tyranny*. Johnson rejected the idea that those who are to be taxed had any claim to representation in government.

Johnson wrote, "The Supreme power of every community has the right of requiring from all its subjects such contributions as are necessary to the public safety or public prosperity."[4]

Johnson compared the power of the ruler over his subjects to "that of obedience of children to the parents, and is not refuted by the assertion, that the consent of those who are required to contribute, is necessary."[5] And as to representation, Johnson argues that many in Britain have no representation and they have to pay. So why should unrepresented Americans whine when "the far greater number of the subjects of England, men who are not freeholders, copyholders, who are a third of the land holders of the kingdom, and all women, were unrepresented in parliament, yet were bound by laws enacted by the representatives of others."[6]

In summary, most people in Britain cannot vote. We tax them. Why should you Americans be any different?

Responding to the colonists' apparent agreement to external taxes, such as duties and tariffs, in lieu of direct internal taxation by the Crown, the British parliament repealed the Stamp Act and responded with the Townshend Acts of 1767, which imposed duties on seventy-two items, including tea (the changes actually reduced taxes on tea originally imported from British colonies to reduce the incentive to smuggle Dutch tea to America). Although the British repealed most of these duties in 1770, they kept the targeted tax on tea to make the point that the Crown could tax whenever it chose to do so. By then, however, the American colonists had stopped distinguishing between domestic and trade taxes and started opposing all taxation and control by Britain, setting the stage for Yorktown.

Our first national government was organized under the Articles of Confederation. The Constitution would come later. The Articles were agreed to on March 1, 1781, and demonstrate the importance Americans placed on controlling the power to spend and tax.

The Articles required that all federal spending and taxation would require a three-fourths, or 75 percent, vote by all the members of Congress. The modern filibuster requires 60 percent. This was a tough climb. And power was dispersed. Congressmen were appointed by the states. The articles imposed what we call "term limits" and what was then thought of as "rotation in office." So that "no person shall be capable of being a delegate for more than three years in any term of six years." One could go in and out of government, but there would be no permanent, professional delegate to this Congress. You would have to have a day job and for at least three of every six years be a taxpayer and not a tax spender.

Article VII stipulated that taxes would be "supplied by the several States in proportion to the value of all land within each State." So after three-quarters of the states agreed to a federal budget and three-quarters of the states agreed to raise the taxes to pay for that budget, then each state would levy taxes and hand the cash over to the federal government. Any amendments to the Articles of Confederation were required to be "confirmed by the legislatures of every State." Unanimity. (Our present constitution allows amendments to whisk through with a simple three-quarters supermajority of the states.)

The first Congress was willing to maintain a tariff to raise money. Beyond that there was little agreement. Any tax would be divided up among the various states based on real property in each state, and the state government would be required to raise the money and send it to the national government.

The states were not exactly falling all over each other to raise tax dollars that would flow to the central government, and in 1787 Congress voted to call a convention in Philadelphia to amend the Articles of Confederation, but there did not seem to be great enthusiasm or commitment to the project.

But then a tax revolt changed American history for the second time.

The US Constitution and Taxation

Massachusetts tax collectors were being annoying raising funds to pay off the states' war debt. Daniel Shay, a veteran of the American War of Independence, led several thousand farmers in a revolt. They were not armed, and failed to capture a federal arsenal. The revolt fizzled and everyone went home. But it certainly highlighted the sense that the central government was weak and unstable. The constitutional convention in Philadelphia was given greater urgency and formally met on May 25, 1787.

The delegates at the constitutional convention had before them both the history of abusive British taxation and the perceived weakness of the Articles of Confederation. They hoped to thread the needle and give the federal government the ability to tax while protecting Americans against the history of governments everywhere abusing that power.

The Constitution attempts to limit the government's power to tax in three places.

Article I, Section 7, stipulates, **"All Bills for raising Revenue shall originate in the House of Representatives; but the Senate may propose or concur with Amendments as on other Bills."** Taxes can only be put forward by the House of Representatives, the lower house, which was viewed as under the closest scrutiny and control by the American people. They were not chosen by the state legislatures. Members of the House are elected every two years. This power was not granted to the president and the executive branch. This power to tax was denied to the executive branch. It was also denied to senators who were chosen by state legislatures every six years.

Article I, Section 8, declares, **"The Congress shall have Power to lay and collect Taxes, Duties, Imposts and Excises, to pay the Debts and provide for the common Defense and General Welfare of the United States; but all Duties, Imposts and Excises shall be uniform throughout the United States."**

While Section 8 listed powers Congress did have. Article I, Section 9 gives the list of things Congress may not do. The following have direct application to tax policy.

No bill of Attainder or ex post facto Law shall be passed.

No capitation, or other direct, Tax shall be laid unless in Proportion to the Census or enumeration herein before directed to be taken. This clause made an income tax unconstitutional. The Sixteenth Amendment in effect repealed this clause. It read, **"The Congress shall have power to lay and collect taxes on incomes, from whatever source derived, without apportionment among the several States, and without regard to any census or enumeration."**

"No Tax or Duty shall be laid on Articles exported from any State."

Note that taxes can only be levied for three reasons: "to pay the Debts" of the United States, to provide for the "the common defense," and the "general welfare." This limitation on legitimate expenditures is a powerful constraint on the federal spending and therefore the taxation required...if it is obeyed by future congresses. Any legislation aimed at the redistribution of income or forcing Americans to buy insurance or pensions is hard to square with this clear language.

And taxation must be "uniform." (This is a powerful argument against "progressive" or "graduated" taxes that tax different individuals at different rates.)

The Fourth Amendment spoke not to taxes but to tax collectors. The Convention delegates remembered how the British had abused the privacy and property of Americans in their drive to collect taxes. It read, **"The right of the people to be secure in their persons, houses, papers and effects, against unreasonable searches and seizures, shall not be violated, and no Warrants shall issue, but upon probable cause, supported by Oath or affirmation and particularly describing the place to be searched, and the persons or things to be seized."**

It seems a tad amazing that after a revolution and war of independence that started around the Stamp Tax, the Boston Tea Party, and No Taxation without Representation, the founding Constitution spent so few words protecting taxpayers. Gun owners got twenty-seven words in the Second Amendment.

But the Founding Fathers believed they did strictly limit taxation though the demand for uniformity of all taxes and apportionment for direct taxes.

"Uniform" Taxation Mandated by the Constitution

In "Federalist No. 10," James Madison laid out the danger of majorities taxing minorities that needed to be defended against in the Constitution he was then promoting: "yet there is, perhaps, no legislative act in which greater opportunity and temptation are given to a predominant party to trample on the rules of justice. Every shilling with which they overburden the inferior member is a shilling saved to their own pockets." One faction taxing another was a grave danger to be prohibited. Is it possible he intended to draft a constitution that failed to protect taxpayers from this danger?

In "Federalist No. 36," Alexander Hamilton, rightly seen as the Founding Father most sympathetic to federal taxation, argued that the danger of majorities voting to abusively tax minorities was prevented by Section 8 of Article I, which requires that taxes "shall be UNIFORM throughout the United States." Hamilton himself put the word "uniform" in all capitals.

When taken literally, if Congress can pass only uniform taxes, they cannot discriminate between classes, regions, or industries or allow the American people to be divided against each other to the advantage of the tax collector dividing and conquering each.

Charles Adams, in his wonderful book *Those Dirty Rotten Taxes: The Tax Revolts That Built America*, highlighted that the choice of the word "uniform" was deliberate and meaningful: "The debates at the convention and the writings thereafter show that the purpose of the 'uniform' command was to prevent discrimination in the tax system. In the first draft on July 23, 1787, the clause read, 'common to all.' This meant, of course, everyone treated the same. Later, on September 12, it was revised to read, "uniform and equal," which was essentially the same thing. This final draft was then sent to the Committee on Style, which strangely enough, dropped the phrase entirely. Madison then rewrote in the word "uniform," which is the way it finally read."[7]

The uniform clause should make any progressive income tax unconstitutional on the face of it. The Constitution does not change. The National Rifle Association has breathed life into the Second Amendment that was long ignored by the courts. The grassroots conservative movements have refocused attention on the Ninth and Tenth Amendments.

The Sixteenth Amendment to the Constitution removes the requirement that income taxes must be apportioned equally among the states, but it did not repeal the requirement that taxes be uniform. That clause and the Founders' intent remain intact, unchallenged, in plain sight, yet overlooked as a treasure to be restored to prominence.

The Constitution was "take two," a mulligan, on creating a limited government that restrained the urge to overtax and overspend. Now what?

It turns out that imposing taxes with representation is not easy. The first effort by the Federalists—our first president, George Washington; his vice president, John Adams; and the first treasury secretary, Alexander Hamilton—did not go well.

The Excise Taxes and the Whiskey Rebellion

Alexander Hamilton, the nation's first secretary of the treasury, convinced Congress to enact a tax on whiskey. An excise tax. An "internal" tax.

The tax was a 25 percent tax on distilled spirits. A tax on a perhaps unhealthy habit and a tax on a "luxury." Except in the then-western part of the United States, farmers turned their crops they hoped to sell for dollars first into whiskey because of the high costs of transportation. Farmers in the suburbs of Philadelphia could take their wheat or corn or apples to market in a horse-drawn cart. Out west, whiskey was used as currency. Easier to carry and ship than bulky agricultural products. Those west of the Appalachian Mountains hoping to sell something to the population centers in the East—Boston, Philadelphia, or New York—faced crossing a mountain range and hundreds of miles in a world where twenty miles a day was a good day's travel.

The excise tax on distilled spirits was viewed as a punitive tax on the West. The West did not have cash crops. Whiskey was the currency or cash they used. This tax truly was a disproportionate burden on the West. It was not uniform.

Today, we are quite aware of the later North/South division of the Civil War but in its early years the nation was deeply divided East versus West. Thomas P. Slaughter brings to life the very real dangers to young America in his book *The Whiskey Rebellion: Frontier Epilogue to the American Revolution*. One could view the Whiskey Rebellion of 1794 as a replay of the American Revolution—new taxes convincing taxpayers that "their" government was too removed from their interests or control. Or the Whiskey Rebellion in reaction to a regionally punitive excise tax could be seen a foreshadowing of the tariff battles that divided North from South in the decades before the Civil War.

The new excise taxes were matches dropped on dry timber.

Slaughter quotes Tobias Lear's prophecy in 1787 that "within fifteen years the inhabitants to the westward of the Alleghany will be a separate, independent people."[8] Western trade naturally flowed west and south down the Ohio and Mississippi Rivers, which linked those west of the Appalachians to the Spanish Empire and possibly Britain, which maintained Canada and the Great Lakes.

Slaughter adds that "as early as 1783, George Mason was predicting that continued neglect of the westerners' needs would 'occasion another war in less than seven years.'"[9] The Whiskey Rebellion came eleven years after Mason's prediction.

Westerners were hoping to create new states that would represent their interests. There had long been a movement for self-government and perhaps statehood for Western Pennsylvania, to be called "Westsylvania," and "Watauga" in western North Carolina. Vermont, which fought for statehood, was denied it for years as Congress worked to keep neighbors New Hampshire and New York happy.

And now the hated excise tax. Fewer than twenty years since the Declaration of Independence, Americans were again tarring and feathering those trying to collect taxes. Liberty polls were erected; and the rebels were not "Sons of Liberty" but "Whiskey Boys." There was talk of succession, and "Loyalists," those farmers who actually paid the hated whiskey tax, found their stills filled with bullet holes. A replay of the first American Revolution. The westerners felt themselves as distant from and unrepresented by Philadelphia as the colonists had felt from London.

And a new tax again sparked violence. Men died as rebels and soldiers fired on each other in Pittsburgh.

By August 1794, Alexander Hamilton convinced President Washington to call out the militia of four states. The rebels had dispersed, but Hamilton wanted the federal government to make a show of force, and so the army marched north. Several rebels were arrested. Two were sentenced to be hanged. The point made, Washington pardoned the two condemned men and granted a general amnesty for all rebels.

Two years later President George Washington retired. He could have run for a third term and most certainly would have been reelected, but he set a tradition by once again retiring from public life. His vice president, John Adams, a Federalist, defeated Thomas Jefferson and took office in March 1797.

In 1798, Congress passed its first direct tax on lands, houses, and slaves. When assessors showed up to determine the value of "property" to be taxed, they were physically attacked. When some resisters were arrested and put in jail, a local auctioneer, John Fries of Pennsylvania, led a march on the courthouse and freed the prisoners. Adams again called out the militia and Fries was arrested, tried, and sentenced to death. Adams's entire cabinet demanded that Fries die. Adams followed Washington's example and pardoned Fries.

Two years later Jefferson defeated Adams with the hated excise taxes front and center in the election.

Our first struggle against taxes defeated the British and ended their claim to govern us.

The second struggle ended the Federalist Party that might otherwise have gone on to govern indefinitely into the future.

Jefferson's vision won in 1800. Still, and this certainly sounds painfully familiar to modern ears, some of Jefferson's key advisers suggested, after he won election, that he not repeal the excise taxes.

It was OK to campaign against the taxes, but it was nice to have the money. Jefferson insisted on keeping his word. Jefferson was rewarded with reelection in 1804 and in fact his low tax promise won six elections. Twice under his name, twice under Madison's, and twice under Monroe's. America liked Jefferson's low-tax vision for America.

Candidates who promise to keep taxes low and keep that promise are rewarded with reelection and the growth of their party.

The hated excise taxes were repealed and only came back temporarily to fund the War of 1812. Unlike in later wars, the excise tax ended soon after the war ended.

The Struggle against the Tariff

The tariff was now the major source of national tax revenue from 1800 to 1861. It was only the Civil War that brought back excise taxes and (for its first appearance) the income tax.

And so the United States entered the period labeled by tax historian Charles Adams the "Struggle against the Tariff."

The tariff raised the price of manufactured imports from Europe and thus allowed Northern manufacturers to raise their prices. The South, more agricultural and less industrialized, was forced to buy manufactured goods from the North at inflated prices protected by the tariffs imposed on imports from Europe. The tariff enriched manufacturers in the North and was a heavy burden on the agricultural economy in the South.

Alexis de Tocqueville saw this and wrote in *Democracy in America*:

> One remembers how excited the Americans were by the free trade–tariff controversy. Not opinions only, but very powerful material interests stood to gain or lose by a tariff. The North thought that some of its prosperity was due thereto, while the South blamed it for almost all its woes. One may say that over a long period the tariff question gave rise to the only political passions disturbing the Union.[10]

De Tocqueville continues:

In 1831, when the quarrel was most envenomed, an obscure citizen of Massachusetts thought of suggesting through the newspapers that all opponents of the tariff should send deputies to Philadelphia to concert together measures to make trade free. Thanks to the invention of printing, this suggestion passed in but a few days from Maine to New Orleans. The opponents of the tariff took it up ardently. They assembled from all sides and appointed deputies. Most of the latter were known men, and some of them had risen to celebrity. South Carolina, which was later to take up arms in this cause, sent sixty-three people as its delegates. On October 1, 1831, the assembly, which in American fashion styled itself a convention, was constituted at Philadelphia: it counted more than two hundred members. The discussions were public, and from the very first day it took on an altogether legislative character: discussion covered the extent of the powers of Congress, theories of free trade, and finally the various provisions of the tariff. After ten days the assembly broke up, having issued an address to the American people. In that address it declared first that Congress had not the right to impose a tariff and that the existing tariff was unconstitutional, and second that it was against the interest of any people, in particular the American people, trade should not be free.[11]

De Tocqueville later focuses on how

The French revolutionary wars and the War of 1812 by preventing free communication between America and Europe, brought into being manufacturing establishments in the North of the Union. When peace allowed European products to reach the New World again, the Americans felt that they should establish a customs system both to protect their nascent industry and to pay all the debts contracted in the war.

The southern states who have no manufacturers to encourage, being exclusively agricultural, were quick to complain about this measure.[12]

In the year 1820 in a petition to Congress, South Carolina declared that the tariff law was *unconstitutional, oppressive, and unjust*. Later on, Georgia, Virginia, North Carolina, Alabama, and Mississippi all made more or less energetic complaints in the same sense.

Far from taking these murmurs into account, Congress in the years 1824 and 1828 raised the customs levels higher and freshly reasserted the principle.

A famous doctrine was then proclaimed, or rather revived, in the South, which took the name of nullification...The whole doctrine of nullification is summed up in a statement made in 1833 before the United States Senate by John C. Calhoun, the recognized leader of the southern nullifiers, who said: "The Constitution is a contract in which the states appear as sovereigns. Now every time there is a contract between parties having no common arbitrator, each of them retains the right to judge the extent of its obligation by itself."

It is clear that such a doctrine would in principle destroy the federal bond and actually bring back that anarchy from which the Constitution of 1789 delivered the Americans.[13]

As the tariff crisis continued, the free-trade convention de Tocqueville noted was held in Philadelphia in 1831, and then another national convention gathered in South Carolina in 1832 "to advise on the extraordinary measures to be taken."

De Tocqueville reports on what followed those efforts:

On November 24 of that year this convention published, under the name of an ordinance, a law that nullified the federal tariff law, forbade raising the duties imposed by it, and forbade recognition of any appeal that might be made to the federal courts. This decree was not to come into force until the following February, and it was intimated that if Congress modified the tariff before that time South Carolina might agree not to follow its threats further. Later on a vague and indeterminate desire was expressed to submit the question to an extraordinary assembly of all the confederated states.

Meanwhile, South Carolina armed its militia and prepared for war.

What did Congress do? Congress, which had been deaf to the complaints of its suppliant subjects, listened to them when they had arms in their hands. A law was passed by which the tariff duties were to be reduced by stages over ten years until they should be brought so low as to not exceed the supplies necessary to the government. Thus Congress completely abandoned the principle of the tariff. In the place of protective duties for industry it substituted a purely fiscal measure. The Union government to conceal its defeat had recourse to an expedient much in vogue with feeble governments: while it yielded the point *de facto*, it remained inflexible in principle. At the same time as it altered the tariff law, it passed another law investing the President with Extraordinary power to use force to overcome a resistance no longer to be feared.[14]

* * *

The May 19, 1828, tariff law, popularly known as the Tariff of Abominations, increased the tariff on clothing to 45 percent and on wool from 15 to 50 percent. Andrew Jackson failed to win the November 1828 presidential election, so the high tariffs remained until 1832, when Jackson was elected and pulled back some of the worst aspects of the tariff law of 1828. Still this was not enough for Senator Calhoun, who pushed forward with the demands for "nullification."

The Compromise Tariff of 1833 further reduced rates. This was supposed to drop the rates over the next ten years to return them to the levels of the 1816 tariff law. But shortly after the tariffs hit that target, the Tariff of 1842, or the "Black Tariff," restoring the policy of protection, and the average rate rose to 40 percent.

Tariffs were brought back down somewhat in the Walker Tariff of 1845, dropped again in 1857, but on March 2, 1861—before Abraham Lincoln was sworn in—the Morill Tariff of 1861 fulfilled a key part of the new Republican Party platform. During the Civil War, Congressman Morrill of Vermont wrote and passed two additional increases to the Morrill Tariff.

Thirty years before the Civil War, states gathered in opposition to the tariff at a new constitutional convention. The tariff was viewed as a violation of the Constitution, the original social contract that created the United States. And South Carolina called out its militia.

Had America been so blessed that had the evil of slavery never taken root on our soil, it is entirely possible that a civil war might have broken out over the tariff issue alone.

But the Civil War did come, and it brought the introduction of the income tax—if only as a wartime emergency measure.

The Long Drive to Impose a National Income Tax

But when a recession in 1894 reduced the federal government's revenues from the tariff, an income tax was reimposed, only to be struck down as unconstitutional in 1895. Then the income tax was viewed by some in the South as a way to reduce the hated tariff and then a new movement, the campaign for prohibition arose and added its voice to an old vice: envy. Others saw the income tax as a way to "tax the rich." Together these breathed life into the cause of a national income tax.

The Sixteenth Amendment to the Constitution, which removed the ban on taxes not equally distributed among the states—at least income taxes—was enacted in 1913 and, later that year, the first constitutional income tax was passed by Congress by a Democrat House and Senate and signed by the new Democrat president, Woodrow Wilson.

The existence of the income tax had two dramatic effects on the history and trajectory of the United States. It made the American entry into World War I possible on a massive scale. Europeans had been killing each other with relish on behalf of their competing kings and empires for almost four years. America might well have stayed clear of the War of 1914 as it did the Napoleonic Wars, the Crimean War, the Franco-Prussian War of 1870, and the various wars of empire in Africa and Asia.

Absent an income tax that could draw cash into Washington with the turn of a spigot, the United States might have stayed out, or decided to defend American shipping by sinking German U-boats, rather than sending 1.5 million Americans to France where 116,000 died. If Britain and France and Germany and Russia and the Ottoman Empire had had to slug it out with their own money and lives, they might have come to a peace that was not as punitive as the one imposed on the German Empire. The inflation and destroyed economy that flowed from the policy of forced reparations set the stage that made it possible for the Communists or the National Socialists to take over Germany in the 1930s and made World War II more likely, if not inevitable.

This is a heavy indictment of the income tax and its powers. The United States did not enter wars of choice promiscuously before the income tax made the funding of wars easier.

And add one more crime to the rap sheet of our newly created income tax: Prohibition. Gangland violence. And the creation of organized crime, which has continued long after Prohibition was repealed.

Social reformers, or busybodies, depending on how you view these things, had been promoting temperance for several decades. Carrie Nation railed against the evils of strong drink in Kansas and across the country. And liquor consumption did fall. But taxes on liquor were 22 percent of federal government revenues in 1880, and 27 percent in 1890, and 32 percent in 1900, and 31 percent in 1910.[15] Making liquor consumption illegal would "bankrupt" the federal government. The tax-and-spenders were not having any of this Prohibition nonsense.

Last Call by Daniel Okrent, a fun book on the history of Prohibition, gives the existence of the income tax equal status with the social reformers in making Prohibition a reality: "The income tax had made a Prohibition amendment fiscally feasible. The social revolution wrought by the suffragists had made it politically plausible."[16]

One could argue that the income tax could not have been passed in the first place if the overlapping Suffragist and Temperance movements had not needed a tax to replace the revenue that would be lost to their criminalizing liquor sales. Perhaps both are true, the income tax made Prohibition legislatively possible and the Temperance/Prohibition campaign made the income tax a reality.

Ironically, it was the collapse in income tax revenues after the Stock Market Crash of 1929 that created the conditions for repealing Prohibition. Because of the Crash, Okrent writes, "Revenue based on 1930 incomes was down 15 percent and the following year was a 37 percent drop, and the year after another 26 percent— compounded it was a vertiginous 60 percent plunge in just three years. Capital gains taxes that have brought $1.5 billion into the treasury between 1926 and 1929 dove into negative territory over the next five years as the allowance for capital losses piled up."[17]

Gangsters, Al Capone, and devastating corruption throughout law enforcement could not convince Congress to repeal Prohibition. A lust for tax dollars did.

William H. Stayton, the founder of the Association against the

Prohibition Amendment, calculated that if Americans returned to pre–World War I levels of liquor consumption and it were taxed at the same rate as in England, the government would raise $1.32 billion.[18] This was a prize worth the chase.

Tax policy really does drive history. It gave us Prohibition and the end of Prohibition, World War I, and thus perhaps World War II, as we will see in chapters five and six.

Tax policy then drove partisan politics for the next decades. Republicans under Eisenhower, Goldwater, and Nixon were balanced-budget "green eyeshade" Republicans dedicated to raising enough money to finance the New Deal and Great Society's spending commitments. They failed to focus on limiting government, both taxes and spending, and instead lusted after the golden calf of a balanced budget—large or small.

The Supply-Side Revolution: JFK to Reagan

It was John F. Kennedy who broke through the stalemate. He proposed a 22 percent across-the-board income tax rate cut and an investment-tax credit that approximated full expensing of new business investment. He argued that lower rates would reduce the disincentive to save and invest. His rhetoric sounded like that of Art Laffer or Jack Kemp or Ronald Reagan in the 1980s. And yet it was Goldwater who voted against the JFK tax cuts. The Kennedy/Johnson tax cuts were passed on February 26, 1964. The House voted 326 to 83 and the Senate voted 74 to 19 for the tax cut.[19]

Thirty-six percent of the "no" votes were Republican.

Nixon raised taxes to pay for the Great Society programs and Vietnam War championed by Lyndon Baines Johnson. Democrats spent and Republicans followed after with tax increases like the circus sweeper who follows the elephant with an oversized pooper-scooper.

But a Republican Party focused on deficits and unable to muster the votes to stop the Democrats from spending was not a likely contender for power. Jack Kemp mocked the "green eyeshade" Republicans, who focused on the deficit rather than creating economic growth. They were, he memorably said, simply "tax collectors for the Welfare State."

And then the tax issue once again rushed to the fore and changed American politics. It created a revolution within the Republican Party and created a new divide between the two parties that continues to this day.

Proposition 13 and the Tax Revolt of 1978

On June 6, 1978, the voters of California went to the polls and voted 62 to 34 to pass Proposition 13, a dramatic cut in property taxes coupled with a requirement that any future tax hikes in the state would require a two-thirds vote of the legislature.

The vote stunned political leaders. This was not a long and confusing piece of legislation that was introduced in the legislature, rewritten by lobbyists and staff, and then again rewritten as a compromise between the version that passed the state assembly and the state senate before being sent to the governor for signature.

Proposition 13 was a one-page law written by two men, Howard Jarvis and Paul Gann, who had been "gadflies" complaining about the increasing cost of taxes in California. They had twice before attempted to get their tax cut/tax limitation measure on the statewide ballot.

This time they collected 1,263,000 signatures with over 1 million being declared valid, significantly more than the 499,846 required by the California Constitution.

Then Governor Jerry Brown led the fight against the tax cut. The entire California establishment opposed this citizen initiative and vastly outspent supporters of Proposition 13. Only a handful of Republican elected officials supported the measure. And the tax rebels won, against all odds. This successful initiative "went viral."

Howard Jarvis was on the cover of *Time* magazine. Citizens had actually cut their own taxes. This gave real meaning to the American Revolution's demand to link taxation to the "consent of the governed."

California was home to one of every ten Americans. Trends started in California and moved East. This tax revolt raged state to state.

Across the nation, in Massachusetts, the home of Concord and Lexington, the Boston Tea Party, and the Liberty Tree festooned with hanging effigies of British tax collectors, a new tax revolt was also moving.

Citizens for Limited Taxation, led by Barbara Anderson and Chip Faulkner, collected signatures to place Proposition 2.5 on the November 1980 ballot. "Prop two and a half," as it was known, limited property taxes to 2.5 percent of assessed value and limited increases in the property tax to 2.5 percent per year, while enacting a series of spending reforms to keep property taxes low.

Proposition Two and a Half was put on the November 4, 1980, ballot and won overwhelmingly 59–41 in "Taxachusetts." And while the Massachusetts proposition was a law—not a constitutional amendment like California's Proposition 13—the state legislature has been afraid to punch holes in the measure over the past thirty years.

In Washington, D.C., the tax revolt focused on how inflation was pushing more and more Americans into higher and higher income tax brackets and forcing them to pay taxes, not on real income but on inflation itself. This drove support for the Kemp-Roth tax rate reduction legislation and the Steiger Amendment cutting the capital gains tax.

The measure to cut the capital gains tax from 50 percent to 25 percent was first introduced by Bill Steiger, a moderate Republican from Wisconsin. It was supported by business leaders such as Mark Bloomfield of the American Council for Capital Formation (ACCF) and Richard Rahn with ACCF and later as chief economist with the US Chamber of Commerce. The bill was supported by the emerging Silicon Valley high-tech sector.

The Steiger Amendment passed the House 362–49 and the Senate 86–4. Carter had threatened to veto the capital gains tax cut but signed the Revenue Act of 1978 that November.

So the hike in the capital gains tax to 50 percent that had been passed by Richard Nixon was finally repealed by a bipartisan effort led by the Young Turks of the post-Nixon-soon-to-be-Reagan Republican Party. Democrats held the House and Senate in 1978, 1979, and 1980. But everyone saw the tax revolt coming, and in addition to the capital gains tax cut that was signed by Carter, both houses passed versions of the Kemp-Roth tax cut, but in classic fashion the Democrats did not allow the bill to go to Carter for signature. In the 1980 campaign George H. W. Bush attacked the central policy initiative of the entire Republican Party, calling tax rate reduction "voodoo economics." Not every Republican was a Reaganite tax cutter in 1980.

In 1981 the Democrats in the House fought to the bitter end to reduce and delay the tax rate cuts. Still, 114 Democrats voted along with all but 1 Republican to pass the bill in the House. Over in the Senate only 7 Democrats voted against the Reagan tax cuts.

In what seems like a lifetime ago, in 1986, Democrats joined Republicans in passing Reagan's tax reform act of 1986 that reduced the number of tax rates to two, 15 percent and a top rate of 28 percent, by a vote of 292–136 in the House and 74–23 in the Senate. Imagine any Democrat politician today voting to drop the top rate from 50 percent to 28 percent.

As late as 1990, when Bush broke his commitment to the American people and voted for tax hikes, he was able to convince forty-seven Republicans in the House and nineteen Republicans in the Senate to join him. Today, try to imagine any Republican president asking Republican congressmen to join him in raising income taxes to spend more—and further, try to imagine a Republican Congress going along.

In 1993, every single Republican voted against the Clinton tax hikes. And fast-forward to the Bush tax cuts of 2001 and 2003 when only one Democrat senator, Nebraska's Ben Nelson voted in support. And in 2009 every single Republican voted against the twenty Obama tax hikes in Obamacare.

Now, we have two political parties. And with almost Ivory Soap percentages you can be sure a Republican will never vote for a tax hike and a Democrat will not vote for a tax cut.

CHAPTER 5

How Government Grows

How did America, a nation created free from many European structures that limited liberties—monarchism, aristocracy, standing armies, a state church—begin to lose its liberty?

We thought we were being careful. We wrote down the Articles of Confederation and then the Constitution, both of which explicitly limited the power of government to spend and tax. We had fifty states that would jealously guard their "rights" against the encroachments of the national government. We were a free and independent people, accustomed to running our own lives.

How did a nation dedicated to low taxes become an overtaxed nation?

Rome was not built in a day. That spare tire over your belt did not arrive over the weekend. Big government does not simply appear inside your home like Goldilocks's home invasion of the Three Bears. The growth of government takes time. And governments, unlike mortals, have plenty of time. They can wait for weakness. Exploit the sin of envy in the many and pride in the few. Always growing.

The state and its Praetorian guard of bureaucrats, government employees, and recipients of taxpayer largesse have never met a problem or crisis that calls for smaller, more focused government. Each new "crisis" cries out for higher taxes, more spending, greater powers concentrated in the state. All politicians know instinctively what Chicago mayor Rahm Emanuel foolishly said out loud: Government grows opportunistically in fits and starts and big government politicians are wisely determined to "never let a good crisis go to waste."

We have watched government grow like a cancer. There are hopeful times of remission. The government probes with bayonets, retreating when it strikes steel, trying the locks on the windows for opportunities to come into our lives, and then is loath to leave. Taxation can change forms like a genie. You don't like the Stamp Tax? How about a tariff?

Politicians looking to raise taxes are like teenage boys on prom night. They have a limitless number of approaches. But always one goal.

You don't like your property taxes? We can replace them—or perhaps some of them—with a tiny, small, manageable sales tax that will not grow. We promise. Not in writing or anything, but a real live political promise by politicians who will be out of office in months leaving you to the tender mercies of new politicians who have made no such promises. And now you have the property tax *and* the sales tax.

Or, this new tax will not be on you. But on the "one percent." On rich people. On "them." Inflation will never push your family's income into higher brackets. This tax is on the "other." People from another state perhaps. Or maybe foreigners will pay your taxes through tariffs. This isn't a tax. It is a fee, a surcharge. Revenue, really. Anyway this tax is temporary, just for a while. It is because of the emergency. A hurricane here in Florida. Who knew? Have you no compassion? And now our nation is at war. We need taxes for that. Are you not a patriot? The war will end. Perhaps the tax will also. We shall see.

Over my many years of fighting big government and its apologists I have begun to see patterns, old tricks that politicians employ over and over again to fool Americans into agreeing to higher taxes. What follows is my list of scams and cons that have worked all too well over the years. Let us learn from them and resolve that we will put as much time and energy and seriousness into fighting to keep our liberty as those before us employed in winning it in the first place.

And, so, dedicated to the rock group The Who, who wrote, "We won't get fooled again," here is...

The list.

One: Replacement of More-Hated Taxes

Before the conflict with Great Britain exploded into a full-fledged war of independence, there was a political dance where the American colonists protested certain taxes such as the Stamp Tax, but hinted that they might find "external" taxes, such as duties and tariffs, acceptable.

And the slogan "No taxation without representation" suggested that higher taxes might be OK if Americans had seats in the British Parliament.

The poor British king and prime minister kept trying to find the tax the colonists would accept. After a while, everyone on our side of the ocean said, "OK, we don't want internal taxes or external taxes and we don't want you taxing us with or without representation. We don't want any tax of yours, Stupid."

Over the years American taxpayers have lost that focus and too often have been tricked into paying new and higher taxes on the promise that the new tax will replace a particularly hated tax.

The state of New Jersey did not have a sales tax until 1966. Property taxes were painful and hated. A sales tax, taxpayers were promised, would fix that. A sales tax would allow the property taxes to be reduced. So on July 1, 1966, the sales tax was imposed. The property taxes remained and, after a temporary feigned retreat, were back on the march upward.

Fast-forward to the 1970s, when the property tax burden was once again the focus of taxpayer anger. Democratic governor

Brendan Byrne proposed an income tax. Only 2.5 percent. It would be less painful than the hated property tax, which would certainly, probably, maybe be reduced a great deal, or some. Someday. The New Jersey income tax was passed by a Democrat Senate (21–19) and Democrat House (43–33). Today, New Jersey has an income tax, a sales tax, and high property taxes.

New Hampshire remains the "Live Free or Die" state without an income tax or a broad-based sales tax because they have resisted the siren song of the state's Democrat Party to impose a state income tax or sales tax in return for the "promise" that this will reduce the property tax.

Of course politicians who want to grow the government at the expense of the people will always be willing to pull back taxes that are too visible, too obvious, too transparently annoying and hated. New, smaller, hidden taxes that have room to grow are added to the existing taxes, which are allowed to go into remission until the tax revolt of the day blows over, and then the original tax can always come back into bloom.

The Value-Added Tax (VAT) in Europe was offered as the solution to other taxes being too high. In each case, after the VAT was imposed, the existing taxes grew more rapidly than before. The state was simply larger, more powerful, and more demanding after being reinforced with the cash flow of the VAT. Feeding the tiger makes the tiger bigger, and after his nap he is hungrier and stronger than before. Every European nation that added a VAT to its tax collectors' quiver still also has a personal income tax and a corporate income tax. They didn't go away.

Herman Cain ran in the Republican primary for president in 2012. He recognized the general anger at the IRS and the federal income tax and put forward his 9-9-9 proposal to have a 9 percent personal income tax, 9 percent business transfer tax (actually a subtraction-method Value-Added Tax), and a 9 percent retail sales tax. It was popular at first as voters focused on the benefits of seeing their federal income tax—now as high as 43.4 percent—capped at 9 percent. There was less focus on the placement of two needles inserted into the taxpayers' veins—the new 9 percent sales tax and the Value-Added Tax.

If you have a tapeworm living in your intestines, what should you do? Is it progress to swallow a new small tapeworm on the theory/promise/hope that the new tapeworm will restrain the existing one? Or might, over time the two tapeworms—despite all their promises—each grow to be larger than the original? Tapeworms and taxes tend to grow over time, despite how they were advertised.

Swapping one tax for another is almost always a mistake for taxpayers. Politicians are willing to reduce or in extreme cases eliminate taxes that are visible and abhorrent to taxpayers. Why? Because highly visible, painful, and unpopular taxes threaten the interests of the state. They make it too clear to taxpayers what they are paying to the government. Painful taxes cannot be raised. What good are they? Best to prune them back like rosebushes, graft new taxes onto the bush, and wait for the next season to have them sprout and grow again.

The paradox for taxpayers is that a visible tax, a painful tax, is the taxpayer's best protection against runaway government spending and taxes. But try putting that on a bumper sticker: "Vote for Me. I Will Support Visible, Annoying (but Difficult-to-Raise) Taxes."

Do not engage in a land war in Asia, nor challenge a Sicilian when death is on the line, and finally, do not play "trade ya" with a politician offering to swap taxes.

Two: "Emergency, Emergency. Everybody to Get from Street"* and Pay More Taxes.

Wars, recessions, once called "panics," and bad weather are emergencies often exploited by politicians to help raise taxes. Taxes in response to such "emergencies" are assumed to be temporary, for a

---

* From the film *The Russians are Coming the Russians are Coming* (United Artists, 1966).

specific purpose, and as an added bonus, anyone raising embarrassing questions is uncaring or unpatriotic.

In 1936, Pennsylvania politicians moved to take advantage of the death and destruction caused by a flood in Johnstown that killed two dozen citizens and damaged three thousand buildings. (This is not the famous flood of 1889. That did not lead to a tax hike. Some politician was asleep at the switch and missed a golden opportunity to exploit death and destruction to permanently hike taxes statewide.)

The Pennsylvania General Assembly passed a "temporary" 10 percent tax on liquor. The rebuilding of the city was completed in the early 1940s, but not only did the tax stick around, it was eventually raised to 18 percent. The tax remains in effect nearly eighty years after the tragedy.

Three: Temporary Taxes

Students of *Saturday Night Live* will remember the land shark that would try over and over to get the hapless apartment dweller to open the door so he could eat him. The land shark would claim to be a friend or pizza deliveryman. The wary victim-to-be would refuse to open the door to the first several lies. But eventually, the land shark would find an impersonation that weakened the suspicions of the target and the door would open and the land shark would have dinner.

Taxpayers wary of tax increases too often fall prey to the promise of a "temporary" tax. The temporary tax is sometimes proffered by the political class as a compromise that avoids a permanent tax. ("Hey, we dodged the bullet...the new tax will phase out over three years.")

In Arizona, Republican Governor Jan Brewer was not willing to fight the spending interests who had already racked up a $3 billion overspending problem. But Republicans controlled the House and Senate and many had signed the Taxpayer Protection Pledge against voting for a tax increase. Most Republicans refused to vote for such a tax hike. But the handful of quisling Republicans needed a fig leaf so they could join her and the Democrats in passing a tax to keep the spending going full steam. Thus a tax hike raising the sales tax from 5.6 percent to 6.6 percent was to be "temporary." It would only last three years. Promise.

At the end of the three years, as suspected, the teachers union led an initiative to make it permanent. All would have gone as planned, but the Arizona state treasurer, Doug Ducey, was a Reagan Republican and he personally led and raised the money for the successful campaign to defeat Proposition 204. (Memo to would-be politicians: Doug Ducey's leadership in opposing the sales tax extension was rewarded by the taxpayers of the state when they elected him governor in November 2014.)

In Massachusetts, Governor Mike Dukakis passed a temporary income tax hike in July 1989. It is still there.

Nevada passed a $600 million "temporary" tax in 2009 because of the recession. Two years later, in 2011, Governor Brian Sandoval extended this temporary tax for another two years. Then, in 2013, another two years. The Recession technically ended in July 2009. When will the temporary tax lapse? In 2015 as promised? Your bet?

Federal income tax withholding was a temporary World War II war measure that is still with us. The death tax was put in temporarily to pay for the Civil War and then World War I. Still there.

President Reagan pointed out that there is nothing so close to eternal life here on earth as a government program. His observation is also true about "temporary" taxes.

Four: Taxation without Representation—Looting Those Who Cannot Vote against You

Given that America won its independence following a war whose early battle cry was "Taxation without Representation Is Tyranny," you might think Americans would honor that principle. But over time the advocates of ever-bigger government learned that taxing people who cannot vote against you is...very good politics.

Every mayor loves taxes imposed on rental cars. Kinda by definition, people who fly into your city's airport and rent a car do not live in your city. They do not vote in your city. They do not know the name of the city councillors who voted for this tax. It's almost perfect. They pay and they go away: the taxpayer version of the "one-night stand."

Or so they think. It turns out that more than half of rental-car customers are actually local folks or companies,[1] people who are having their cars repaired or who need a bigger car for a day. But that doesn't stop the add-ons from politicians who still remain convinced they are fleecing taxpayers who can't turn them out of office.

This writer has a receipt taped to his desk for a car rental at Boston's Logan International Airport. Cost for the rental was $20.49 for one day. Total bill after taxes and fees including sales tax as well as the customer facility charge and tax and the parking-ticket surcharge and the convention center surcharge and the energy surcharge was $43.90. Half was taxes beyond the normal Massachusetts sales tax of 6.25 percent.

Hotel taxes have the same wonderful—"Let's tax them there outsiders who don't vote in our municipal or state elections"—advantage. Of course, Los Angeles loots New Yorkers who visit, and New York City loots Los Angelinos when they come to the Big Apple. The government always wins, and travelers, consumers, and taxpayers lose.

There is a solution to some of this cross-border looting and it can be found in the 4R Act, passed in 1976, which prohibits discriminatory taxes on railroads, pipelines, and other transportation firms. In the past there was a real fear that Utah (to choose a state at random) would pass higher property taxes on railroad property running through Utah and owned by "out of state" railroad companies. Utah residents who could vote for state legislatures would pay one rate, and railroad land, owned by "outsiders" and quite immobile, would pay a higher rate. And "Mr. Railroad Guy, now that you built your railroad through our state, it would be rather expensive for you to move your railroad tracks—so pay up." This was viewed as highway robbery at the expense of interstate commerce—something mentioned from time to time in the Constitution—and the 4R Act was passed to protect against such discriminatory taxation. Each state can tax property 1 percent, or 2 or 10, but you cannot tax the locals 1 percent and out-of-state nonvoters 10 percent.

This is similar to speed traps where the small-town cops know to give warnings to the locals and stiff fines to outsiders who live and vote in another county or state and are just driving through.

The 4R Act can and should be extended to car rentals and hotels. The bill to prohibit such looting of people who rent cars has been introduced in 2013 in the House by Missouri congressmen Steve Cohen and Sam Graves. A similar law can and should soon protect travelers from highway robbery in hotel taxes and fees beyond the normal state sales tax on services.

For the past fifty years there has been a campaign by the tax-and-spenders to allow one state government to tax businesses in another state who have the audacity to sell stuff through catalogs or more recently over the Internet. L. L. Bean has a store in Maine. It sells through catalog sales to all fifty states. It has "Nexus" in Maine. That is a legal term meaning it lives there. It has buildings and employees there. It pays property and income and sales taxes in Maine. Maine chooses not to impose sales taxes on products L.L. Bean sells to consumers in other states. It could legally tax every sale at the 5.5 percent Maine sales tax. It doesn't. The L. L. Bean employees work and live and *vote* in Maine.

There was an effort by loser politicians in North Dakota who wanted to tax "the other" in 1992, demanding that everyone who sells stuff through catalog sales had to collect the North Dakota sales tax. The Supreme Court, in *Quill Corp. v. North Dakota*, ruled that no, North Dakota cannot tax businesses in other states.

Now that Al Gore has invented the Internet, the government-worker unions have begun a campaign to tax Internet sales across state lines so they can increase pay and benefits and pensions for government workers, who already earn more than the taxpayers in each of their states.

Here is how the scam works. The union bosses go to the mayors demanding more money. The mayors point out they have stripped the taxpayers bare. The union bosses suggest they tax the big shopping mall down the street that cannot move and therefore is a great target for property taxes. The union boss and the mayor go to the shopping mall owner and say, "If you don't lobby the governor and state legislature and your congressman and senators to allow us to 'export' our sales taxes by collecting sales taxes on Internet and catalog sales, we will have to raise taxes on you. You have a nice business here, it would be a shame if something bad were to happen to it—like a tax hike."

The nice Republican retail store owner is frog-marched down to lobby his Republican congressman, governor, or state legislator (the Democrats are already on board with the union bosses' demands, surprise, surprise) to pass a law to allow taxes on Internet sales.

To entice politicians to allow such cross-border taxation, the advocates of taxing Internet sales have claimed that state and local governments are missing out on $23 billion in taxes each year. In fact, now that Amazon has changed its corporate strategy and is building a series of warehouses across the nation, the actual amount of sales taxes not collected from businesses in other states has been estimated at $2–3 billion by the eMainStreet Alliance.

Why do the tax-and-spenders commit so much time and energy to changing the law in order to pick up pennies, a tiny fraction of state revenues? Because then all the energy and focus directed at picking up the last coins between the pillows in the sofa are not directed at reforming government to cost less. This campaign deflects questions of whether government spending is effective to "Hey look, over there, a penny we have failed to tax." The spending interests want no one looking at how they spend and everyone up in the crow's nest scouting for new and more taxes.

The other team is not stupid, they are evil.

One Republican governor was visited by a group of Republican retail merchants who explained that all they wanted was "fairness." Would he sign legislation to tax goods sold into his state bought over the Internet? The governor thanked them for visiting and said he would be willing to consider taxing such Internet sales. Just how many billions of dollars in additional revenue would this change rake in for the state? he asked. They gave the inflated figure retailers have peddled, and the governor said, "Fine, we will cut our state sales tax by the same amount so you have full tax equality with Internet sales and your sales taxes go down." The retailers who had been sent into the governor's office tasked with getting him to agree to an overall tax hike (to please the government workers unions and the mayors the unions own) looked at their feet and each other and left. No bill to create a revenue-neutral "reform" was drafted. That wasn't the real goal. It was just the sales pitch. The governor, who knew full well what their game was, offered fairness when what was really being demanded was a tax hike...on people and businesses in other states.

The nonnegotiable demand of the government union bosses is called the Marketplace Fairness Act. Fairness? Well, a bookstore that sells $100 worth of books in Utah pays $106 because Utah has a 6 percent sales tax. But you or a small business selling through eBay charges $100 because the commerce clause of the US Constitution does not allow Utah to tax your business based in a different state. Rather than fight to reduce the Utah sales tax imposed on their customers, the local bookstore owner suggests it is unfair that Utah citizens could buy $100 of books from you. To make you less competitive, you should have to pay the Utah sales tax. But why should you pay a Utah sales tax? What "services" do *you* living in, say, Washington State, get from Utah? *You* do not send your children to Utah schools (half the cost of Utah government) or get police protection or fire protection. When UPS delivers a package for *you* to a customer in Utah, the nice UPS folks already pay gasoline taxes for road building and maintenance.

The cost of shipping one hundred dollars' worth of books is more than the six dollars in tax demanded by Utah if you buy from a Utah bookseller. Transportation costs are greater than the "tax advantage" for Internet sales for all but very expensive goods, such as cameras.

But politicians lust after the Holy Grail of taxing businesses outside one's own state. Nonvoters. At present, Supreme Court decisions and the Commerce Clause of the Constitution protects us from such cross-border tax raids. But the government unions, often using as human shields Republican businessmen suffering from Stockholm syndrome, keep coming back demanding taxation of those completely without representation.

The only thing better than taxing people who live in another state is the ability to pretend that taxes are being paid by people in another country. Tariffs or custom fees have long been dishonestly advertised as a tax on foreigners. In fact if France wants to sell perfume for a hundred dollars, and the US government tacks on a fifty-dollar tax or tariff, consumers pay that fifty dollars when we buy perfume. France doesn't pay it. We do. Raising customs duties raises taxes on American consumers. Now, someone does win when tariffs are raised. Those American businesses that make similar perfume may now raise their prices by up to fifty dollars and yet remain competitive with the French perfume. Consumers who buy French perfume pay an extra fifty dollars in taxes. Consumers who buy American perfume (much better, I am sure) pay an additional fifty dollars to the nice businessman who makes perfume and must spend at least ten dollars a bottle of perfume contributing to congressmen who keep tariffs high so he can pocket forty bucks a bottle of sheer politically manufactured profit. This has traditionally been popular with politicians who gain campaign contributions (or direct payments in suitcases, in less fastidious nations) and can pose as patriotic supporters of domestic manufacturers, who vote unlike those French-type people.

Another one is the "jock tax," which hits successful baseball, football, hockey, and basketball players, as well as rock stars and the less famous people who tape their cords to the floor. They all find states and cities claiming a piece of their annual incomes based on their appearing in a stadium once a year playing sports or instruments. A small percentage of a big salary is worth the effort, and these people don't stick around to vote in your elections.

One variation on the theme of taxing folks who live in other states and cannot vote against you is to follow taxpayers fleeing your jurisdiction and taxing them. California competes at the Olympic level at this sport. They followed an inventor, Gilbert Hyatt, for years after he fled to Nevada (no income tax) and claimed he thought of his invention—which was worth hundreds of millions—while still in California. They sent police into his new state to spy on him. This irritated Nevada and the whole thing went to the Supreme Court, and in *Kappos v. Hyatt* California lost. Still, California has refused to pay the fines levied by the court. California has not given up on the quest to pursue tax refugees.

Five: The Perfect Tax

The federal excise tax on long-distance phone calls, imposed to pay for the Spanish-American War in 1898, is the quintessence of tax increases. A golfer's hole in one. A trifecta at the track. Erica Jong's "zipless" tax hike. Everything a young, budding politician longs to achieve. Michelangelo's *David*. A thing of beauty. Perfection itself.

The tax was "on the rich." It was a tax on long-distance phone calls billed by time of call and distance. In 1898 only 680,800 Americans had phones.[2] The phone had only recently been invented in 1876, by Alexander Graham Bell. They cost a bundle. As much as $44 to rent one phone for a year (around $1,222 in today's dollars), not including usage costs. Thus only "the rich" had phones. Only the really rich made long-distance phone calls. And the tax would be stuck on your phone bill, so it was not very visible. And this was a tax to pay for a war. The nasty Spanish had attacked us (or something) and we certainly had to defend ourselves by conquering Cuba, Puerto Rico, and the Philippines and Guam and Saipan. It was national defense. It was patriotic. And because wars against "empires" as weak as the Spanish one don't last very long...this would be a temporary tax. Promise.

A tax on the rich. (check) A hidden tax. (check) A tax for war. (check) A temporary tax. (check)

All this fun was ruined by the Republican takeover of the House and Senate in 1994. Most of the new congressmen had gone to public schools. But someone had been watching one of the History Channel shows and learned that the Spanish-American War had been over for some time. And as politicians, they also noticed that what was once a tax on the rich was now a tax paid by almost every single American. Over 95 percent of Americans now had phones. So the Republicans passed a law to end the temporary wartime measure tax on the rich. And Bill Clinton, tribune of the masses, vetoed it. So the tax remained. It was well hidden in the cluster of small print at the bottom of our phone bills. It was the FET—the Federal Excise Tax.

Remember the film *The Hellstrom Chronicle*, where they tell us that cockroaches will survive even a nuclear war? The Federal Excise Tax on phones to pay for the Spanish-American War gave the cockroaches a run for their money in the immortal department.

Eventually, the phone companies that had the privilege of collecting the federal excise tax from their consumers and shipping the cash—about $6 billion a year—to the wise stewards of our national treasury noticed something. The wording of the law that imposed this phone tax said the tax was to be levied on phone bills charged by distance "and" length of call. By 2000, calls were billed by the length of the phone call, not the distance. The federal government went to court fourteen times arguing that while the law said "time and distance," what they really meant was "time or distance." These are the guys who made fun of Bill Clinton's "it depends on what the definition of 'is' is." Eventually George W. Bush's secretary of the treasury, John W. Snow, threw in the towel and stopped trying to collect the tax.

There was some talk by the political class that it should be buried in Arlington National Cemetery as the longest-lasting survivor of the Spanish-American War. Others at the IRS wanted to replace the statue of Nathan Hale, now uncomfortably close to the IRS building, with a tribute to this almost perfect tax.

Six: Sin Taxes

One of the great tricks of the tax collectors is to present their lust for your money as a virtue. They will now tax "sin." Being "against sin" suggests the tax collectors are themselves virtuous. Taxes on liquor, beer, wine, cigarettes, gambling are taxes on sin. They will help you—or others—fight temptation. Taxes can make you healthy. Thin. They are your friend. They are an active good. Learn to love the bridle.

Two problems with this narrative: A government that heavily taxes liquor is a silent partner in every liquor company. If liquor is not sold in massive quantities, the government is short on cash. When the stock market crashed in 1929, and income tax collections fell, it only took the cash-starved politicians four years to repeal the Eighteenth Amendment, which had created Prohibition, and bring back legal spirits, beer, and wine. It wasn't about sin. It was about money.

Cigarette companies net *63 cents profit* on every pack of cigarettes.[3] The federal government "earns" $1.01 on a pack of cigarettes in federal taxes, and every state has a state tax averaging about $1.54 cents per pack. Who has the greater interest in cigarette sales?

In state after state the advocates of "public health"—and unsurprisingly, the beneficiaries of spending on same—demand higher taxes on tobacco to stop teen smoking. When the then-governor of South Carolina, Mark Sanford, insisted that a tobacco-tax increase advertised as a means to depress demand for cigarettes be married to a cut in the income tax—so that there would be no net tax hike on citizens—those who pretended to care about teen smoking bared their teeth and lost all interest in the "health" of citizens. They refused the revenue-neutral tax trade. They wanted the money and "health," or "teen smoking" was a smoke screen.

This was most recently and clearly exposed when companies invented "vapor" products such as e-cigarettes which do not put smoke in your lungs. Ninety-plus percent of the health concerns of tobacco were eliminated by the new products. And now two states are already taxing e-cigarettes. They are taxing the healthier alternative. To discourage health? They want the money. They fear citizens will shift from taxed and less healthy cigarettes to untaxed vapor products—and those patrons of our public health are unhappy with this. State legislators who once demanded higher taxes in the name of public health are now demanding higher taxes at the expense of public health. They don't care. They could have starred in the 1996 film *Jerry Maguire*. "Show me the money!"

And as the appetite for your paycheck grows, the number of deadly and therefore taxable sins also grows. Now they want to tax plastic bags. Glass bottles. Soda pop. Candy. Fatty foods. E-cigarettes.

Seven: Lotteries

Government-run lotteries have many advantages as a way to part taxpayers from their money. They are "voluntary." Sort of. First the government bans privately run lotteries. Private lotteries that continue to exist outside the law—like the numbers racket run by organized crime—tend to have higher payouts. Government does not like competition. So if you wish to "play the numbers," you have one choice—the government's rigged game.

True, the mathematicians tell us that lotteries are a tax on people who cannot do math. Or less generously, a tax on stupid people. The payout is very small. The expected value is negative.

Still, most lotteries are sold to voters promising that they will bring in millions of dollars for, say, education and they are also sold as an alternative to other tax hikes.

Lotteries have a long history in America. During colonial times local governments would ask the governor for permission to run local lotteries to pay for a specific road or bridge. The lottery paid for what might otherwise have been paid for by taxes collected by the colonial government.

In Britain, lotteries paid for the Westminster Bridge, the British Museum, and part of the navy. About 7 percent of the cost of Britain's war against our independence was raised through lotteries.

In the United States lotteries were used to fund roads, canals, and bridges, as well as hospitals and schools. Economic historians Donald W. Gribbin and Jonathan J. Bean write, "Lotteries were so popular in the early 1800s that eight eastern states raised a total of $66.4 million in 1832. This amount was four times the federal expenditure of the same year."[4]

In the late 1880s, states began to phase out lotteries. Louisiana was the last in 1895. Gribbin and Bean give three reasons: First, stronger state governments had access to money from direct taxation. Second, there was revulsion to public scandals where there were exposés of lotteries being fixed or fake tickets sold. Third, religious and social reformers opposed lotteries because they were a form of gambling.[5]

State lotteries returned first in 1964 with the New Hampshire lottery. Other states followed. Illinois presents a good example of how the lottery was sold. It was promised the money would flow to education, but in fact it went into the general treasury. Money is fungible. And lotteries are no longer used instead of taxes. Lotteries in modern America are an add-on rather than a replacement for existing taxes.[6]

Eight: War Taxes . . . War Is the Health of the State

The history of wars saddling new taxes on the American people deserves its own chapter. And our next chapter does just that. But here let us simply note that "We must raise your taxes because of the war" is one of the more successful arguments for tax hikes. It wraps together the "emergency" excuse; hints that it is temporary, as wars are supposed to end at some point; deploys patriotism as a tax collector; and makes questioning of a new or higher tax an act of disloyalty. Powerful stuff. For this reason, writer Randolph Bourne wrote an essay during World War I titled "War Is the Health of the State."[7]

And one notes that politicians demanding sacrifice (read higher taxes) often employ the rhetoric of war to build support for their demands. Jimmy Carter wanted to raise taxes on energy and demanded we view the "energy crisis" as "the moral equivalent of war." We pay taxes to fund a "War on Cancer" begun by Richard Nixon and also Nixon's "War on Drugs." Declaring war is how a politician clears his throat to prepare for the next sentence—"and you will pay for it in higher taxes."

This was all predicted, and recommended by the American philosopher William James, in his 1910 essay, "The Moral Equivalent of War," where he notes with admiration that "war taxes are the only ones men never hesitate to pay, as the budgets of all nations show us." James then urges statists everywhere to replicate the ability of war to demand tax increases and the limits on individual liberty in order to fund and enable other nonmilitary demands and goals of the government.

Nine: Envy

Envy is one of the Seven Deadly Sins, falling sixth on the list, which includes wrath, avarice, sloth, pride, lust, envy, and gluttony. But the modern Democrat Party sees envy in a different light—as a political program.

Many new taxes or tax increases are imposed as taxes on "the rich." Not you. Them. The rich. Those we envy. Let's tax the lifestyles of the rich and famous.

One remembers Jimmy Carter ranting against the three-martini lunch as an argument for raising taxes by reducing the tax deductions for business lunches. Democrats in 1990 insisted on taxing yachts and expensive cars as part of the Bush 1990 "grand compromise." Obama talked a great deal about corporate jets.

Envy is a double-edged sword, able to be employed to either keep taxes high or raise them. Almost every tax cut proposed in the past thirty years has been attacked as cutting taxes "on the rich." Tax increases are sold as simply insisting that the rich "pay their fair share." The Reagan tax cuts were supposed to be tilted "to the rich," and the Clinton and Obama tax hikes were "only" on the top 2 or 1 percent.

The Reagan tax cuts, which cut marginal tax rates across the board roughly 25 percent for each bracket, were attacked as pro-rich. The left's argument became that all tax cuts are by definition tax cuts for the rich, even if everyone benefits.

The Reagan tax cuts spurred growth and actually increased both the total and the relative tax burden on higher-income earners. Now, this might lead smart liberals whose goal was to maximize tax revenue and government spending to support lower tax rates, because it does shift the burden to higher-income earners. But it doesn't. The goal isn't simply money to pay for government, it is to punish higher-income earners for the sin of achievement.

Or look at the George W. Bush tax cuts of 2001 and 2003. The 2001 tax cuts slowly rolled back the tax rate hikes of Clinton, and in 2003 the capital gains tax was cut from 20 percent to 15 percent and the second tax on dividends (already taxed once at the corporate level) was dropped from 35 percent to 15 percent.

In the first four years of the combined Bush tax cuts, from 2003 to 2007, the total dollars paid by Americans earning more than $1 million a year increased from $132 billion to $310 billion.[8] Looking only at the superrich, those earning more than $10 million, the tax take jumped from $35 billion to $111 billion in the period from 2003 to 2007.[9]

Looking at the sweep of history from just before Reagan to 2004 after the Bush tax cuts were fully in effect, the top tax rate for individuals fell from 70 percent to 35 percent, and the top 1 percent increased the percentage of total taxes they paid from 19 percent to 36 percent. The top 10 percent saw their share of the tax burden jump from 49 percent to 68 percent.[10]

In 2007, just before the Fannie Mae and Freddie Mac financial collapse, the top 1 percent of income earners were earning 22 percent of all income and paying 40 percent of all income taxes.[11]

Envy helps to sell tax increases and to oppose tax reductions of any sort. But given the reality of the tax burden today, it doesn't pass the laugh test.

The reason a politician says he will tax only "the rich" is to convince most Americans they should pay no attention to a coming tax. This won't hurt you.

The many taxing the few is easier in a democratic system, where we have rule by the majority. Fifty-one percent could always vote to loot 49 percent. But that doesn't give a politician much room for error. Better to think along the lines of 98 to 2, as Clinton did, or even more cautiously 99 to 1, as Obama did.

Of course, "the rich" are not a fixed small group of people.

Two factors have a big impact on whether you are in the top 20 percent, the top quintile of earners, or the bottom.

Your age and how many people in your family work.

Think of your own life and that of your parents and children. How much did you earn when you were twenty, how about when you were fifty, and how much after you retired? In 2006, the median family income for a head of household age twenty was about $20,000.[12] At age fifty it tops $70,000. And by seventy-eight it was just below $30,000. The same person is poor, rich, and then poor as he or she passes through life. So how would a politician peddling envy instruct that voter to cast his or her ballot?

And within a family, if the wife and husband both work, that family is likely to be denounced—and taxed—by Obama and

Clinton as rich when they are simply two quite hardworking married people. The top 20 percent of families with the highest income have an average of 2.1 workers in the family. The bottom fifth has half a worker per family on average. The second quintile has 1.1; the third, 1.45; and the fourth, 1.8.[13] The more workers per family, the higher the income of the family. This is not a plot by the Rockefellers.

The rich are not always rich. Looking at those Americans who reported and paid taxes on incomes over $1 million between 1999 and 2007, we find that half of those reporting at least $1 million in income did so in only one of the nine years.[14] Fifteen percent earned $1 million for only two years. Maybe they sold a business, a home, or a stock. They are not the Kennedy kids clipping coupons. Only 6 percent of those reporting $1 million in income did so in every year between 1999 and 2007.[15]

And how do we compare with other nations? The share of taxes paid by the richest 10 percent of Americans is 45 percent. In "socialist" Sweden, 27 percent. Japan, 29 percent. Britain, 39 percent. Those Bolsheviks to our north in Canada: 36 percent. The average of all OECD nations is 32 percent.

The United States has a more "progressive" tax structure than any of the major nations in Europe.[16]

Ten: Trickle-down Taxation

In his 1984 acceptance speech at the Democratic National Convention, Walter Mondale announced that if elected president, he would raise taxes. He lost the Electoral College 525–13, carrying only the District of Columbia and his home state of Minnesota.

Since then the two Democrats who won the presidency have promised that to pay for larger government, they would only raise taxes on "the rich." Bill Clinton defined the rich as the top 2 percent of income earners.

In September 2008, candidate Barack Obama said, "I can make a firm pledge. Under my plan, no family making less than $250,000 a year will see any form of tax increase. Not your income tax, not your payroll tax, not your capital gains taxes, not any of your taxes."[17]

In the 2012 election year, President Obama again promises to only target individuals earning more than $250,000—but his public statements on raising taxes focus on those earning more than $1 million a year. In theory this could be a winning political argument. The many might be convinced to allow the politicians to tax the few.

Yet the GOP congressional landslides in 1994, 2010, and 2014 suggest that American voters have figured out that politicians are once again practicing "trickle-down taxation." They're getting elected by promising to tax only the rich and then extending new and higher taxes to the middle class.

During the 2011 debate on combining tax hikes and spending to reduce the deficit by $2.5 trillion, Scott Rasmussen's polling found that 75 percent of Americans were convinced that any deal in Congress would actually increase taxes on the middle class.[18]

Even with the president promising to tax only the rich, why did 75 percent of Americans believe they were the ultimate targets of any threatened tax hike? The history of trickle-down taxation over the last hundred years and the last two Democratic administrations suggests an answer.

The Alternative Minimum Tax was imposed in 1969 because 155 households investing in municipal bonds reportedly paid little or no federal income tax. This tax on the rich, who were paying what the president and others call a "fair share," now affects four million households. The budget Obama put forward for 2013 anticipated the Alternative Minimum Tax would hit fully 31 million taxpayers—raising $120 billion—when the Bush tax cuts lapsed. This was largely avoided by the legislation that made 85 percent of the Bush tax cuts permanent for 99 percent of Americans. Yet here a tax on 155 rich people has trickled down to hit millions—and almost tens of millions—of Americans.

The personal income tax, made possible by the Sixteenth Amendment, also promised to be a tax on the wealthiest Americans. It began in 1913 with a top rate of 7 percent, which hit only those with a taxable income of $500,000 or more. (According to the Bureau of Labor Statistics inflation calculator, that would be $11.5 million now.) Fewer than 4 percent of Americans paid income tax in its first years. Today, roughly half of American families pay the personal income tax. The bottom rate is 10 percent. Higher than the top rate in 1913.

Politicians at the state level have also played trickle-down taxation. Maine imposed an income tax in 1969, and the tax that once only hit folks earning more than $308,000 in today's dollars now hits Mainers with a rate of 8.5 percent and kicks in at $19,950. Almost everyone in Maine is now "rich."

More recently, Bill Clinton's promise to tax only the top 2 percent lasted about six months before the administration demanded tax increases on every single American in the form of a tax on electricity and a tax on gasoline. Mr. Clinton then replaced those taxes with a gasoline-tax increase of 4.3 cents per gallon. Everyone who drove a car was suddenly, magically rich.

Barack Obama's promise to tax only the rich in the 2008 campaign had a shorter shelf life: He signed his first tax increase sixteen days into the presidency—on cigarette smokers, a group whose average annual income was $36,000.[19] One year later, Obamacare imposed at least seven new or higher taxes that directly hit middle-income Americans—including the individual-mandate excise tax, the "medicine cabinet tax" on health savings accounts and Flexible Spending Accounts, and even an indoor-tanning tax.[20]

When a proposal for higher taxes goes directly to the people, voters often recognize trickle-down taxation for what it is. In Washington State—which has no income tax—voters were asked in November 2010 if they wanted to create an income tax, but one that would hit only individuals earning more than $200,000. They voted no to this virtual carbon copy of Mr. Obama's definition of the rich, and it was a landslide: 64 percent to 35 percent.[21]

One hopes that more American taxpayers focus on this pattern of trickle-down taxation. Such tactics do have a shelf life. There is a reason the Greeks did not conquer the rest of Asia Minor with the Trojan horse trick that worked so well the first time.

Eleven: Economic Downturns: Permanent Tax Hikes

Politicians raise taxes during economic downturns, "to maintain public services." But then when the economy recovers the government gets a bump up in its revenue that is permanent. Recessions, like wars, tend to become arguments for higher taxes that become permanent hikes in total taxation and spending. The recession of 1894 brought back the Civil War income tax for a trial run. It would have stayed forever—even though the economy recovered by 1897—if it was not struck down in 1895 by the Supreme Court. The Great Depression became an argument for hiking taxes to make up for lost revenue due to a weak economy. Hoover increased income taxes from the post–World War II top rate of 25 percent to 75 percent. Later, under FDR, a constitutional amendment was rushed through to end Prohibition so that liquor taxes could return.

Almost every recession has seen the federal government and states increase taxes. Then, when the economy recovered, the new taxes and higher tax rates stayed higher and sucked up a larger percentage of the national economy.

In the 1982 recession, twenty-one states raised taxes. In Washington D.C., the Democrat House and the Bob Dole Republican Senate pushed through the 1982 set of fifty-five tax hikes past Reagan.[22] The economy rebounded in 1983, and those "recession" tax hikes remained.

The economic slowdown of 1969 saw Nixon and the Democrat House and Senate pass "tax reform" that was a tax hike, the creation of the Alternative Minimum Tax (AMT) and the extension of the income tax surtax. America got a recession and all I got was this stinking AMT tax.

Twelve: The New Tax Will Provide More Services

In 1960, nineteen states did not have a statewide income tax, thirty-one did. Over the following thirty-one years eleven of the nineteen decided to impose one: West Virginia in 1961, Indiana in 1963, Michigan in 1967, Nebraska in 1968, Illinois in 1969, Maine in 1969, Pennsylvania in 1971, Rhode Island in 1971, Ohio in 1972, New Jersey in 1976, and finally Connecticut in 1991.

One state, Alaska, went the other way, ending its state income tax in 1980.

How did the eleven states get sold on enacting a state income tax?

One of the strongest arguments for a state income tax was to wax eloquent about all the government services that would flow from the income tax revenues. More money would improve education, health and hospital services, police protection, reduce poverty and build more roads. To reread these promises one gets the impression the salesmen were double and triple spending the same anticipated tax dollar over and over again but before different audiences.

But in a wonderful new book, *An Enquiry into the Nature and Causes of the Wealth of States*, economists Art Laffer, Steve Moore, Travis Brown, and Rex Singquefield and company decided to look at the facts. What did happen to spending and quality of services in the eleven states after they crossed the river Styx and became income tax states?

Did imposing an income tax improve education in the eleven states? The study looks at reading and math test scores for fourth graders and eighth graders. Ranked against the other states, three of the new-income-tax states improved on fourth-grade reading and seven worsened,[23] three by more than 2 percent down.[24] For math three states improved, seven got worse, four much worse.[25]

And for eighth-grade mathematics scored relative to other states, seven of the new-income-tax states worsened.[26]

Looking at the number of health and hospital personnel per 10,000 state citizens, we find that of the eleven states four improved their ratios compared with those of other states and seven lost ground, four of the seven rather dramatically.[27]

Maybe crime went down in the new-income-tax states relative to other states now that there was so much more money for police? Three of the states saw their violent crime rates as measured by the FBI fall, eight had increases.[28] And on the measure of property crimes, such as robbery, four saw a reduction in the rate of property crimes compared with the national average, one (Illinois) was unchanged, and in six, property crimes increased.[29]

OK, maybe all the money was spent alleviating poverty so there wasn't any for education or police. Of the eleven new-income-tax states, three saw their relative levels of poverty decline, eight saw them increase.[30]

Now, don't leave us yet. Maybe the money was all spent on highways. Looking at Reason Foundation's comparison of state highway systems, we learn that five states saw their highways improve relative to those of other states. Six saw declines. The declines were larger than the improvements.[31]

The income tax did not bring noticeable improvements relative to the other states—and some decline—in education, crime reduction, poverty, and highways.

Higher taxes do not translate into more services or better services or better outcomes compared with those of other states. Why?

Higher tax rates—particularly on income—do bring in more money from every dollar earned in the state. The state used to get zero in income tax, and now it would get 1.5 percent in Connecticut and 5.25 percent in Rhode Island the first year the income tax was imposed. But over time taxes slow economic growth, and the state's gross state product—total income of its citizens—declined relative to the other thirty-nine states after the eleven imposed an income tax. The new-income-tax states saw their economic growth decline relative to the other thirty-nine.[32] By 2012 every single state was producing a smaller percentage of the national income than it was before. Every one. The drop ranged from 18 percent in Connecticut, which had lived with the new income tax only since 1991, or for twenty-one years.[33] This compared to Pennsylvania, which declined 38 percent after thirty-one years with the income tax, and West Virginia with forty-one years of a new income tax fell by 50 percent.[34]

And total tax revenue in the eleven states also fell relative to the other thirty-nine states.[35] Every last one of them raised less revenue compared with the other states in 1992 than when they first imposed the new income tax. Again, Connecticut and New Jersey, which were the most recent additions to the state income tax club, fell "only" 4 and 3 percent.[36] By 2012, Pennsylvania's total tax revenue compared with the other thirty-nine states fell 28 percent, Illinois 24 percent, and Michigan 46 percent compared with where they stood on the day they first imposed an income tax forty-one, forty-three, and forty-five years earlier, respectively.[37] The British used to hang pirates near busy seaports and leave the corpses to rot over time as a disincentive to would-be pirates. The eleven states that were fooled by politicians into imposing an income tax with sweet promises of more spending on the "general welfare" now serve the same purpose in warning the remaining "no-income-tax states" against such false advertisements.

Thirteen: The Forgotten Man—the Taxpayer

A key part of most schemes to raise taxes is to focus the public's attention away from the taxpayers who will foot the bill. The taxpayer becomes "The Forgotten Man" of Yale philosopher William Graham Sumner's essay of January 1883.

Sumner's essay explained how the progressives of his day tricked citizens into paying for the social programs of the elite:

As soon as A observes something which seems to him to be wrong, from which X is suffering, A talks it over with B and A and B then propose to get a law passed to remedy the evil and help X. Their law always proposes to determine what C shall do for X or, in the better case, what A, B, and C shall do for X. As for A and B, who get a law to make themselves do for X what they are willing to do for him, we have nothing to say except that they might better have done it without any law, but what I want to do is to look up C. I want to show you what manner of man he is. I call him the Forgotten Man. Perhaps the appellation is not strictly correct. He is the man who never is thought of...He works, he votes, generally he prays—but he always pays....[38]

Amity Shlaes wrote a powerful history of the Great Depression and how Hoover and FDR raised taxes and federal spending to new peacetime heights, which she titled *The Forgotten Man*. She writes in the book's introduction that "in 1932, a member of Roosevelt's brain trust, Ray Moley recalled the phrase, although not its provenance. He inserted it into the candidate's first great speech. If elected, Roosevelt promised, he would act in the name of the 'forgotten man at the bottom of the economic pyramid.' Whereas C had been Sumner's forgotten man, the New Deal made X the forgotten man—the poor man, the old man, labor or any other recipient of government help."[39]

Clever to put the focus on the beneficiary of the spending—the person or group whose political support you wish to purchase and, through misdirection, avoid any focus on the taxpayer who foots the bill for the politicians' vote buying. If you listen to most tax-and-spend politicians, it certainly sounds as if the politician himself was the benefactor. How often have you read that a politician like Teddy Kennedy or Franklin Roosevelt was "generous" and "caring" because he took money from taxpayers and gave it to others for the political benefit of themselves? Charity would have been spending some of their own considerable wealth.

Franklin Roosevelt's adviser Harry Hopkins was quoted in the *New York Times* in 1938 by reporter Arthur Krock as outlining the FDR administration's game plan: "We will spend and spend, and tax and tax, and elect and elect."[40]

This strategy works best if the attention of the nation is focused on the recipient of government spending and simultaneously directed away from the true forgotten man—the taxpayer.

Fourteen: Energy Taxes

Energy taxes are sin taxes, emergency taxes, and taxes on the other (Arabs, oil companies, blue-collar workers in red states such as Alaska and Texas), all rolled into one. They show the dexterity of tax hikers. My favorite trilogy began with the demand by the *Washington Post* editorialists that taxes on energy be increased because there were shortages and high energy prices. (Higher taxes would make people use less energy, and this would drop the cost of energy. Mind you that is what free-market prices do, but statists only like high prices mandated by the government.)

When Reagan did exactly what the editorialists did not want him to do—he deregulated oil prices—and the oil prices did just what the statists knew would never happen—they fell, the editorialists demanded we raise taxes on energy because lower energy prices would no longer force people to conserve in order to save money, because the prices had fallen. Later the price of oil was steady for several years, and the editorialists demanded we raise taxes on oil because prices were unchanging and therefore the market was not forcing people to do what their intellectual and moral betters (them) knew should be done.

High energy prices: raise taxes. Lower energy prices: raise taxes, Stable energy prices: raise taxes. Gee. At some point you might think they had a tax hike policy, not an energy policy.

CHAPTER 6

Even Good Wars Breed Taxes

War is the health of the State.

—*Randolph Bourne*

War and taxation are inextricably linked.

In ancient times the best way for a king to raise money was to conquer a neighboring kingdom and take over the business of taxing the subjects of the new kingdom as well as his own. Rome grew and got rich through conquest and plunder. In the Hundred Years' War between England and France the whole point was to take over more land and extract the taxes on the peasants there for one's own treasury rather than the other guys'. In the short term you did not have to be very nice to your new taxpayers. Smarter kings and emperors learned a rudimentary form of supply-side economics— you get more tax money by treating your tax subjects with some restraint. Overtaxation in America can lead to tax evasion and politicians losing the next election. In ancient Rome overtaxation by "tax farmers" led to rebellions that required the same people to be "reconquered" at great expense. Overtaxation could also be expensive for the tax collectors. In Asia Minor a tax revolt began with the assassination of eighty thousand Roman tax collectors. Low tax rates keep the peace, raise some money, and keep the cost of tax collection (paying your army) lower. The Roman legions were the business end of Rome's IRS.

Over time political leaders learned that you could make more money trading with other nations than attacking them, defeating them, and occupying and taxing them. Wars and occupations cost money. Maybe more than you could gain from taxing the losers of the war. And, one must remember, sometimes those who start wars of conquest lose. Risk is bad. High front-loaded costs of wars are bad. The world moved to trade rather than conquest as a means to wealth. Looting one's own citizens is easier and cheaper than building an empire. It is called taxation, and it is legal, and no one holds war-crimes trials.

In modern times, the connection between wars and taxes is that wars cost money. Lots of money. If you want to fight a war—or are attacked and not quite given much of a choice in the matter—then you must shift present government spending to the military, raise taxes, and/or borrow money. If you choose to borrow, the day will come when those debts must be paid back—-with tax money.

American history began with an example of this. Britain fought a twenty-year war with the French and had to borrow heavily to do so. At the conclusion of the French and Indian Wars in the Western Hemisphere (cannot say "America" yet) the British government was heavily in debt and was looking to raise taxes on someone to pay for the sunk costs of victory. The relatively wealthy and "undertaxed" American colonists seemed like a good target. When Britain passed the Stamp Act requiring that a stamp be bought (a tax paid) and affixed to all legal documents, it began the conflict with the American colonists that led to the war for American independence.

The War of 1812

Before the American Civil War most money raised to pay for the costs of the United States national government came from tariffs collected on imported goods and the sale of land owned by the federal government to settlers moving west. There were some internal taxes—taxes on distilled spirits, and even a Stamp Tax—but those were unpopular and were abolished. They came back briefly to pay for the War of 1812—the war's costs trumped the unpopularity of those taxes—but then they lapsed again when the war ended.

The Civil War

The Civil War brought the first income tax to America. Twice. The Union first imposed an income tax on August 5, 1861. The Confederacy followed on April 24, 1863, creating a progressive individual income tax, which taxed "unearned" income higher than wages and a progressive corporate income tax. And income tax withholding made its first appearance for government employees of the North. (Britain had imposed an income tax back in 1799 to pay for the war with Napoleon.) Certainly had there been no Civil War, there would have been no income tax in the 1860s in the North or the South.

The Union imposed the first death tax.

The Union's income tax was increased to 10 percent of all income over $10,000 with the June 30, 1864, tax hike. Tying taxes to national patriotism, Congress returned on July 4 and hiked all tax rates on income over $600 by 5 percent on top of the previous week's tax increase.

First the South and then the North reached back into the medieval past and brought back an ancient form of tax: forced labor. Conscription for the military, the draft, was imposed by the South in 1862, and then by the North in March 1863, and subjected all men between the ages of twenty and thirty-five to the draft. One must serve or pay a $300 tax. The government needed the money more than it needed the extra man. Remember that taxation paid in coin had been a great leap forward over conscripted labor—the serf worked a day a week for the lord and was required to fight in his wars for free. Taxes paid in currency leaves the taxpayer alone to decide how to raise the cash. Conscripting labor does not. Opposition to the draft led to the New York Draft Riot of 1863, which left more than one hundred dead.

The Civil War put the income tax, the idea of income tax withholding, the death tax, and forced labor—the draft—into American history. They all ended with the end of the war...but they would be back. The South's taxes died with the Confederacy. The Union income tax continued until 1870. The Union's death tax died in 1871. The bulk of the excise taxes lapsed in 1871. We were largely returning to normalcy, but the body politic was infected. Politicians learned that Americans will pay new and dramatically higher taxes in time of war for national survival.

The government grew. Federal government employment before the Civil War in 1861 was 5,837 and the federal budget was $63 million. Six years after the war ended, in 1867, federal employment was 15,344 and the federal budget was $358 million.[1] This time, the government did not completely shrink back to its previous size as it had after the War of 1812.

World War I

World War I saw the federal government grow in power and taxing authority to unimagined levels. And when the war was over, the government once again stood larger than ever before.

The income tax was made constitutional in 1913 with the enactment of the Sixteenth Amendment, and Congress moved with some speed to enact the first income tax that year. The early income tax was cute...like a baby lion. The top rate (including surtax) was 7 percent. The first $4,000 was exempt from tax; $600 was an average year's pay. So less than 2 percent of Americans were required to pay the income tax, and it raised less than 10 percent of the federal government's revenues.

World War I influenced American tax policy before America

entered the war. The disruption in trade with Europe reduced tariff revenue, and so the War Revenue Act of 1914 raised stamp taxes and alcohol taxes. The tax was to sunset on December 31, 1915. The war in Europe continued, and the Revenue Act of 1916 raised the top income tax rate from 7 to 13 percent. The War Revenue Act passed on October 3, 1917, increased the top income tax rate from 13 to 50 percent. The Revenue Act of 1918 raised the income tax to a base rate of 12 percent on incomes above $5,000 and the top rate was 77 percent. Peacetime and the election of Republicans Harding and Coolidge along with Treasury Secretary Mellon cut taxes each year to bring the top rate down to 25 percent.

Before World War I, in 1913, 358,000 Americans paid the income tax. The top rate was 7 percent. In 1920, two years after the war was over, 5.5 million income tax returns were filed in a nation with 106 million citizens. And the top income tax rate in 1925 stood at 25 percent, three times as high as in 1913. War is the health of the state. More Americans were paying income taxes and rates were higher long after the war ended.

America was not better off for having entered World War I, but the government was.

The First World War was not a war for national survival as was the War of Independence and the Civil War. It is therefore all the more powerful to watch the campaign to conscript the entire nation into a sense of self-sacrifice and obedience in service of the war. Patriotism, President Wilson knew, could bring a nation under his control. In the 2008 book *War and Taxes* authors Steven A. Bank, Kirk J. Stark, and Joseph J. Thorndike summarize their study of taxes and World War I with "It was the war, though, that brought the income tax to the forefront in modern public finance. The transition from an almost exclusive reliance on customs duties to a substantial reliance on internal revenues, such as the income tax, the estate tax, and excise taxes, could not have occurred without the demand for fiscal sacrifice that accompanied wartime politics. But this process did not flow naturally from the public mood in support of the war. Rather for the first time, the notion of wartime fiscal sacrifice was cultivated, marketed, and sold to the American public."[2]

One effort, run by the "Committee on Public Information," was a PR campaign in which the "Four Minute Men," hundreds of volunteers organized by newspaper editor George Creel, went out to give four-minute speeches in movie houses—it took four minutes to change the reels of film—-linking the paying of income taxes with victory in the war.

The draft was brought back in May 1917, but deliberately given a "kindler, Gentler" name: "Selective Service." President Wilson said this was to change how conscription was viewed from "a conscription of the unwilling" to a "selection from a nation which has volunteered in mass."[3] Two million and seven hundred thousand Americans would be drafted for World War I.[4] And politicians used the conscription they voted into existence to argue for higher taxes on those not drafted. If they must sacrifice their bodies, you should be willing to sacrifice your income. In a phrase echoed by many politicians, Kansas Republican Edward Little argued that conscription of the young should be matched by conscription of wealth. "Let their dollars die for their country too."[5] Others referred to income taxation as "conscription of income."

Columbia economist Edwin Seligman pointed out that unlike the taxes raised to pay for the Civil War, 74 percent of the taxes raised in 1917 targeted wealth and another 13 percent hit "luxurious or harmful consumption."[6] While Wilson was funding his war, he used the tax code to divide Americans by income class and targeted excise taxes in an early version of both the politics of envy and the nanny state.

World War II

World War II saw the income tax, once a tax on the few, become a tax on almost everyone. By 1945, 90 percent of American workers were filing income tax returns. For comparison, in 1929, when times were good and before the stock market collapse removed many from the tax rolls, only 3 percent of Americans over the age of twenty were paying income taxes. The top rate would jump to 94 percent for the highest income earners. The corporate income tax, which had the advantage of being invisible to consumers—the taxes paid by companies silently increased costs and dropped wages— also gained in size and cost. By 1943 a combination of the corporate income tax plus the "excess profits tax" could hit 95 percent on the marginal dollar earned. Corporate income taxes raised about a third of total wartime taxes.

Franklin Delano Roosevelt campaigned in support of new and higher taxes just as had Woodrow Wilson in World War I. He said, in his Four Freedoms speech on January 6, 1941, "I have called for personal sacrifice…a part of the sacrifice means the payment of more money in taxes." One notes the "four freedoms" highlighted in the speech were the selling points for the actual goal of the speech: reducing freedom through higher taxes.

While demanding unity in fighting the Axis, Roosevelt used the war and its annual tax-increase bills as part of his campaign to divide Americans by "class" and use that division to demand more progressive taxation. He even floated the idea of putting an overall limit on what an American could earn: On April 27, 1942, he said to Congress, "In time of this great national danger, when all excess income should go to win the war, no American citizen ought to have a net income, after he has paid his taxes, of more than $25,000 a year."[7] Ideas put forward in wartime return in peacetime. Thirty years later George McGovern would argue that every American should have any of his life savings above $500,000 confiscated by the government through the estate tax.[8]

And as in World War I, the government ran an extensive propaganda campaign, not dropping leaflets over occupied Europe but instead here at home. The government had Irving Berlin write a song, "I Paid My Income Tax Today" with the lyrics

I paid my income tax today
I never felt so proud before
To be right there with the millions more
Who paid their income tax today
I'm squared up with the U.S.A.
You see those bombers in the sky?
Rockefeller helped to build 'em, so did I
I paid my income tax today.[9]

And it worked. In February 1944 a Gallup Poll asked, "Do you regard the income tax which you will have to pay this year as fair?" It was answered yes by 90 percent of Americans.[10] Compare with today when the same question gets 54 percent.[11] The separate income tax of 5 percent on income over $624, enacted in 1942, was named the Victory tax. "Victory" sounds better than "income." Later we would have the "Patriot Act."

The draft was reinstated in 1940. This was a peacetime draft. America was not at war. Emergency measures passed in war tend to become viewed by government as their rightful power. The wartime draft of the Civil War and World War I became the peacetime draft enacted in 1940 when Roosevelt was running for reelection on the boast that "he kept us out of War." Forced labor—once viewed as part of the barbarism of the Middle Ages and replaced by the advance of civilization with taxes paid in coin—returned.

Mr. Roosevelt's peacetime draft would become a wartime draft in 1941–45. World War II would end, yet the draft continued through 1973, when it was ended by President Nixon. To this day, advocates of massive government expansion look to the draft as a cheap way to increase the number of government workers. Now it is proposed as "national service."

And as in World War I, the draft was used to explain why your taxes are so high. We draft your son, so now we "draft" your income.

World War II also left a lasting legacy in implementing "withholding" of income taxes. Before 1943 Americans had to save up what they expected to owe in federal income taxes and write a check on April 15. But now millions more Americans were being pushed into the income tax system. Could people really be expected to save ahead for their full income tax liability, particularly given how much the government planned to increase that burden? Withholding both hides the true cost of taxation and makes it easier to collect more taxes from more taxpayers.

Withholding was not a new concept in 1943. The 5 percent Victory tax of 1942 was withheld by employers at the source, as were Social Security taxes. Initiating the withholding of income tax at the very same time that it was to explode in its number of "participants"—and total burden—has had lasting effects. Withholding did not end with the war but continues to this day. Imagine the size of Tea Party rallies if every American had to walk to the post office on April 15 with a check (and actually have that much money in their checking account) for their entire income tax and Social Security tax liabilities. The present level of government taxing and spending would not be sustainable. Congressman Dick Armey (R-Texas) once suggested that taxpayers send in their tax payments on a monthly basis as we do our electric bills. Everyone got the joke that this would lead to riots.

Before World War II, in the year 1940, 14.7 million Americans paid income taxes. In 1948 after the war was over, 52 million Americans were filing income tax.[12] The top income tax rate was 79 percent before the war, and 94 percent both during the war and at the end of it.[13] The top tax rate was 91 percent in 1963—eighteen years after the end of the war. Withholding is still with us.

Before the war, in 1940, after a decade of Hoover/Roosevelt peacetime spending, the federal government employed 699,000 Americans[14] and spent 9.6 percent of GDP.[15] After the war, in 1946, the federal government employed 2.2 million Americans[16] and spent 24.2 percent of GDP.[17]

Men are wounded and die in wars. The state thrives.

The Korean War saw taxes jump up, but also Truman demanded

some across-the-board spending restraint in the rest of the government. Most of the Korean War tax hikes have been rescinded since.

The Vietnam War

The Vietnam War has a bitter tax legacy. Johnson was loath to raise taxes to pay for his escalation from 189,000 to 500,000 American troops[18] in Vietnam because he thought it might discredit his recent massive new government programs, specifically Medicaid and Medicare in 1965. Richard Nixon inherited the Vietnam War when he won the 1968 election. Reinforcing the notion that he was a foreign policy president who brilliantly divided China from the Soviet Union but had little or no understanding of domestic economics, Nixon begged Congress to continue the 10 percent surtax put in place temporarily in 1968.[19]

The liberal Democrats in Congress demanded "tax reform" in return for their support for such a tax hike. (Does this sound a tad strange for those of us used to the post-Reagan partisan alignment of the parties on the tax issue? Can we imagine a Republican demanding higher taxes from a Democrat Congress to continue the policies of a previous Democrat and being willing to make taxes even more "progressive" and higher to buy their support?)

As strange as it sounds, this is what happened. Nixon agreed to impose a "Minimum Tax"—now known as the Alternative Minimum Tax—as part of the 1969 "tax reform" bill. This soak-the-rich tax was supposed to hit 155 high-income Americans who paid no income tax. These are people who invested all their savings in government bonds, whose interest payments are exempt from taxes (as a favor to the national, state, and local governments). The AMT soon grew to hit millions of families. In 2001 a patch was placed on the AMT to hide its true breadth and temporarily keep it from hitting tens of millions. And without the Bush tax cuts becoming permanent, the AMT would have hit 27 million in 2013.[20]

Iraq and Afghanistan

And now we come to the wars in Iraq and Afghanistan and the subsequent occupations of those two nations. Together they cost $620 billion between 2001 and 2007. They cost $170 billion in 2006 alone. All told, by the 2014 official date of Americans leaving Iraq, the cost of the two wars and the occupations was nearly $2 trillion.[21]

The wars cost money and lives. The occupations that followed for a decade were the bulk of the financial cost.

One noticed during those wars that the Democrats were beside themselves attacking George W. Bush for not raising taxes to pay for the wars. The loudest voices for higher taxes to "pay for the wars" came from left-of-center politicians who opposed the wars in the first and second place. They didn't want to pay for the wars. They wanted higher taxes that would continue after the wars and occupations had ended.

Obama telegraphed his plans to do just this on the spending side when he promised in the 2008 election that he would not spend an additional dollar on any new spending without reducing existing spending by a similar amount. Given his plans to dramatically increase government spending, how could he possibly say this? He was telling the truth—given one big assumption. He claimed to assume that spending on Iraq and Afghanistan—estimated at $2 trillion over the next ten years—would continue unchanged. So he could "cut" spending simply by leaving Iraq and Afghanistan on the same time schedule Bush had proposed.[22]

By this reasoning Jimmy Carter "cut spending a great deal" by not continuing to spend at the rate the federal government spent money in World War II. It was a ridiculous assertion. But one the establishment press accepted for the duration of the campaign.

After he was elected, Obama tried to use the savings from leaving Afghanistan and Iraq—again on the Bush timetable—as part of the Republican demand that he cut $2.5 trillion in spending if he wanted his $2.5 trillion debt increase.

At the time this author wondered what the heck Bush was doing in 2004 through 2009 by including the wartime spending in an "emergency spending" bill as if it was a flood or some unexpected expense. Why was a known and expected expenditure paid for outside the regular budget and why was it called an "emergency supplemental"? It wasn't an emergency. It was a wholly anticipated expense.

But here Bush was wise. Very wise. If he had put the spending for the Iraq and Afghanistan wars and subsequent occupations in the regular Pentagon budget, it would have gone into the "baseline budget," and after the wars and occupations ended, any future Congress and president could claim—with technical honesty—that they were not increasing spending beyond the projected budget.

Had the costs of Iraq and Afghanistan been in the baseline budget, they would have increased the total federal budget $1.6 trillion by 2015 alone.[23]

Bush may or may not have been wise to occupy Afghanistan and Iraq. But he was very wise not to raise taxes or put the extra spending into the baseline budget.

There was a further budget cost to the wars and occupations of Iraq and Afghanistan that lasted long after Bush left office. And that was the Republican loss of the 2006 House and Senate elections that put Harry Reid and Nancy Pelosi in control. The economy in 2006 was in its fourth year of strong economic growth, averaging 3.2 percent a year.[24]

But polling showed that the nation—and particularly Independents—had tired of the wars, and this cost the Republicans control of the House and Senate in 2006 and the presidency in 2008. Wars continue to be expensive. The Iraq and Afghanistan wars, certainly the occupations that followed, brought a Democrat Congress that resulted in TARP, the Stimulus, and Obamacare.

PART III

How We Restore Limited Government, Individual Liberty, and Economic Growth

CHAPTER 7

Stopping the Bleeding: The Taxpayer Protection Pledge

The Taxpayer Protection Pledge, the sword and shield of the Reagan Revolution, has been a powerful weapon against the tax-and-spenders in Washington, D.C., and state capitals.

One reason we know this is because we hear the screams of frustration when the Pledge stops them from getting more tax money to spend. They howl into the wind, damn the greedy taxpayers who would deny them their due, and lash out at those congressmen who stand with taxpayers against them. They have spent millions on dishonest television ads attacking signers of the Pledge. And when they cannot break pro-taxpayer congressmen, they have raged and whined at me for creating the Pledge.

"If only we could abolish, crush, or break the Taxpayer Protection Pledge," they believe, then "we" could get back to the business of bipartisan tax increases each year to fund ever bigger government.

They have a point. The Pledge *is* a strong guardrail against higher taxes and the higher spending that higher taxes would permit.

So, what is the Taxpayer Protection Pledge?

The Pledge is a simple written commitment signed by elected officials and candidates for office publicly promising the American people that they will "oppose and vote against" any efforts to increase taxes. (And not that we don't trust anyone, but the Pledge has space for two witnesses.) It is only fifty-eight words. Short. Simple. Easy to understand.

In 1985, Ronald Reagan asked me to run Americans for Tax Reform, the national organization created to support his drive to cut tax rates and simplify the tax code. I had started my life in Washington, D.C., as associate director and then executive director of the National Taxpayers Union in 1978, just as the tax revolt spread state by state from California's Proposition 13 across to Massachusetts's Proposition 2½. This was a dream job that became a life's work.

Reagan wanted a tax reform bill that was not a Trojan horse for tax increases. He wanted lower tax rates. Fewer special-interest tax deductions. No net tax hike.

Before 1986, "tax reform" was a code word for higher taxes. It was a favorite tactic of the left. Inside a promised reform would lurk a massive tax increase. With thousands of pages in the tax code, politicians could move around deductions, credits, rates, and exemptions like street hustlers playing Three-Card Monte. Each voter could imagine/hope that reform meant his or her taxes would go down. The spending interests had a goal, they planned for an end game that raised taxes to enable more spending. Politicians could campaign as tax reformers and govern as tax increasers. It worked too often: tricking American voters who wanted a simpler and lower tax burden into voting for congressmen and senators and governors who did the opposite once safely past the election and secure in power. Politicians could campaign promising to simplify and lower taxes, but in reality the changes would leave the government richer and the American people poorer.

But Reagan was determined to change this dynamic. He had campaigned in 1980 promising to cut tax rates 33 percent across the board. He meant it. The legislation he endorsed, the Kemp-Roth tax cut, was designed by New York congressman Jack Kemp and

Delaware senator William Roth. Reagan won the 1980 election on this platform. The bumper sticker read, "Republican Tax Cut: 33 percent." But after the 1980 election, Speaker Tip O'Neill and the Democrat majority in the House of Representatives opposed his tax cut. Rates were only cut about 25 percent, not 33 percent. The top rate did fall from 70 percent to 50 percent and the lowest rate fell from 14 percent to 11 percent. Unfortunately, the full tax cut did not take place immediately. Rather the cuts were delayed and only fully phased in over three years. This delayed the recovery.

Unemployment fell from 10.4 percent in January 1983, the month the tax cut was fully in place, to 8 percent in January 1984, 7.3 percent in January 1985, and 6.7 percent in January 1986. More than 3,458,000 jobs were created in 1983; 3,880,000 more in 1984; 2,502,000 in 1985; and 1,902,000 in 1986.[1]

Because he kept his word and cut taxes, and because those tax cuts created jobs and economic growth, Ronald Reagan was reelected in November 1984 with 59 percent of the vote, carrying forty-nine states with 525 electoral votes. Every state voted for Reagan except the Democrat candidate Walter Mondale's home state of Minnesota, which voted 49.72 percent for Mondale to 49.54 percent for Reagan.

Now it was 1985 and Reagan was determined to cut rates again.

I became the president of Americans for Tax Reform in the summer of 1985. Our goal was to pass what became the Tax Reform Act of 1986. The intention of the act was to reduce the complexity of the tax code, to eliminate many of the special-interest tax breaks that had accumulated like barnacles over the years, and to again reduce marginal tax rates on all Americans.

In the final version of the Tax Reform Act of 1986 the eleven tax rates in 1985 ranging from 11 to 50 percent were reduced to two tax rates, 15 and 28 percent. The personal exemption was increased so that a married couple with two children would pay no taxes on the first $13,000 in income.

But many congressmen still feared that at the last minute—despite the promise of revenue-neutral tax reform—the final package would emerge from a smoke-filled room with tax increases secreted inside the "reform."

I created the Taxpayer Protection Pledge to protect taxpayers from just this understandable concern.

The pledge reads as follows:

I, _____ pledge to the voters of the State of _____ and to the American people that I will:
    ONE, oppose and vote against any effort to increase marginal tax rates on businesses or individuals, and
    TWO, oppose and vote against any effort to eliminate further deductions or credits unless matched dollar for dollar by further tax rate reductions.

There is space below the pledge for a signature by the congressman or candidate for office and the two signatures by witnesses.

Before the final bill was brought to a final vote in the House on September 25 and in the Senate on September 27, 1986, one hundred congressmen and twenty senators signed the Taxpayer Protection Pledge promising the people of their states that they would oppose and vote against any legislation that was a net tax hike. Hundreds more candidates for office in 1986 ran making the same written commitment. Reagan promised to veto any net tax hike.

The Tax Reform Act of 1986 was passed. No net tax hike was hidden inside.

The power of the pledge was noticed.

In 1988, all the Republicans running for president signed the Taxpayer Protection Pledge—except for Senator Robert Dole of Kansas. Jack Kemp had signed the pledge as a congressman and cheerfully signed as a presidential candidate. Pete du Pont, the former governor of Delaware, who cut income tax rates in half as governor, signed the pledge on the steps of the New Hampshire capitol. Vice President Bush said he had a policy of not making pledges. But he recognized that the Taxpayer Protection Pledge was different. Powerful. And necessary. He wrote the exact Pledge wording in a public letter and signed it. He later famously announced it in this acceptance speech.

Senator Bob Dole won the Iowa caucuses, and many believed he was on his way to win the GOP nomination that year. But in the final debate before the New Hampshire primary on February 16, 1988, Pete du Pont handed Senator Dole the Taxpayer Protection Pledge, pointing out that all the other candidates had signed the pledge. On national television Dole recoiled from the Pledge as if someone had tossed a cross in a vampire's lap. The voters of New Hampshire were not happy to learn that Dole was open to higher taxes, and he lost the New Hampshire popular vote by nine percentage points, and went on to lose the nomination to Pledge taker George H. W. Bush.

While the Taxpayer Protection Pledge was not yet well known nationwide, in New Hampshire "The Pledge," a commitment by candidates for governor to oppose and veto any state income tax or broad-based sales tax, had long been a staple of New Hampshire politics. Meldrim Thomson Jr. served three terms as governor of New Hampshire from 1973 to 1979, created New Hampshire's Pledge, and first took it when running for governor in November 1972. Since then no one had ever been elected governor or won the Republican nomination without taking the Pledge.

I grew up in Massachusetts just south of New Hampshire and certainly had that successful and effective example in the back of my mind when I created the Taxpayer Protection Pledge for federal candidates.

Bush was losing the nomination until the Taxpayer Protection Pledge became front and center in that debate. Bush publicly committed to opposing all tax hikes. Dole refused. Bush won New Hampshire and changed the course of the primary elections.

Bush then won the Republican nomination, but he was running behind Massachusetts governor Mike Dukakis when he announced at the convention that he would run for Ronald Reagan's third term. "Read my lips," Bush said on August 18, 1988, standing before more than 2,200 Republican delegates in New Orleans: "No new taxes." The promise to oppose tax increases was now front and center in the general election.

Bush went on to defeat Dukakis, 54 to 46 percent.

Lesson learned. Sign the Taxpayer Protection Pledge, win the primary. Repeat your commitment to oppose tax hikes and win the general election.

Bush had truly been elected to Ronald Reagan's third term just as James Madison was elected to Thomas Jefferson's third term on his opposition to excise taxes. George H. W. Bush promised to govern as Reagan had. But he failed to learn from eight years of Reagan's success. He allowed spending to drift upward. The cost of regulations exploded. By the end of the Bush term, House Majority Leader Dick Armey calculated that fully one-quarter of the total costs of government regulation in the United States were imposed during Bush's one term.

George H. W. Bush was nominated and elected having promised to oppose and veto any tax hike. But Bush appointed Richard Darman to be the director of the Office of Management and Budget. Darman wanted to negotiate with the Democrat House and Senate to trade tax hikes for promises of spending cuts. He thought he could avoid the mistakes of 1982 and this time, because he was just so darn smart, actually get real spending cuts for real tax hikes. (*He* hadn't promised not to raise taxes.) Darman's wrongheaded self-confidence reminds us that even the "smartest man in the world" cannot put tax hikes on the negotiating table and walk away with real spending restraint.

Parents who whine that their children learned little in four years of college should reflect that George H. W. Bush learned nothing about the politics of tax-and-spend from eight years as Reagan's understudy. He didn't learn the lines. He didn't even read the script.

In 1982 we all watched in horror as Reagan was promised three dollars in spending cuts for every one dollar in tax increases. He was cheated. Reagan referred to this as the biggest mistake of his presidency. The promised spending cuts didn't happen. Eight years later, in the spring of 1990, Bush was offered two dollars of phony spending cuts for every dollar of tax hikes. Evidently, Bush was viewed as a cheaper date than Reagan. It was a public display by the Washington Establishment of contempt for Reagan's vice president. Since the Democrat Congress was trading in counterfeit currency that they had no intention of redeeming, they might at least have flattered Bush before they humiliated him. They could have offered a ten-to-one ratio of imaginary spending cuts for the very real and very painful tax hikes. If you are going to cheat someone, there is no reason not to feign respect.

Bush raised taxes and the economy slowed. Higher tax rates are not healthy for economies and other living things. When he ran for president in 1980, he had called supply-side economics—the recognition that tax rates matter when people decide how much to work, save, and invest—"voodoo economics." This was not simply a cheap shot at Reagan. By 1980, support for the Kemp-Roth tax cut was a Republican Party position. Amazingly, Bush thought that attacking tax cuts would win Republican primary votes. It didn't in 1980, and he lost to Reagan. Even after being given a ringside seat to watch the explosion of jobs from January 1983 to January 1990 (20 million)[2] and real GDP economic growth (4.4 percent annual average)[3] following the implementation of the Reagan tax rate cuts, Bush had not learned. In 1988, George H. W. Bush was defeated for reelection by a little-known governor from Arkansas named Bill Clinton. One reason was that Ross Perot ran as a third-party candidate and this divided the Reagan vote. Reagan won in 1984 with 58.8 percent of the vote. In 1988, Bush, running for Reagan's third term, won 54 percent. In November 1992 the Bush and Perot vote together totaled 56.4 percent. But Bush alone won 38 percent of the vote, losing to Clinton, who won only 43 percent of the 1992 vote, fewer votes than Dukakis earned when he lost in a landslide.

The country still wanted to vote for a Reagan Republican. The votes were certainly not there for Dukakis's vision of liberal Massachusetts governance. Or for a tax-hiking Republican.

We can pinpoint the tax issue as central to Bush's defeat in 1992. Without the tax hike a Ross Perot presidential run would have been a joke. There would have been no reason for Republican-leaning Independents to jump ship. To add salt to the wound, Democrat nominee, then Arkansas governor, Bill Clinton ran a devastating ad attacking Bush for violating his pledge and instead raising taxes. ("He gave us the second biggest tax increase in American history. Bush increased the gas tax by 56 percent. Can we afford four more years? Bill Clinton, a different kind of Democrat.")

Bush had, on the foreign-policy front, been a strong and successful president. He drove Saddam Hussein out of Kuwait without getting stuck occupying Iraq for ten years. Bush got the Japanese, the Saudis, and the Kuwaitis to pay for much of the short and limited war. Bush managed the collapse of the Soviet Union as it broke into fifteen parts, ending its forty-five-year occupation of Eastern Europe without a great deal of blood on the floor. Yes, Reagan broke the back of the Soviet Empire with his policies of denying Russia loans and putting teeth into our containment policy with a stronger defense. But there were a hundred ways the Cold War could have continued or ended very badly. There Bush ran a masterful foreign policy.

He lost because he raised taxes. Because he broke his pledge.

The rules had changed dramatically in American politics. For generations political leaders throughout history and across the globe have lied their way into power, promising to keep taxes low until they had secured power.

In the past both Republicans and Democrats often answered the "tax question" by observing, "This is not the time to raise taxes." Or "The last thing I want to do is raise taxes," or "Raising taxes in this weak economy would be bad." Voters may have thought they were promised no tax hikes, but those politicians really only stressed how painful it would be for them to be forced, in the future, when things changed, to raise taxes.

This was the power of the Taxpayer Protection Pledge.

It is a written promise to voters. It cannot be changed. It is a simple sentence. Easy to understand. There are no caveats. No weasel words.

Politicians like to cover their lies by insisting that "if you listened to my statement in context..." Or "I said at the same time..."

But the pledge has no context. It stands alone. You sign it as a candidate or you refuse to sign it. Yes or no. On or off. Binary.

If you ask about a candidate and your friend says that "he has promised not to raise taxes," you don't really know anything about that candidate. What was the actual phrasing of this so-called "promise"?

But if you read in the newspaper that a candidate has signed the Taxpayer Protection Pledge, you know exactly what he or she has committed to.

Bush failed to learn about the power of the tax issue in both policy and politics. But the rest of the Republican Party learned a great deal from Bush's failure.

Bush signed the Pledge against tax hikes and won the GOP nomination. He promised, "Read my lips, no new taxes," and won the general election. He broke his pledge and threw away a perfectly good presidency in 1992.

Bush taught us: Take the Pledge, win. Break the Pledge, lose.

No one's life is a complete waste; some people serve as bad examples.

And the Republican Party learned quickly. Not a single Republican voted for the Clinton tax increases, which passed the House by one vote on August 5, 1993. Republicans all opposed the Clinton/Gore drive for higher energy taxes, which was defeated in the Senate.

In the 1994 midterm elections, almost every single Republican House and Senate candidate signed the Pledge. The Republican promise to oppose tax hikes and the Democrat record of voting or Clinton's tax hikes were central to the election. It was a landslide, as Republicans gained 54 House seats and 8 Senate seats to establish a 230–204 majority in the House and a 52–48 majority in the Senate.

The Democrats had held the House for forty uninterrupted years, from 1955 to 1995. They had held the Senate for thirty-four of those forty years. American politics had changed.

When the dust settled, a majority of the members of the House had signed the Pledge. For the next six years the Republican Congress passed a series of tax cuts. Clinton signed a cut in the capital gains tax, from 28 to 20 percent. Clinton vetoed efforts to abolish the death tax as well as the tax on long-distance calls, put in place in 1898 to pay for the Spanish-American War. The Pledge-taking majorities in Congress never passed a tax hike. The Pledge held.

In 2000, George W. Bush signed the Pledge as a candidate for the presidency. He defeated John McCain, who had signed the Pledge as a senator but would not make that commitment as a presidential candidate. George W. Bush served for eight years. He made many mistakes. But he never raised taxes.

For fourteen years, from 1995 to 2009, Pledge signers held the House, the Senate, or at least the presidency. They kept the Pledge, and no tax hike became law for sixteen years—from 1993 to 2009—the longest period without a tax hike in modern US history.

Before Obama won the presidency in November 2008, the Democrats had already captured the House and Senate in the November 2006 elections. President Obama joined a 257–178 Democrat majority in the House and a 59–41 majority in the Senate and the first thing they did together was raise taxes two weeks and two days after his inauguration. Then, in early 2010, twenty taxes that, when fully phased in, would cost $1 trillion over a decade, were passed under the banner of "Obamacare."[4]

The victorious Democrats were able to raise taxes, but not a single Republican joined them in voting for Obamacare and its twenty taxes. Smart Democrats in Congress remembered how voters punished the Democrats who voted for the 1993 Clinton tax hikes by electing a Republican majority in the House and Senate in 1994. They were worried. This way lay danger.

To protect themselves, Obama and the Democrats wanted company. Politicians and small children know that when you are doing something wrong, it is wise to have someone you can point to and say, "He did it too."

The Plot to Trick Republicans into a Bipartisan Tax Hike: Scene One

A trap was set for the Republicans.

Democrat senator Kent Conrad talked several Republicans into cosponsoring legislation that would have created a bipartisan commission to write up "deficit reducing" legislation that would both increase taxes and reduce spending and then—here was the sharp edge of the rat trap—whatever this commission came up with would be scheduled for a vote that could not be filibustered. Voilà. The one remaining defense Republicans had—the now forty-one senators who, when they acted together, could stop legislation (other than budget reconciliation)—would be moot.

In the House of Representatives this Rube Goldberg contraption for creating an inevitable "bipartisan" tax increase in the name of deficit reduction was sponsored by Democrat Representative Jim Cooper (Tenn.) and Republican Frank Wolf of northern Virginia. Wolf was a pre-Reagan Republican and an appropriator who measured his success in Congress by how many millions of dollars in earmarks he dragged out of taxpayers back to his northern Virginia congressional district. Such spenders need revenue...aka taxes.

In the Senate many Republicans cosponsored the legislation to create the commission unaware that it had teeth. Many assumed it was simply a feel good "Message: I care about the deficit" measure that was not actually expected to become law. But in January 2010 Senate leader Reid brought the legislation up for a vote and sensing the trap that had been built, seven of the original Republican cosponsors of the commission legislation voted no and the plot failed 53–46.

The whole point of this exercise was to get Republican fingerprints on the legislation. The bill and the commission had to be "bipartisan." In the House, Wolf had trouble getting Republicans to cosponsor his legislation. Many Republican members reported to me that they told Wolf that they had signed the Taxpayer Protection Pledge and would not support the legislation because the whole point of the bill was to raise taxes and make it appear bipartisan. Wolf was quite unhappy, and there was reportedly a fair amount of shouting and whining at his anti-tax-hike fellow Republicans. They would not budge.

Eventually Wolf asked me to come by to chat. He seemed to think that his problem was not that every other Republican in the caucus opposed tax hikes but that I opposed his bill. He hoped to talk me into supporting his bill. Congressman Wolf said he was not for raising taxes and that he hoped that the commission would only recommend spending cuts. I smiled and said we were then in full agreement. All he had to do was rewrite the legislation so that the commission was required to recommend a collection of spending cuts—not tax hikes—to then go to a vote of both houses of Congress. I offered to help get cosponsors for such a bill. In fact I had worked years earlier with then–budget chairman John Kasich (later governor of Ohio) on just such a piece of legislation aiming at proposing $25 billion in spending reductions. Kasich's bill was to recommend spending cuts, and not tax hikes, to be fast-tracked for a vote of Congress.

Wolf frowned and said no Democrats would cosponsor or vote for such legislation. Of course not. They wanted a bill with Republican support that would force tax hikes.

Democrats could have created and voted for legislation creating a tax-hike and spending-cut commission all by themselves. They had strong majorities in the House and Senate for two full years in

2009 and 2010. But that would have undermined the goal of creating Republican co-ownership of the hoped-for tax hikes.

Hardworking burglars keep trying other windows when the first one is locked. Teenage boys reword the question when confronted with no.

Take Two: The Simpson-Bowles Stratagem to Get a Bipartisan Tax Hike

Obama decided to push forward with the commission concept. It would not have the force of law, but if the establishment press cooperated and said "bipartisan" enough times on the Sunday talk shows, it might give the Democrats some cover.

So Obama established the National Commission on Fiscal Responsibility and Reform through Executive Order 13531. He had that "pen and phone" thing going way back then.

Obama chose two compliant Republicans and five loyal Democrats to put on his commission. He invited the Republican and Democrat leaders in Congress to each appoint three congressmen and three senators.

So the deck was stacked with seven Obama-appointed votes, six congressional Democrat votes and six Republicans that included three Republican senators who Obama correctly assumed could be had.

There were no surprises. The commission moved forward like a familiar play. You know that Macbeth is not going to beat Macduff. You are reasonably certain that Romeo and Juliet are not going to sit down and think this thing through calmly before doing anything rash. Othello is not going to apologize for leaping to conclusions and recommend "make-up sex." And the Simpson-Bowles Commission was going to recommend a replay of the 1982 and 1990 budget "compromises" that permanently raised taxes and made a head fake toward spending restraint.

Had the Democrats lost only a few seats in the House and Senate in November 2010, the Simpson-Bowles Commission might have worked. It was a clever plan.

But on Election Day the Republicans, fueled by national anger over Obamacare, the Stimulus, and massive spending and debt, gained sixty-three house seats to capture a majority of the House, and gained six Senate seats for a total of forty-seven. Enough to filibuster.

The Simpson-Bowles Commission failed to win the supermajority of fourteen votes they needed for a formal commission recommendation. But because the commission report was only a recommendation and not legally binding, Simpson and Bowles wisely chose to simply report out their own two-man plan. The press treated it as a full commission report anyway. And Simpson was a Republican former senator from one of the square states out west, so that made it "bipartisan."

I wrote an open letter on December 2, 2010, to the three Republican senators on the Simpson-Bowles-Obama Commission, Senators Greg, Coburn, and Crapo urging them to oppose the chairmen's report.[5]

The letter read:

> **Sens. Gregg, Coburn, and Crapo:**
> You have today announced that you will support the Simpson-Bowles-Obama debt commission report on Friday. This report contains a ten-year net tax hike of over $1 trillion and increases tax revenues from their historical 18 percent of GDP to a record and permanent 21 percent. **This report shifts the debate from where it properly should be—spending—and onto deficit reduction, and thereby tax increases.**
>
> **This report opens the door to a third round of disastrous budget summits.** In 1982, President Reagan agreed to $3 in spending cuts for every $1 in tax hikes. The tax hikes became law, but spending went up. President Reagan called this the worst mistake of his presidency. In 1990, President

George H. W. Bush broke his "read my lips" Pledge when he agreed to $2 in spending cuts for every $1 in tax hikes at the infamous Andrews Air Force Base summit. He later lost re-election largely on the tax issue, and actual spending was higher than CBO predicted it would be before the deal.

All the tax hikes in Simpson-Bowles are real—they become law upon the bill being signed. Many of the spending cuts are simply promises to do better on appropriations bills, and have been historically impossible to enforce.

The tax increase in question is not "tax reform" along the lines of the 1986 Tax Reform Act. That bill lowered marginal tax rates and broadened the tax base, just as the commission report does—but with one essential distinction. That 1986 bill was tax revenue-neutral, whereas the commission report is a massive, $1 trillion-plus net tax hike on the American people. It's a tax increase that is merely disguising itself as tax reform. Real tax reform would lower the rates, broaden the base, and be at worst tax revenue-neutral. Again, this plan has a stated goal of raising tax revenue to 21 percent of GDP indefinitely, a record never hit in any one year, and higher than the historical level of 18 percent of GDP. The plan raises the gas tax and raises the Social Security payroll tax. **Taxpayers may have lower marginal tax rates under this plan, but they will have a bigger tax bill to Uncle Sam.**

I urge you to only support a plan that is tax revenue-neutral.[6]

*   *   *

Simpson-Bowles called for increasing total federal taxation to 21 percent of GDP.[7] Taxation in 1776 was 2 percent. Federal taxes before 1930 were less than 4 percent of GDP. Federal taxes in 1940 were 7 percent of GDP.[8]

And federal taxes in the previous forty years had averaged 18.5 percent. Simpson-Bowles was urging a permanent increase in the

tax burden of 2.5 percent of GDP. Congressman Paul Ryan calculated it was a $2 trillion tax hike over the coming decade. The Heri-
tage Foundation said that it was, in its first ten years, $3.3 trillion
in higher taxes.[9] Certainly when fully phased in, it would be at least
a $500 billion-a-year tax increase, or a $5 trillion tax hike over ten
years.[10]

In return, Simpson-Bowles suggested spending be reduced from
its 2014 level of 23.8 percent to 21.6 percent in 2015, and 21 percent
by 2035. That looked like progress, but before Bush and Obama and
TARP and the Stimulus spending, the federal government spent on
average 21.6 percent throughout the 1980s, 20.0 percent throughout the 1990s, and 19.6 percent throughout the 2000s.[11] This only
looked like a spending cut because of the recent spike in spending.
It was really about locking in the "progress" from the tax-and-
spenders' point of view of the previous three years.

Spoiler Alert. In the real world, Republicans steered away from
the siren song of bipartisanship, thwarting all that determined effort
to lure them onto the shoals of higher taxes. Taxes were not raised.
Planned spending was reduced. And in 2014 spending was 20.4 percent of GDP.[12] This was achieved twenty-one years earlier than
promised by the Simpson-Bowles "plan." And without tax hikes.

But this future was not yet known or won.

Obama needed a very large increase in the debt ceiling to get
him past the November 2012 election. He reckoned he needed a
$2.5 trillion debt-ceiling increase. Obama cleared the decks. He
had his Democrat House and Senate extend the expiring Bush tax
cuts for two years—past the 2012 election. He could deal with those
annoying, but thankfully temporary, tax cuts later. After he was
safely reelected. A continuing resolution was passed to keep spending going at present levels through the spring. Now, back to getting
that debt-ceiling increase. He would need Republican votes in the
House. To do this, he would have to talk to Republicans. He lacked
experience in that zone.

The Boehner Rule Appears

John Boehner, who was just elected to be Speaker of the House by his 243-member Republican caucus, changed the future when on May 9, 2011, he announced the "Boehner Rule." The Republican caucus will vote to increase the debt ceiling $2.5 trillion if, and only if, that legislation also reduces real spending by $2.5 trillion over the next decade. One dollar of spending restraint for one dollar of debt increase: "So let me be as clear as I can be. Without significant spending cuts and reforms to reduce our debt, there will be no debt-limit increase. And the cuts should be greater than the accompanying increase in debt authority the president is given."[13]

In negotiations Boehner said he would be willing to count revenue that flowed from economic growth as part of the $2.5 trillion. Obama and company immediately assumed that "revenues from growth" meant tax hikes. Boehner and the GOP leadership made it clear they meant Ronald Reagan–style tax-rate reductions that spurred growth and would actually bring in more revenue. Dave Camp, the Michigan Republican chairman of the Ways and Means Committee, drafted a tax reform package three years later, in 2014, that was scored by the Joint Tax Committee as revenue neutral, using static scoring, and as a $700 billion revenue increase from growth that flowed from cutting the corporate rate to 25 percent and the individual rates to a top rate of 35 percent.[14] Such a tax reform/tax cut would have produced $700 billion more in revenue, and Boehner and the Republicans were willing to include that in the effort to get to $2.5 trillion in deficit reduction. The rest would have to come from spending reductions.

But the Democrats do not consider revenue from growth to be real money. They wanted "real" tax increases. Ones that draw blood.

The ploy to create an automatic-tax-hike vote through the Frank Wolf/Judd Gregg legislation to create a bipartisan tax commission to enact tax hikes failed.

The Simpson-Bowles Commission failed.

So now those hoping for higher taxes moved to plan C.

Third Try: The Gang of Six

Senator Durbin of Illinois set up a "Gang of Six" to once again create a "bipartisan" deal that would mask tax hikes. The three Republicans chosen were Senator Coburn of Oklahoma, Senator Chambliss of Georgia, and Senator Crapo of Idaho. The Democrats were Dick Durbin of Illinois, Mark Warner of Virginia, and Kent Conrad of North Dakota.

Obama did not like being forced to negotiate directly with Boehner. In this fight Boehner was his equal. Both had to agree. He could not push Boehner or the House GOP around. Obama really needed some Republicans in the Senate to open a second front against the House Republicans so that the fight would be three against one. Obama, the Senate, and the Washington press corps against the new Republican majority in the House.

I had long conversations with Senators Coburn, Chambliss, and Crapo, and all three in private recognized the failures of 1982 and 1990 and swore they would not be taken in again to trade imaginary spending restraint for tax hikes.

They knew they had each made a commitment to the voters of Oklahoma, Georgia, and Idaho when they signed the Taxpayer Protection Pledge promising in writing to oppose and vote against any net tax increases.

The Republicans in the Gang of Six Hold Firm, for Now

I was very pleased when the three wrote an open letter to me on February 17, 2011, recommitting themselves to keeping their pledge to the American people to oppose any net tax hikes and agreeing that any "revenue" being discussed was only that from higher rates of growth.[15]

They wrote:

The solution to our economic and fiscal problems will be
based on both spending reduction and economic growth.
Like you, we believe tax hikes will hinder, not promote,
economic growth. And, as you know, the current tax code
has become burdensome and complex and filled with provisions which only benefit a limited portion of Americans, at
the expense of higher rates for all Americans. Proposals that
simplify the tax code, broaden the base, lower all individual
and corporate tax rates, and make our corporate tax code
more competitive for US business will create a surge in economic growth, which will not only generate more income for
the American people and businesses, but more revenue to the
federal Treasury, which, as your website notes, is not only
allowable, but greatly desired.

And the final, key sentence of the letter read:

If and when there is a legislative proposal to be presented to
Congress and the American people, we look forward to again
working with you and all interested parties to support a proposal where any increase in [tax] revenue generation will be
the result of the pro-growth effects of lower individual and
corporate tax rates for all Americans.

On February 22, 2011, I wrote back thanking them for clarify-
ing their position publicly and thereby knocking down assertions
by some in the press that they were open to tax hikes as part of a
debt-ceiling deal.[16]

The Gang of Six negotiations dragged on and on. I spoke on the
phone again with Senator Coburn, concerned that he would be pressured into agreeing to a "grand bargain," as in 1982 or 1990, with
real tax hikes and soft or temporary or nonexistent spending cuts.

Press reports suggested that the Republicans on the Gang of Six might be willing to raise taxes. Certainly the three Democrats— Durbin, Conrad, and Warner—wanted nothing else.

Senator Coburn assured me on the phone that while he was willing to put possible tax hikes on the table for discussion purposes, he had no intention of ever voting for a tax hike. This was simply to keep the Democrats at the table and get them to put real spending cuts on the negotiating table. "Grover," Coburn told me breathlessly, "you can't imagine how much spending reduction Durbin is putting on the table."

I suggested that Senator Durbin might be having a similar conversation with his Democrat caucus: "Hey guys, I hint at spending cuts we would never really agree to in legislation and let me tell you about all the tax hikes Senator Coburn is willing to concede."

Senator Coburn assured me that Illinois Democrat senator Dick Durbin would never be that dishonest. "So, let me get this straight," I said to Senator Coburn. "Your position is that you are misleading Durbin about possibly raising taxes but that Durbin would never be so dishonest as to lie to you about his and his caucus's willingness to cut spending." I suggested that I found it quite likely that Senator Durbin was lying and I worried that Senator Coburn was not really that comfortable lying. I thought at some point he would end up believing his own "bluff" on tax hikes.

Senator Coburn did learn how phony the Durbin spending-cut conversations were. He eventually realized there were no real spending cuts being offered and he walked out of the Gang of Six negotiations on May 17, 2011. "There's mandatory spending that was not addressed to my satisfaction," Coburn said. "It's got to be balanced, and I didn't perceive where it was balanced."[17]

Senator Coburn Changes Teams

The Stockholm syndrome, identified by Swedish psychiatrist Nils Bejerot, describes how someone kidnapped by criminals or other annoying people can over time begin to identify with their kidnappers. It is named after what happened during and after a 1973 bank robbery in Stockholm, Sweden, where bank staff were held hostage from August 23 to August 28. The hostages came to identify and empathize with the bank robbers *even after being freed.* This same phenomenon also happened with Patricia Hearst in 1974, when she was kidnapped by the Symbionese Liberation Army (SLA) gang and, instead of hating her captors, actually joined them in a bank robbery.

The FBI finds that about 8 percent of hostages suffer from Stockholm syndrome. Eight percent suggests that if forty-six Republican senators were told that they could not have spending cuts without meeting the demands of the Democrat majority holding deficit reduction hostage to higher taxes, as many as four senators might be expected to begin to identify with the Democrat and take their side, even when released from the confines of the Gang of Six negotiations.

This happened to Senator Coburn, who said he was willing to abandon his written pledge to the voters of Oklahoma that he would never vote for a tax hike and his emphatic restatement of that commitment just before he went deeper and deeper into the Gang of Six closed-door "negotiations." After the Gang of Six negotiations were exposed as a phony ploy by Durbin to extract tax hikes without any real or permanent spending restraint, Senator Coburn decided that the real problem was not the Democrats who would not cut spending. Rather the real enemy was the "near enemy": his fellow Republicans who would not raise taxes.

Here Senator Reid played a clever card. He belittled Republicans, suggesting that their unwillingness to raise taxes was not based on principle or even the experience of 1982 and 1990. No. The reason Republican senators would not raise taxes was because they had signed the Taxpayer Protection Pledge—"to me." I was bossing Republicans around. I would not allow them to raise taxes. He, Democrat leader Reid, was trying to free them from my evil grip.

On November 1, 2011, Harry Reid said, "My Republican friends, those poor folks, are being led like puppets by Grover Norquist. They're giving speeches that we should compromise on our deficit. Never do they compromise on Grover Norquist. He is their leader."[18]

Dialing up the hysteria two weeks later, Reid suggested, on November 15, that the American public should "impeach" me because Republicans were holding the line on taxes.[19]

Barack Obama had been reading from the same script: On September 19, 2011, President Obama said, "The last time I checked, the only pledge that really matters is the pledge we take to uphold the Constitution."[20]

CBS's *60 Minutes* did a profile of me and Americans for Tax Reform and the Taxpayer Protection Pledge. One question the interviewer asked six or seven times was, "Harry Reid says you are the most important man in Washington. Are you the most important man in Washington?" My answer helped tamp down the Left's attacks: "The tax issue is the most powerful issue in American politics today and throughout our history." It was never about me. It has always been about the power of the tax issue to affect every American.

This suggestion that the Pledge was made to me was nonsense. The Pledge is made to the voters of each senator's state and to the entire American people. It is written down. There is no mistaking that. The Pledge is not made to Americans for Tax Reform or to me personally. The Republican senators knew that. They had signed the Pledge and campaigned on it election after election. They had read it. Still, a few less confident senators were bothered that anyone might think they were "taking orders" from a taxpayer leader— or anyone. Reid was not wrong to push that button in a few cases. It just didn't work with Republican senators who were comfortable in their own skin.

In Senator Coburn's personal situation there was another common error in play. Senator Coburn was trying to solve the wrong problem. He confused spending reduction with deficit reduction. We were working to reduce federal spending by $2.5 trillion over ten years. He thought we were trying to reduce the deficit by $2.5 trillion over ten years. The American people, and particularly the Tea Party movement wanted spending reduced by $2.5 trillion as the price for Obama's debt hike. Cutting spending $2.5 trillion would reduce the debt/deficit by $2.5 trillion. Problem solved. Tax hikes—to replace any or all of the spending cuts—might in theory reduce the deficit/debt (if the tax hike did not slow economic growth), but the tax hikes would simply displace spending cuts.

Tax hikes are not part of spending cuts. They are the alternative to spending cuts.

After conversations with Senator Coburn where he used the terms "spending cuts," "deficit reduction," and "tax hikes" interchangeably I called Steve Moore, then with the *Wall Street Journal*, who had run the Club for Growth in 2004 when it spent $675,130 supporting Tom Coburn's election to the Senate.[21] Could Steve help me and speak with Senator Coburn, who on most days is our hero in fighting against government spending? Well, said Steve, Coburn had never understood the difference between spending reduction and deficit reduction. Steve had tried years ago and felt it was not possible to get Coburn to see that any tax hike was undermining the effort to reduce spending and that a deficit reduction through tax hikes did not cut spending. It enabled it. Steve could not help here. My advice to all the political groups is to do a better job of vetting candidates in the future. It is not brain surgery or nuclear physics. Tax hikes are not the same thing as budget cuts.

It's like being color-blind.

Senator Coburn had now decided the Republicans were the problem. They would not vote for a tax hike. He knew from months of negotiations that the Democrats would not actually contribute any real spending cuts to a deal. So the Republicans must be made to raise taxes. Patty Hearst now understood the real concerns of the Symbionese Liberation Front. Winston Smith, the protagonist of George Orwell's *Nineteen Eighty-Four*, had finally learned to love Big Brother.

In a May 29 interview on C-SPAN's *Newsmakers*, Senator Coburn exploded. "Why will I take on those that are against tax increases for Republicans? Because it's the right thing to do to save our country."[22] Later in the same interview he said, "I've been just as vocal supporting revenue increases after I left the (Simpson-Bowles) Commission as I was before."

On June 9, Coburn turned to the liberal cable network MSNBC to announce, "Do I believe we have to raise taxes to be able to get a deal to cut spending? Yeah."[23]

But there was that damn pledge, which almost every Republican in the Senate had signed. (Never mind the House. Like many senators, Coburn seemed to think that if the Senate cut a deal with Obama, the House of Representatives would have to fold and do what they were told.)

Senator Coburn's Plan to Destroy the Taxpayer Protection Pledge

So how could Coburn break the Pledge and the resulting Republican unity behind spending cuts rather than a tax hike?

If you are counting, we are now relating the fourth effort, Plan D, to break the Pledge and get a tax increase so that the debt ceiling can be raised and the spending can continue.

Senator Coburn prepared an amendment to end the ethanol tax credit several months before it was scheduled to expire on January 1, 2012. The tax credit cost the government $6 billion in revenue each year. Ending it several months early would raise the total tax burden $2.4 billion (out of a federal budget that year of $2.5 trillion).[24] A vote to eliminate a tax credit or deduction without reducing taxes elsewhere by the same amount at the same time is in fact a tax hike. In this case a rather silly and small tax hike, but it would in fact increase the total tax burden on the American people. If one really wanted to get rid of the tax credit—which was disappearing anyway under existing law in six months—one could simply attach a very small marginal tax rate cut of equal or larger value and the elimination of the ethanol tax credit would not be a "tax hike." Problem solved.

But Coburn wanted to "trick" Republicans into voting against a politically driven tax credit (without an offsetting tax cut) and then announce that since every Republican had now voted for a tax hike, they were no longer virgins but rather harlots who could now cheerfully vote for trillions in higher taxes. Breaking the Pledge once—even with a tax hike this small, temporary, and silly—would, he hoped, free the entranced Republicans from their anti-tax-increase position and we could get back to repeating the grand bargains of 1982 and 1990.

It didn't work. It wasn't ever going to work.

Republican senators saw this coming a mile away. So did taxpayers. Senator DeMint of South Carolina realized this vote on ethanol was an effort to "defeat" the Taxpayer Protection Pledge and open the door to future tax hikes. So DeMint announced he would offer the repeal of the death tax as an amendment to the same bill Coburn planned to attach his ethanol-repeal amendment to. Republican leader Mitch McConnell, also alerted to Coburn's plot, announced that he would not allow the underlying legislation to move forward unless it had both the Coburn small tax increase and the much larger death tax elimination attached. Every Republican could vote for Coburn's tiny tax hike knowing that it would never move out of the Senate unless it was firmly attached to the elimination of the death tax. (The death tax cut would have been a permanent annual tax cut of $50 billion each year.) This would have been a wonderful trade for the onetime $2.4 billion tax hike on gasoline using ethanol.

Why did Coburn believe he would fool anyone with this ploy? It was not completely stupid. The ethanol tax credit was disliked for many reasons. It was a targeted tax credit. It was politically driven. So why had it been put forward, even if only temporarily in the first place? Answer: The liberal environmentalists liked the idea of forcing Americans to put ethanol made from corn into our gas tanks. They had a theory—now largely discredited—that this was somehow better for the environment. And using ethanol mixed with real gasoline in automobiles lured otherwise sensible and decent farmers into support for this crony-capitalism trick because it helped them by raising the price of their corn. But there was a problem. Ethanol is more expensive than real energy. That is one reason people do not do this in the free market. And if the Greens forced us to buy gasoline with more expensive ethanol mixed in, then consumers might be understandably angry at the idiot congressmen and senators who thought this up. So those congressmen and senators created the tax credit to hide the true cost of their little social experiment.

But getting rid of the tax credit would not end the expensive use of ethanol There was a law, a mandate, forcing gasoline refiners to use a fixed amount of ethanol each year.

Many conservatives wanted to end the ethanol mandate. Coburn's plan was to direct this animus at the meaningless and expiring tax credit. The mandate would stay in place so the Greens and the subsidized farmers would still get what they wanted and consumers would continue to be looted when they went to the gas pump.

The Coburn plan to get conservatives to support ending the political tax credit for ethanol and thereby unknowingly vote for a small tax hike and break their pledge fell apart quickly.

I wrote an open letter to all Pledge signers letting them know that a vote for the Coburn Amendment was not a violation of the Pledge because, as Republican leader, McConnell had made crystal clear that the small, temporary tax hike Coburn was pushing would never move forward unless DeMint's abolition of the death tax also passed.[25] Therefore a vote for Coburn could never been construed as a violation of the Pledge.

Things got worse for Coburn. He hoped to use the conservative revulsion over the ethanol mandate to drive support for ending the tax credit. (And this did confuse one writer for the editorial page of the *Wall Street Journal*—for a brief moment, not permanently.)

On the floor of the Senate on June 13, Coburn stated that he supported the mandate forcing consumers to use ethanol in their gas and that he, Coburn, would vote against Senator DeMint's amendment to end the destructive ethanol mandate.[26] Free-market conservatives around the nation had assumed Coburn was against the mandate and were appalled to learn differently. No one on the Right was fooled any longer by his "End the ethanol tax credit" ploy into thinking he now opposed this very expensive and destructive ethanol mandate.

Americans for Tax Reform was joined by the American Conservative Union, Americans for Prosperity, the Competitive Enterprise Institute, and many other free-market groups in sending a letter to all senators urging them to vote for Senator DeMint's amendment to Senate bill 782 ending the ethanol mandate and the tariff that kept out lower-cost imported ethanol and also for Senator Coburn's original ploy Amendment 426, which ended the temporary tax credit a few months early.[27]

Senator Coburn's bluff had been called. Everyone was free to vote to end the counterproductive tax credit without ever being attacked for violating the Pledge—because the death-tax-repeal tax cut dwarfed the small Coburn tax hike. And it was now clear Coburn was not actually against the destructive ethanol regime.

Americans for Tax Reform sent a letter applauding the passage of the Coburn Amendment and another praising the Senate for killing the underlying bill.[28]

The reason all this was so important was that it exposed as silly and dishonest one of the Democrats' arguments against the Pledge. The Pledge does not stop anyone from eliminating any particular credit or deduction inside a tax cutting or revenue neutral bill.

The Democrat Party's Political
Attacks on the Pledge

In 2010, Democrats running for Congress were confronted with a problem. Their candidates wanted to raise taxes once elected. Again. The incumbent Democrats had already voted for twenty taxes in Obamacare. They were running against Republicans who had signed the Pledge. This was not healthy.

So the DCCC (the Democrat Congressional Campaign Committee) designed ads claiming that anyone who signed the Pledge could not ever vote to eliminate any tax credits. They would highlight a tax credit they claimed they opposed and then assert that any Pledge signer was somehow wedded to protecting that tax credit.

But of course the Taxpayer Protection Pledge allows any tax credit to be thrown on the tax heap of history as long as there is an accompanying tax cut of the same size and duration in the same legislation. The Coburn fiasco showed how contorted he had to get to try—and fail—to create a vote to end a political tax credit that had no offset. The Reagan Republicans in the Senate simply attached an offsetting tax cut. Problem solved.

Worse for the Democrats in 2010 was that two of the fact-checking columns—both run by folks who tended to be friendlier to the liberal side—found that these attack ads were completely false. FactCheck .org ruled against a DCCC ad against Republican House candidate Charles Kong Djou in Hawaii. The Democrat ad claimed that the Pledge "protects tax breaks for companies that send jobs overseas." FactCheck pointed out, "It's an ad that the Democrats could run against nearly any Republican House candidate, all but a few of whom have signed the anti-tax pledge in question. But the ad is not true."

PolitiFact made a similar ruling against an almost identical Democrat ad against Republican Robert Hurt in Virginia. PolitiFact summarized their criticism of the ad: "So we find the claim false."

*   *   *

The establishment press was on the hunt for Republicans who would vote for a tax hike. Partly because it was a break from boring stories that the Republicans won't raise taxes and partly to undermine Republican unity and convince the grassroots that the GOP would once again (remember 1982 and 1990) betray them in search of a Washington grand bargain that was "grand" only for people who made their living in Washington.

The *Hill* newspaper noted in the summer of 2011 that while most Republicans in the House of Representatives had signed the Taxpayer Protection Pledge, there were seven Republicans who had not formally signed the Pledge. When a reporter from the *Hill* called them, it turned out that one of the seven assumed he had signed the Pledge and immediately made sure he had one formally signed and witnessed. And of the remaining six, fully five of them had repeatedly stated they would never vote for a tax hike. They each had some reason they were uncomfortable signing a pledge, but they were adamant to the *Hill* that they would never vote for a tax hike. This left the lone Republican open to higher taxes as Frank Wolf, a pre-Reagan Republican appropriator. Wolf retired in 2014, to be replaced by a strong anti-tax Congresswoman, Barbara Comstock.

The 2011 Debt-Ceiling Battle over Taxes Comes to a Conclusion

So what happened? Did the Taxpayer Protection Pledge and a Republican House majority committed to a "no tax hike" position destroy a golden opportunity for bipartisan compromise that would "reduce the deficit" by raising taxes and restraining spending growth? No.

We moved to the brink with the establishment press and the Democrat leadership shouting in our ears that we were about to sail over the edge of the world. But the final agreement was reached on August 2. It rolled back much of the massive planned spending increases Obama, Reid, and Pelosi had put into the 2010 budget plan for the decade. One trillion dollars in planned spending increases for domestic discretionary spending was eliminated. This was painful for the Democrats, but they were not losing any spending they were presently "enjoying." They just were not getting the second dessert after dinner that they had hoped for. There was no weight loss here. Just a failure to gain weight. Still, it was real progress to take off the table the winnings the interest groups of the Left believed was their due from the 2008 election.

The second part of the budget deal was where the scalpel cut. Obama's staff came up with an idea. How about a sequester that would limit spending on domestic discretionary spending by law over the next decade? It didn't reform Social Security or Medicare or Medicaid or Food Stamps or Obamacare or any of the "entitlement programs" that the establishment kept saying (correctly) was the real cause of our long-term budget problems. The Sequester would reduce the planned spending over the next ten years by $1.2 trillion. That was real money. Those were real cuts. This would "hurt" the spending interests. Not just hurt their feelings, but they would have to change behavior. Prioritize. Learn to say no to old "friends."

Now, this Sequester would go into effect only if a "supercommittee" of six Republicans and six Democrats could not agree by December 2, 2011, on alternative "deficit reduction" legislation that totaled $1.2 trillion. Note that the Sequester was all spending cuts whereas the supercommittee could replace those spending cuts with a combination of spending cuts and tax hikes or all tax hikes.

Here is where Barack Obama, the guy who thought he was the smartest person in his 2008 campaign and the smartest guy in his own White House, made a boneheaded mistake. The guy conservatives believed was a clever follower of the political strategist Saul Alinsky was too clever by half.

Obama believed the Left's caricature of conservatives and Republicans. He truly believed that the Pentagon ran the Republican Party. He bet his presidency on the belief that conservatives were enthralled to weapons manufacturers and would oppose any restraint on Pentagon spending. (Now, to be fair to Obama, the Bush years sometimes did make that buffoonish assertion ring somewhat true.)

Obama and his team believed that once the Republicans noticed that half the $1.2 trillion in Sequestration savings over the next decade would come from the defense budget, they would come crawling back to the Democrats demanding that we raise taxes rather than make any reforms in Pentagon spending.

The Sequester was $1.2 trillion in spending restraint. Obama wanted to replace it with a mix of tax hikes and spending restraint. Exactly how much tax hike and how much spending cut did the president hope to win? What ratio were Obama and the Democrats looking for? Was it the three-to-one-ratio promise to Reagan in 1982? Or the less generous two-to-one trade promised to George H. W. Bush in 1990?

Or was Obama willing to offer ten dollars of spending cuts for every dollar of tax hikes, the ratio offered by Fox News's Bret Baier when he asked all of the GOP presidential candidates in a debate if they would accept or reject such a hypothetical budget deal? One remembers that the candidates were all smart enough to know it was a fool's errand to trade real tax hikes for promises of spending cuts.

I ran into then-senator John Kerry of my home state of Massachusetts in the hallway of the Russell Senate Office Building during the end days of the supercommittee deliberations. (Someone had decided that "supercommittee" sounded better than Gang of Twelve.) The senator politely greeted me and suggested that our wives really should get together soon. He said that he thought an agreement was possible, likely, and forthcoming but that he could use my help talking to the Republicans on the supercommittee.

"What is it you want?" I asked. Well, he wanted the Republicans to agree to $1.4 trillion in higher taxes. I interjected that I had understood that the goal was to replace $1.2 trillion in spending restraint found in the Sequester…where did $1.4 trillion come from? Well, the president insists on another round of stimulus spending of $400 billion. So if we raise taxes $1.4 trillion, add $400 billion in Stimulus (*Part Deux*), and accept $200 billion in cuts that "everyone agrees with," we hit the $1.2 trillion mark. I was so flabbergasted by the idea of another $400 billion in spending in the middle of a deficit-reduction package that I forgot to ask about the very interesting idea that there were some simple, easy-to-achieve, $200 billion in spending restraint. Where had that collection of low-hanging fruit been all my life?

I promised to do what I could. No harm in being polite. But I was struck at how wrong the establishment press was in believing the Obama administration wanted some sort of "grand bargain" to reduce runaway entitlement spending and how off base they were in thinking Obama and the Democrats were willing to reduce spending at all. All they wanted was tax hikes. There was no discussion of entitlement reforms. Even at a time the Democrats could tell their "base" they didn't have a choice. Everything I had thought about these characters was true. Not mostly true. More true than I had thought. Obama and the Democrats' idea of a balanced spending-cut/tax-hike package was *increasing spending and increasing taxes*. Not a trade of spending cuts for tax hikes at some ratio. Not ten to one, or three to one, or two to one…but—and let's do the math—$200 billion in spending hikes in return for $1.4 trillion in tax increases. The deal is more spending for more taxes. No spending restraint at all. We never heard that proposed on CNN as an option.

Republicans said no. The Pledge held against the establishment media, the White House, the Senate, and a handful of Republicans who had not actually ever voted to break the Pledge but certainly had "impure thoughts" about same.

On March 1, 2014, the Sequester took effect.

Taxes were not raised. The Boehner Rule was intact.

Federal spending stood at 20.2 percent of GDP in fiscal year 2008, the last fully Bush budget. This was increased to 24.4 percent in 2009, mashing together Bush's plans and the Obama Stimulus and TARP part two. Federal spending was 23.4 percent of GDP in 2010, and 23.4 percent in 2011. Then, reflecting the budget deal, federal spending was 22 percent of GDP in 2012, 20.8 percent in 2013, and 20.4 percent of GDP in 2014. If present law remains in place, if the Sequester holds for the next ten years, spending will be 21 percent of GDP in 2016 and 21.5 percent in 2020.[29]

In November 2012, Republicans maintained control of the House. Remember that cutting spending is supposed to be wildly unpopular. Not only had they gone head-to-head with the White House, forcing spending restraint, they voted in 2011 and 2012 in support of the Ryan budget plan, which would reduce federal spending by $6 trillion over one decade and trillions more over time by reforming Medicaid, food stamps, and Medicare. Voting to reduce federal spending, indeed voting to reform entitlements, was not the "third rail" of American politics—deadly to the touch. Heck, the Republican House had fondled that third rail and won reelection in 2012. (They would vote again for the Ryan budget in 2013 and 2014 and again win a majority of the House.)

In the 2012 election every single Republican candidate for president signed the Pledge, with the exception of former Utah governor Jon Huntsman. Bright, articulate, well funded, he could not win a single primary. If you want to show that you are a "moderate" Republican, it's probably best not to lead with a willingness to consider tax increases as your one vice. Better to go with adultery or cocaine use.

After the 2012 election Republicans were understandably unhappy with losing the presidency. There was not a Tea Party bump in voter turnout in 2012, as happened in 2010. The AEI study argued that the Tea Party rallies drove up the GOP vote in 2010 by between 3.2 and 5.8 million votes.[30] The total GOP house vote in 2006 was 35,674,808, and in 2010, 44,827,441, a total increase of 9,152,633 votes.[31] That is why it mattered that the IRS played smashmouth with the Tea Party and denied most of the new grassroots groups the tax status that would have given them legal protection and the ability to raise money and grow between 2010 and 2012. The GOP vote for president increased less than one million votes between McCain's 59,948,323 votes in 2008 and Romney's 60,933,500 vote in 2012.

A more complete measure of how Americans view tax-and-spending issues can be found by looking at a map of the fifty states after the 2012 election, when the *New York Times* suggested the modern Republican Party had ceased to exist—as they had previously asserted in 1964, 1974, 1986, and 1992.

Twenty-five states, with 165.7 million citizens, fully 53.98 percent of the nation's population, had a Republican governor and a Republican House and Senate. Only thirteen states, with 82 million citizens and only 26.7 percent of the American population, were completely run by Democrats in both the governor's mansion and the House and Senate. One of those was West Virginia, where in 2014 Republicans captured control of both houses of the legislature.

Still, in Washington, D.C., conservatives and Republicans were in a foul mood after November 6, 2012. Why the depression? Republicans held the House majority and could stop any legislation Obama wanted. Republicans had forty-five votes in the Senate—enough to filibuster any Democrat initiative in the Senate.

All true. But the Bush tax cuts passed in 2001 and 2003 were enacted inside "budget reconciliation," a legislative process that only requires fifty-one votes in the Senate and cannot be filibustered. But the flip side is that tax cuts passed inside "budget reconciliation" cannot last longer than ten years. The 2001 and 2003 Bush tax cuts were originally scheduled to end on December 31, 2010. Why didn't they? Well, the Republican Party, energized by the Tea Party reinforcements, had just won a resounding victory in capturing the House in November 2010. Dazed, and concerned about the 2012 presidential election, Obama and company simply agreed to continue all the Bush tax cuts from 2001 and 2003 for two years. They would all lapse without another vote on December 31, 2012.

Immediately after the November 2012 election, the Democrats were riding high, and December 31, 2012, was now less than two months away. Republicans in Congress held no cards. None. If no vote was held, taxes would increase by $500 billion in 2013 and by $5 trillion over the next ten years. It was called the "Fiscal Cliff" by the media, and it certainly was an avalanche of threatened tax increases. Without a vote, the following tax hikes would occur: The top rate would jump from 35 percent to 39.6 percent. The tax on dividends alone would jump from 15 percent to 43.4 percent. The tax on capital gains would jump from 15 percent to 23.8 percent. Both these numbers include the Obamacare surtax. Protections against the marriage penalty would evaporate. The per-child tax credit would fall from $1,000 to $500.

All in all a $5 trillion tax hike over ten years.

Speaker Boehner and the House Republicans passed legislation through the House to make all the Bush tax cuts permanent. Obama announced he would veto any such bill, and the Harry Reid Senate refused to even consider it.

Obama offered to continue the Bush tax cuts for anyone earning less than $250,000 a year. This would protect 82 percent of the Bush tax cuts for 98 percent of the population.[32] He would have his "tax the rich" pound of flesh.

Americans for Tax Reform campaigned to make the entire tax cut permanent, but the Senate and the White House could block that effort, and we needed a vote from the House and Senate and a signature by the president to save any of the Bush tax cuts. Not to act was to lose everything. Worse, if the Bush tax cuts were allowed to lapse, the Democrats could, with some justification, blame the Republicans and then only dribble back some of the Bush tax cuts. They could spend two months passing small tax cuts—restoring only a fraction of the Bush tax cuts—and at the end of that period, with the help of CBS, be remembered as the party of a dozen tax cuts.

Boehner put forward a measure to continue the tax cuts for all

Americans earning less than $1 million a year. Some outside groups in Washington denounced this as a tax hike. Well, on January 1, 2013, if nothing happened, taxes were going up by $500 billion on everyone. If Boehner's legislation passed on January 1, 2013, taxes would have only increased $35 billion a year. Not perfect, but 35 is a smaller number than 500—and better than what we ended up with.

A handful of Republicans in the House decided they would rather watch a $5 trillion tax hike hit Americans than be in the room when we saved only 85 percent of the tax cut for 98 percent of the people. Not the best choice, but the choice we faced.

By denying Boehner a 218 majority to make most of the Bush tax cuts permanent and then negotiating from relative strength with the Senate, the House's backbencher Republicans made the House majority impotent in the rest of this fight. Some of the traditionally most pro-taxpayer congressmen absented themselves from the fight of the decade. They went AWOL.

Action and power and decisions moved to the Senate, where the Democrats had control. They decided that Obama's $250,000 was too low and voted instead to continue the Bush tax cuts permanently for all those earning less than $450,000. House "conservatives" who refused to engage forced McConnell in the Senate to negotiate up from $250,000 to $450,000. A House vote protecting all earning less than $1 million would have forced the White House and Democrat Senate to negotiate down from $1 million. Senators of both parties believed at the time that the number would have been $750,000 if the House had acted. Pouting by some members in the House cost American taxpayers more than $100 billion over the next decade. An expensive display of ideological purity detached from the real-world implications.

As expensive as that hiccup was, the larger picture was not the dollar amount of where the Bush tax cuts would remain or lapse. It was the word "permanent."

Bush had only won those tax cuts for ten years. Obama, back to the wall in 2010, continued them only for two years. This time, when Obama was riding tall, most of the tax cuts were made permanent. Before, the tax cuts died if they were not re-voted. Now, to take away these tax cuts would require a vote in both the House and the Senate and a presidential signature.

Obama had just made his second huge mistake. Had he simply agreed to continue all the Bush tax cuts for a year, he would, one year later, have held the power of a disappearing $5 trillion tax cut that could be continued in whole or in part only if the GOP folded on their spending-limiting sequester. The Republicans in the House, undermined by some of their own appropriators, would not likely have saved all or even much of the Sequester when faced with the threat of losing much or all of the Bush tax cuts.

Obama threw away his leverage for the rest of this presidency. He gave away control over spending when he proposed and then signed the Sequester. He then gave away the ability to unilaterally raise taxes by making 85 percent of the Bush tax cuts permanent.

For those who thought he was Machiavelli, this was an eye-opening moment. He was more like a child on the beach who held a huge pearl in his hand—the power to grant or take away $5 trillion in taxes over a decade—and he threw the pretty thing away back into the ocean's waves. He had held real power. He did not understand it and he threw it away.

After the president had agreed to make 85 percent of the Bush tax cuts permanent, but before he actually signed the legislation stripping him of the power to deny the extension of the tax cuts, I was on CNN discussing the matter and was tempted to explain how this was the president of the United States slashing his own tendons and rendering himself largely powerless for the rest of his administration even before he was inaugurated for his second term. He had given up control over total government spending in the 2011 Sequester deal and was about to give up control over taxation weeks before his second inauguration. Had any president ever shorn himself of such power? On TV, I sort of choke as I realize that there was just the teensiest chance that he had missed this and some staffer over at the White House might say, "Hey Boss, wait on signing that." I shifted my comments to something anodyne and un-useful to the other team.

Not long after this, I shared my analysis and that story at a conference sponsored by the *Atlantic* magazine and hosted by the unstoppable Steve Clemons and, as I walked off stage, was met by Robert Kuttner, the copublisher of the *American Prospect*, who is depressingly left-wing and even more depressingly smart. He shouted at me that I was completely correct in my analysis that the president had already given away his power before his second term started when he made the better part of the Bush tax cuts permanent. Why, I asked Mr. Kuttner, did the president and his advisers agree to this permanent deal, then?

Mr. Kuttner shared a rather uncharitable view of the mental capacities of those advising the president in this case. One of the brightest men of the Left in America saw the correlation of forces and the available levers of power just as I describe it here in these pages. And Obama missed it. Obama gave away power he had worked his entire life to accumulate. That has got to be no fun to contemplate in the retirement home.

Is a Grand Bargain an Option? Was It Ever a Possibility?

Might Obama, Reid, and Pelosi agree to a grand bargain that dramatically reduces unfunded liabilities and future debt by reforming entitlements and at the same time increases taxes? It is not impossible to imagine. Many in the media imagine this with some regularity. From time to time some Republicans believe such a deal would be very advantageous to Democrats and that therefore they might actually pull the trigger on the to-date-illusory "grand bargain."

But we do not have to guess about what Democrats think. We don't have to channel John Lennon and his song "Imagine." We can look to history. Not the Middle Ages or the Roaring Twenties.

We can look to two full years of 2009 and 2010 when Obama was president and the Senate was run by Harry Reid and fifty-eight (and briefly fifty-nine) more Democrats and Nancy Pelosi had an eighty-six-seat Democrat majority in the House. They could have reformed as much or as little of our runaway entitlement spending as they wished. They could also have raised taxes at the same time. They could pass any "grand bargain" with any ratio of spending restraint and tax hikes their little hearts desired. Ten-to-one reductions in long-term entitlement reform in return for more cash now in higher taxes. Or three to one. Heck, one to one. Whatever.

Given this opportunity, the Democrat leadership woke up every morning for two years, 728 days, and did not draft legislation, hold hearings, or give a speech about such a deal. When they had the power to do the "grand bargain" and did not need a single GOP vote...they did nothing.

If someone tells you they "really, really, really" want to go to the gym and exercise and lose weight, but for two full years they never step foot in the gym, you may decide they have no interest in actually slimming down.

Why do we believe the Democrats want to do something now when they could have done it by themselves at any point for two years?

Or go back to the Clinton years...they had complete control in 1993 and 1994. They raised taxes, increased spending, and increased entitlement spending. Or in the eight years of Kennedy and Johnson. They did not reform entitlements, they expanded them.

And when Obama, Reid, and Pelosi were given as close to ultimate power as a party is granted in the American constitutional system, they chose in 2009 and 2010 to not reform any of the entitlements that are driving a $84 trillion unfunded liability but instead to add to that by passing an unread Obamacare bill of three thousand pages that will increase taxes and spending by more than $1 trillion each decade in the future.[33]

So Republicans, conservatives, taxpayers, random observers with above-room-temperature IQ can be pardoned for believing that media elites speaking for Democrats and explaining their undying devotion to a "grand bargain" to hike taxes and reform entitlements significantly are either delusional or fibbing.

The offer of a grand bargain of tax hikes for spending cuts was made in 1982 and 1990 as a way to convince Republicans to walk down a dark alley with the promise of massive spending restraint only to be mugged once again and left with tax hikes and no spending restraint.

In 1990, the Taxpayer Protection Pledge punished those who were seduced, used, and fooled by the "grand bargain" ruse. By 2011, the Taxpayer Protection Pledge was strong enough to protect all taxpayers from this all-too-predictable "sting."

The Taxpayer Protection Pledge made it possible for the House majority to stand up to President Obama, and it kept the Senate caucus united despite some impure thoughts about tax increases on the part of a surprising few. The Pledge saved the American people $2.5 trillion in spending over ten years. And the Pledge stopped both the $5 trillion in tax hikes threatened by Simpson-Bowles and the $1.4 trillion in higher taxes later demanded by President Obama and Senator John Kerry.

Not bad work for a fifty-eight-word sentence and a tradition only thirty years old.

CHAPTER 8

Focus: It Is the Spending, Stupid

If you want to reduce taxes, you have to restrain government spending.

When the government spends a dollar, it is committed to taking that dollar from taxpayers today, or to borrowing the dollar and having future taxpayers pay it back with interest, or to inflating the currency so the dollar of debt is worth less and less. (As is your paycheck.)

The inflation route was used to pay for much of the Revolutionary War. The expression "not worth a Continental" stemmed from the lost value in printed money not backed with gold, land, or taxes. Confederate currency met a similar fate. Fully 75 percent of the funding of the first year of the South's cost of the Civil War was either borrowed money or printed currency.[1]

It is unlikely that modern lenders will tolerate our government inflating debt completely away. A dollar spent today will be paid by taxes now or taxes later.

If we are to reduce the tax burden, we must reduce the cost of government spending.

Easier said than done.

Every dollar spent has political support from the fellow who grabbed it. And the more wasteful and silly the spending, the harder the recipient knows he has to fight to keep it coming. There is no strong political constituency for wise and necessary spending. That kind of spending does not spawn the massive buildings on K Street that today "protect" cash flow to organized spending interests.

In the past, taxpayer movements have risen up to oppose tax hikes. But those tax hikes often came years after the overspending that made them necessary. Why didn't voters act at the start? Why didn't we see increased spending leading inexorably to higher taxes? Good questions. People are busy. They have lives. The tax-and-spend interests do a good job of trying to hide the connection between spending and taxes. The new spending, we are told, will come from "the government" or "revenue." Rarely, if ever, do the big spenders accurately label their new programs and admit to voters who will be paying the bill. Many taxpayers may assume (or hope) that "someone else" will pay the coming taxes.

I would have told you—I certainly said it to myself—that I *knew* we were screwed in 2008 as soon as Obama was elected and combined the power of the White House with the already Democrat House and Senate. I knew the wily Obama would cleverly pile up spending with little effective opposition and we would only be able to begin to turn things around when his tax hikes—wisely delayed until he and his Congress were reelected—spurred a tax revolt.

But I was wrong. After thirty years of fighting for limited government, I, and the entire country, saw something new. An anti-spending revolt. I was as surprised as I was delighted.

On February 19, 2009, Rick Santelli unleashed a powerful rant on CNBC against Obama's massive explosion in new spending and debt. By the week of April 15, 2009, there were between six hundred and a thousand Tea Party rallies with between 440,000 and 810,000 attendees.[2] Unbelievable. Unprecedented. America had seen many tax revolts. This was the first revolt to focus on spending.

The Republicans in Congress in January 2009 felt the mood change. Before the Tea Party rallies, before the Santelli rant, the House Republicans held together to vote against the $800 billion stimulus spending. Can you imagine the temptation hovering over Republican appropriators? The deal was obvious: "How would you like $40 billion (five percent of the spending spree) divided among forty Republicans to give to your favorite friends?" All Faust wanted was forty Republican votes for the Stimulus plan. The payoff would be somewhat larger than thirty pieces of silver. The Democrats didn't need the GOP leadership or even a majority of Republican members. They only needed to buy off a few Republicans. Then the spending would be "bipartisan," which is Washington talk for "there is no one identifiable target to blame." But the ground had shifted. Something big was afoot. Every Republican in the House voted no on the Stimulus. Later every single Republican in the House and Senate voted against Obamacare. After the 2010 election, earmarks were abolished by the House on January 5, 2011, and by the Senate Appropriations Committee on February 11.

The 2011 budget reduced Obama's plans for federal spending by $2.5 trillion over the next ten years. The Sequester put a legal cap on domestic discretionary spending. This was not a promise that congressmen would vote to reduce government spending in future years. This was real. Previous promises to cut spending in the future were left to the tender mercies of the appropriations committees, and they turned out to be lies in 1982 and 1990.

Federal spending had been 19.0 percent of GDP in 2007, before the Fannie Mae and Freddie Mac collapse. Obama drove the spending up to 24.4 percent of GDP in 2009. Thanks to the GOP takeover of the House in 2010 and the sequester in 2012, by January 2015, federal spending as a percentage of GDP had fallen back to 20.4 percent of GDP.[3] In wrestling, this is known as a reversal.

How much easier would it be to downsize the IRS and reform taxation if the federal government were only "required" to take 10 percent of everything Americans earn? Not 20 percent, but only half that. Tax reform is difficult, if not impossible, when reformers must raise the same amount of money as under the old regime. How much progress can be made with those rules? But if we can reduce the total tax burden, then tax reform is easier and more likely to pass political muster.

So, what is to be done? Here follow ten ideas to help us reduce total government spending.

One: Focus on Spending as Percentage of the Economy...not the Deficit

Step one is always to focus on the right metric. If we wish to keep an eye on government spending, if we wish to limit and reduce government spending, we should then measure and focus on government spending. This sounds obvious. It is. But the big spenders work like magicians employing legerdemain who try to distract us and trick us into focusing on the wrong numbers. Such as the deficit.

Spending is how much money the government spends. The federal deficit is the difference between how much money the government takes in taxes this year and how much it spends this year.

When I was in college at Harvard, all the smart liberal professors explained that the deficit did not matter. "We owed it to ourselves." Talk about the deficit was, I was told, a trick by Republicans to oppose wonderful new spending programs.

It is true that conservatives in the 1950s and '60s often criticized deficit spending. They thought they were using "deficit" as an intensifier, as in "really, really big" or "way too much" spending. Deficit spending was meant to convey that the crazy government was spending so much money that it overran their tax take. It also played to the American antipathy to debt. This level of spending is not only higher than our taxes, but it also increases debt.

While Democrats pooh-poohed criticism of "deficit spending," Republicans made a different mistake. As Americans are wont to do, they shortened the phrase from "deficit spending" to "deficits." So now, they were arguing against deficit spending but calling them "deficits." This allowed Democrats to sound like Republicans by railing against "deficits" when they were actually calling for higher taxes to continue the spending.

Republicans had screwed up. They lost the focus on total government spending. Heck, they lost the focus on spending at all. Now everyone was talking about "deficits," and there are two ways to fix that: raise taxes or cut spending. The Democrats and the media had no interest in reducing spending. The establishment media jumped in and said, "Great, now that we all agree that the problem is the deficit, let's raise taxes. Problem fixed." This is what allowed the 1982 and 1990 "deficit reduction" budget agreements to turn into tax increases to pay for higher spending. The press and the Democrats went so far as to call tax hikes "fiscally conservative" because they promised to reduce the deficit. That is how backward the conversation got.

When we fight to reduce "spending," we have to say it loudly and clearly. "Spending." Better yet is to measure and focus on total government spending as a percentage of the economy. Then one can compare one year to another over the decades. This has averaged just below 21 percent for the past forty years.[4]

There are only two ways to reduce spending as a percentage of the economy, or GDP. One, reduce spending. Two, increase the size of the overall economy through economic growth. Now, center-right politicians support lower spending and pro-growth policies such as lower tax rates, less regulation, and tort reform. Our friends on the Left oppose real spending restraint and are prevented by their political masters—the unions, beneficiaries of government spending, and trial lawyers—from supporting any pro-growth policies that actually create permanent private-sector jobs. This is not an exaggeration. The national Democrat Party does not support any single proposal that would increase real economic growth. The ideas they toss out—taxing Peter to pay Paul, and pretending that the entire economy has grown—do not work. All they do is move wealth around. Peter has it taken from him. The dollar is given to

Paul. If you take a bucket of water from one side of a lake and then pour it back into the lake—in front of TV cameras—is the lake any deeper?

Why would conservatives ever move from measuring and debating spending as a percentage of the economy, a debate for which the conservatives have two answers: less spending and pro-growth tax reform, and the liberals have no answers at all that either grow the economy or reduce spending?

Let us place our feet firmly on the battlefield of reducing government spending as a percentage of the economy and challenge the Democrats to come to the table with something that moves that meter in the right direction.

Two: Expand the Success of BRAC Spending Reform to Other Areas

The Grace Commission, created by President Reagan to identify opportunities to save taxpayer dollars, reported that there were at least $2 billion a year to be saved by closing unnecessary military bases. Dick Armey, the conservative congressman from Texas, introduced legislation to close down several useless bases and forts that dated back to the War of 1812. This sounded like an easy, simple, small, but useful step forward in reducing unnecessary spending. Not. The congressmen in the districts with forts scheduled to be closed went to work to build political opposition. They got their senators involved. They traded their votes to other congressmen who were defending different wasteful spending efforts. Here was the deal: "You vote to protect my unnecessary military 'base' and I will vote for your counterproductive sugar subsidy. You win, I win, and the taxpayers lose." A well-meaning effort to save a few bucks actually backfired and created more support for wasteful spending than had existed before. Ouch.

Then, in 1987, Dick Armey had a moment of genius. He recruited liberal Democrat Philip Sharp of Indiana to cosponsor his bill entitled the Base Realignment and Closure Act (BRAC). Here is how it worked: Congress would appoint a commission filled with military experts and folks from both parties that would work with the Pentagon to prepare a list of bases that the Defense Department did not need or agreed could be scaled down. (The Pentagon participation protected any bases that appeared wasteful but were in reality housing some supersecret weapon system.)

Then this list would go to Congress, and unless Congress voted down the recommendation and the president signed the rejection legislation, the closures and realignments would go forward. Stopping the commission's recommendations would take a majority of the House and Senate and the president's support, or two-thirds of the House and Senate to override a presidential veto.

Why did we have to go through this rigmarole? After World War II, defense secretaries closed down hundreds of bases that were no longer needed. But when the Nixon administration attempted to have the secretary of defense organize a similar reorganization of US military bases after the Vietnam War—when the active armed services reduced in number from 3,064,760 to 2,128,120 between 1969 and 1974—the Democrat Congress passed legislation taking that authority away from the Defense Department.

When Dick Armey first introduced his base-closing legislation in 1987, it was narrowly defeated. (It tells us a great deal that one of the most innovative and important ideas for reducing what everyone knew was wasteful spending was voted down the first time Congress looked at it. However, the following year, Reagan's defense secretary, Donald Carlucci, ignited support for the measure by nominating a BRAC commission anyway. The Defense Authorization Amendments and Base Closure and Realignment Act was then passed on October 12, 1988, with overwhelming support.[5]

The commission recommended the closure of eighty-six installations and the realignment of fifty-nine others. A resolution of disapproval was sent to Congress. It failed 381–43. The first BRAC was a success.

Four more BRACs followed.

The BRAC process is particularly effective because it allows unneeded bases to be closed while protecting elected officials from attacks that they failed to "keep federal dollars flowing." The BRAC allows every congressman to vote against waste in general while defending his or her own unneeded base unsuccessfully. Once the list of closures and realignments was out, everyone whose home base was not targeted could bravely welcome the savings. Those on the cutting block were not numerous enough to stop the process. The independent commission was able to make decisions on the merits.

When the 1991 commission recommended the closing of a base in Pennsylvania, Senator Arlen Specter challenged the legality of the commission, arguing the case himself in front of the Supreme Court. The court rejected his case, but Specter was viewed as a champion by those communities profiting from the unnecessary bases. The senator looked good for the locals. The savings took place.

The 1993 commission recommended the closure of 130 bases and 45 realignments. These were estimated to have a onetime cost of $7.43 billion and netted $3.8 billion in additional annual savings. The 1995 round also required an upfront cost of $3.6 billion, and saved an estimated $1.6 billion each year. There were also BRACs in 2001 and 2005.

Five times Congress has gone through the difficult process of passing legislation to set up a new BRAC. One way to save more money more quickly would be to make the BRAC an annual event that continues until Congress votes to stop the annual process.

The BRAC structure could be also used to stop other wasteful spending that is otherwise defended by local congressmen. Such as? Well…today there are 31,135 post offices in the United States. By comparison, FedEx has 1,800 regional offices and UPS has 4,700 regional offices. Just like they love their military bases, many local politicians love their local post offices. They may be named after a fellow local pol. Maybe even the congressman's father. The Post Office believes it could save billions by closing some post offices and consolidating others—just as the military has done. What would it take to stop wasting billions? One solution would be another BRAC, this time for post offices.

And states should look at the BRAC structure as ways of saving money by reducing or eliminating white elephants at the state level.

Three: Re-create an Anti-appropriations Committee

There are fifty-one members of the House Appropriations Committee. There are twelve subcommittee chairmen. In the Senate, there are thirty members on the Senate Appropriations Committee and twelve subcommittee chairman. That is 14 percent of the House membership and 42 percent of the one hundred senators. It is a small army of congressmen whose job in Washington is to spend other people's money. Like professionals who work in mortuaries or slaughterhouses or law firms, you can get used to anything. Even conservatives who come to Washington promising to rein in spending can get used to spending money that doesn't belong to them. Millions blend into billions and now trillions. Every day, they meet people who lobby for the spending interests. They rarely meet taxpayers who say, "Enough." An appropriator who says no many times is still saying yes too often.

Indulge my fantasy for a moment. What if Congress created an "Anti-appropriations Committee," a committee just like all the other committees, but this committee could only pass laws that cut spending and ended spending programs. They couldn't spend a penny. Their jurisdiction would be "spending cuts."

While the BRAC process provides immunity for politicians who fear the political consequences of doing the right thing, the Anti-appropriations Committee would provide institutional incentives for championing spending reform. Candidates for Congress could run for office proclaiming, "I want to serve on the Anti-appropriations Committee." They could get famous holding hearings on the failures of programs that have been unquestioned for years. This could change the culture of Congress. It could change the world.

There has actually been legislation introduced in Congress to create this thing of beauty and wonder—the Anti-appropriations Committee. Is it all a dream?

No. Here in the United States there actually once was such a committee. It did great work from 1941 to 1974. It saved billions in wasteful spending and killed programs that, if allowed to continue, would have grown over the years. Let's look back at a glorious but forgotten part of our history and see what we can learn in order to re-create such a committee.

The "Joint Committee on Reduction of Nonessential Federal Programs"—roll that name around on your tongue, doesn't it sound sweet?—was first proposed in the Seventy-Seventh Congress by Senator Harry F. Byrd, Sr. (D-Va). Later known for its creator, the "Byrd Committee" could only recommend reducing or eliminating existing government programs.

The committee was a bicameral body made up of fourteen members: three from each of the House and Senate Appropriations Committees, three from the House Ways and Means Committee, and three from the Senate Finance Committee. The treasury secretary and the director of the Bureau of the Budget also served on it. The committee had the ability to subpoena officials to compel them to testify on wasteful government expenditures.

Following years of New Deal growth, the committee had a "target-rich environment." It can be credited with abolishing the Civilian Conservation Corps in 1943, saving $240 million. In the same year, the committee slashed the size of another New Deal project, the Work Projects Administration. A year later, the committee convinced Congress to end the program completely, saving taxpayers $106,168,499 in 1944 dollars. In 1944, the committee also axed the National Youth Administration, saving another $57 million. By 1945, the committee reported it had amassed savings totaling $3 billion, or roughly $40 billion in today's dollars.

It was unique and successful in its simplicity: Given no authority to increase the burden of government, it was left only to cut the size of the state or do nothing at all. The Anti-appropriations Committee was helped by the fact that the government wanted to spend money on the war effort and this helped create pressure for savings elsewhere that is less evident in times of peace.

Sadly, once the war and the budget pressures it presented began to wind down, the committee's recommendations were largely ignored by Congress. It devolved into a mainly academic body, providing detailed reports on government waste. The committee was discontinued in 1974, when Congress transferred its responsibilities—but not its authority and power—to a newly created Congressional Budget Office. The CBO remains as an important if imperfect scorekeeper for Congress, but lacks the ability to impel Congress to vote on cost-saving legislation.

Restoring the Anti-appropriations Committee would allow congressmen to campaign and govern as pro-taxpayer reformers. The previous model available for a new congressman was to excel at "constituent service," which meant stealing money from other congressional districts and appearing at the resulting ribbon-cutting ceremonies in their own districts. Of course, the cost of having access to the taxes paid in other districts was to have to stand by silently as the other 434 congressmen looted your own district. But congressmen rarely put out press releases celebrating the despoiling of their neighbors and voters.

One of the few funny jokes about Congress is that there are three political parties: Republicans, Democrats, and Appropriators. An Anti-appropriation Committee could create a fourth party, uniquely dedicated to protecting taxpayers and campaigning not on the ability to deliver pork but on the courage to oppose it.

Four: Term-Limit Membership on the Appropriations Committee

The term-limits movement has had some great victories. Today thirty-six states have term limited their governors to one or two terms.[6] Fifteen states have term limited their state legislators to terms of six, eight, or twelve years.[7] The federal government term limited the president after Franklin Roosevelt insisted on running for a third and fourth term despite the two-term tradition set by Washington and despite his own failing health. How selfish to have run in 1944, knowing he would not serve through a term that would face monumental challenges. FDR died eighty-two days into his fourth term. The slogan against Roosevelt in his 1940 drive for a third term was "Washington Wouldn't, Grant Couldn't, and Roosevelt Shouldn't." Washington, of course, could have been reelected as often as he wanted. King George III said Washington's decision to walk away from power made him the greatest man in the world. He was right. It put the nail in the coffin for anyone thinking of reestablishing a monarchy. Grant wanted to run for a third term but was stopped by his own party. When the Republicans took control of the House and Senate in 1947, they wanted to make sure this would never happen again. Politicians are lousy judges of how indispensable they are to the republic.

The modern term-limit movement ran state initiatives and defeated the efforts run by incumbents and their friends in the lobbying field. In 1992, eight states passed initiatives installing term limits, winning an average of 67.8 percent of the vote.[8]

Those initiatives also created six-year term limits for US congressmen and twelve-year terms for senators. A divided Supreme Court voted 5–4 to disallow states from imposing term limits on federal officeholders. So right now there are no binding limits on average congressmen. But the logic of term limits did arrive in Washington. The incoming Gingrich Republican class of 1994 demanded that committee chairmen be term limited. They didn't want to work in a Congress where the twenty committee chairs held court for decades at a time, bullying younger members to vote for lousy bills under the threat of having any legislation they cared about killed in the committee chair's jurisdiction. The Senate reluctantly followed in 1997.

This meant that every six years there would be a new chairman for each committee. The moment they became chairman, their power would begin to melt. It was term limited. It had a sell-by date. All congressmen were more equal. No longer a collection of peasants driven by lords.

But there are some congressmen, other than committee chairs, who wield excess power. Those are the members of the Appropriations Committee in the House and Senate. It is past time to term limit membership on this committee. Would such a move be unprecedented? No. When the Budget Committee was created in 1974, it was believed that the power of the purse would flow from this committee. To limit this power, membership on the Budget Committee was limited to six years. Still is. But they missed the target. The excessive and dangerous power was actually in the Appropriations Committee.

Six years on the Appropriations/Spending Committee should not ruin a healthy young man or woman who arrives in Washington wishing to do good. But with no term limits, initiates arriving at Reagan Airport to join Congress eventually come to see themselves first and foremost as appropriators and only secondly as Republicans and Democrats.

Five: Keep the Ban on Earmarks

We are now, thankfully in the post-earmark era. A congressman's ability to procure earmarked spending for some of his constituents used to be proof of the congressman's vigor and virility. Now it is seen as boorish and corrupt, as publicly acceptable as farting at the dinner table.

But there is always a danger that earmarks could return. Apologists for earmarks point out that the amount of earmarks in a given year was small. In 2004, for instance, earmarks amounted to $3.1 billion—a tiny fraction of total spending that year of $2.3 trillion.

Why focus on earmarks? Three reasons.

First, regular congressmen could not stick earmarks into the budget. They had to ask an appropriator to do this for them. This required a favor. Favors, for those who watched *The Godfather* and *The Godfather Part II*, come with obligations. Someday. Someday soon. Those outside the Appropriations Committee were perpetually and increasingly "in debt" to the appropriators. They were hardly in a position to oppose the massive spending bills the appropriators churned out each year. Earmarks were hostages. Vote against the budget and your earmark bites the dust.

Second, earmarks were the broken windows of the overspending problem. If every congressman was scurrying around to grab a few million dollars in wasteful spending for his campaign contributors' favorite charities, it is difficult for anyone to take seriously that there is any interest in large-scale reforms and spending restraint. If everyone is busy shoplifting, no one reports the embezzler.

Third, earmarks have traditionally been the currency of Washington corruption. If the president or the congressional leadership wanted you to vote for legislation that violated your sense of decency—and for a Reagan Republican, that would be legislation that included a tax hike or too much spending—you would be offered, or denied, an earmark. Earmarks were payoffs to do the wrong thing. Earmarks, small as they were, bought tax hikes and spending that did real damage to the economy and the congressman's soul.

Six: Require All Emergency Spending to Be "Paid For" by Cuts in Present Spending Across the Board

When Bill Clinton was president. the Republican House and Senate did not trust the administration. This was wise. Congress insisted that any "emergency" spending because of a disaster such as a hurricane, flood, or drought be offset in the same legislation by across-the-board cuts in other programs. This stopped Congress itself from turning a targeted emergency piece of legislation into a "Christmas tree," with spending not only for the flooded state but for the friends and relatives of congressmen and senators in the other forty-nine states. Any spending had to be offset. This forced the existing beneficiaries of spending to fight against new folks pushing their way to the trough. This falls into the category of "it takes a thief to catch a thief." The best guardian of the henhouse is a fox who doesn't like competitors. Unfortunately this internal rule was abandoned by the Republican Congress when Bush was president. It should return as a law, not just a rule of thumb.

Seven: Measure Outputs, Not Inputs

Whenever we engage in a political debate, we should be clear just what we are asking/demanding the federal government to do. If we simply ask them to "do something" about education, the response will be to spend money. Perhaps we should explain that we want children to be able to read. Then the measure of whether a spending program works is whether reading skills advance. All political debates should focus on what the goal is *and* how we measure it. If this is not crystal clear, the spending interests will impose their metric: How much did "we" spend? Spending then becomes the measure of success. And if you are unhappy with the results of our little program, the problem must be we failed to spend enough money. Taxpayers actually want to know that crime is falling or education is actually happening. If there is no metric, there should be no spending program. If those demanding more money cannot explain what they will do with it—and how you measure that they told the truth—then it is clear they are just asking for money with no real reason beyond wanting more money. And they should be pushed down a stairwell.

Eight: Reduce the Number of Government Employees through Attrition

Much of the cost of any "program" is personnel. Twenty-eight percent of the army's budget, for example, is pay and benefits and pensions for soldiers.[9] Personnel accounts for 42 percent of the budget for Congress,[10] and for 34 percent of the budget for the White House.[11]

It follows that one of the best ways to reduce government spending is to reduce the number of government workers. The great conservative writer Frank Chodorov, who authored *The Income Tax Root of All Evil*, pointed out during the McCarthy period that the best way to reduce the number of Communists employed in the federal government is to hire fewer people in the government. True enough. It's also the best way to keep costs down, period. But the Washington establishment makes it difficult to impossible to fire government "workers."

The Ryan budget plan calls for reducing civilian government employment through attrition, replacing only one of every three workers who retires—no one gets fired. The downsizing takes place over time, and the bureaucracy has time to get used to what is coming. Congressman Ken Calvert (R) of California has introduced legislation to downsize the Pentagon civilian workforce by 15 percent over current levels beginning in 2021. It minimizes disruption, reduces the political opposition, and as the average federal employee costs $120,000 a year in total compensation costs—pay, benefits, pensions—the savings are substantial.

Nine: Make All Government Spending—at the Federal, State, and Local Levels—Completely Transparent

Every check written, every contract, grant, pay stub, expense account, should be online and searchable by any American—heck, even the odd Canadian or two. The official government watchdogs looking for waste, fraud, and abuse have not done the job. How about using 300 million volunteers—the American people—to look at how money is spent to see who has a "no show" job, who gets multiple checks, and whether contract payments are reasonable and competitive.

Ten: Move All Government Pensions from "Defined Benefit" to "Defined Contribution"

Decades ago most pensions in the private sector and the government were "defined benefit." You were promised that after you retired, you would receive, say, half your salary until you died. Several problems: What if your employer, General Motors or the city of Detroit, goes broke—then what?

A "defined contribution" pension is one where what is defined is how much money your employer—a business, city, or federal or state government—put into your Individual Retirement Account (IRA) or personal savings account or 401(k). Every year a portion of your salary goes directly into your personal savings account, which you, not the government or a business, controls. When you leave your job, you take it with you to another job or retirement.

When a politician promises state or city employees he will raise their defined- benefit pension, he is making promises that will be paid out long after the present politician is out of office or dead. Think Mayor John Lindsay of New York City. Or all of the Chicago mayors. It is not surprising to learn that many business leaders in the private sector—for example, GM—sign contracts with unions that bankrupt their business only after the lazy CEO has retired and sold off all his GM stock. It buys temporary labor peace and a nice feature article in the *New York Times*.

No politicians should be able to make promises to spend money in the future. It is too corrupting. It is too tempting to give away the store in return for votes, a union endorsement, or campaign contributions. This is why we have run up $3 trillion in unfunded liabilities by state and local governments. Making such promises seemed so easy years ago. But we are approaching the time when more and more of those promises fall due, and some cities have gone bankrupt and a state or two might also. Illinois and California are nominating themselves. Some states are moving in the right direction: Utah passed a law in 2010 requiring that all new hires in the state—state, local, school district, and country employees—will have 10 percent of their salaries put into their personally controlled IRA. Police and firefighters get 12 percent. This ends the accumulation of new unfunded liabilities. Michigan did it for state (not local) employees in 1998 and this has already saved the state $1 billion in real dollars and $3 billion or $4 billion in what would have been unfunded liabilities.

Insisting that all pay, benefits, and pensions be online and transparent to voters is a good first step. Requiring that all pensions be defined-contribution stops politicians from being able to hide spending in the future. It ensures that it is impossible to promise unbelievable benefits today for the few tomorrow, benefits that will bind millions of taxpayers in involuntary servitude to pay pensions that are not available to those who work for a living in the real economy.

In the past few years most real businesses have made the shift from defined-benefit to defined-contribution systems. Now smart states and towns are doing the same. This needs to move forward more quickly.

Eleven: Kill the Davis-Bacon Law

Some laws are stupid. Some laws are evil. Other laws are both stupid and evil. That is the story of Davis-Bacon. The Davis-Bacon Act was enacted in 1931 and named for Congressman Robert L. Bacon of New York and Senator James J. Davis of Pennsylvania. It was a deliberate effort to keep Southern—read "black"—workers from moving North and competing with white union labor.

Davis-Bacon requires that federally funded contractors pay "pre-vailing wages," which not surprisingly are determined to be union wages, higher than market rates. This makes it difficult to hire younger, less experienced workers and train them. If contractors have to pay union wages by law, they simply hire larger, unionized companies and not new firms and young workers. Those trying to get a start in life would find themselves without a first rung on the economic ladder. South Africa did the same thing with job reservations, which kept blacks out of higher-paying jobs. All the economic damage done to the young and vulnerable by minimum wages happens on steroids with the more powerful, targeted, and destructive Davis-Bacon.

Davis-Bacon laws increase the annual cost of federal construction of army bases, houses, and highways by an estimated 25 or even 40 percent. It runs into the billions in overspending each year. By abolishing this antiquated and mean-spirited law we could save taxpayers a great deal of money, or we could spend the same amount and have more, better, and safer highways and bridges.

Thirty-two states have state versions of the federal Davis-Bacon law that drive up the cost of everything they build at the state level. Eighteen states function quite well without such laws. They competitively bid public-works contracts to lower costs. Step one would be for the thirty-two states to save money by repealing their state anticompetitive Davis-Bacon laws.

Twelve: Audit the Pentagon

What? Are we picking on the defense budget? No. The CFO Act of 1990 requires federal agencies to pass an independent audit. Some departments have done better than others.

Having an audit doesn't mean you are spending wisely. It just means you can show how much you spent and where. And that if you claim you spent money on a car or tank, you can point to it. However, our friends at the Pentagon have never actually passed an audit. In fact, they have never even begun one. They tell Congress that they shouldn't insist on an audit, because the Defense Department could not pass it. That is actually a very good reason to do an audit, and a very lousy reason to postpone an audit. Americans who understand that we need a serious national defense in a still-dangerous world should be the first to insist that the Defense Department undergo an annual audit so that taxpayer dollars spent on defense are actually being spent on national defense and not the defense of entrenched spending interests, yesterday's priorities, and bureaucratic turf.

Thirteen: Ban Politicians from Naming Things after Themselves

This is an obvious follow-on reform to the banning of earmarks. Politicians like to name things after themselves. This goes back to the days of Rome and emperors who filled the public square with projects named after them and paid for by taxpayers. Robert Byrd, longtime appropriator from the state of West Virginia, filled the state with government buildings named after himself.

Banning the naming of any building, road, airport, or government-funded anything while a politician serves in public office would reduce the present incentive to use tax dollars to create the modern equivalent of mausoleums and pyramids to commemorate the vanity, pride, and corruption of those who use the tax dollars of others to build monuments to their egos. This ban should be enacted at the state, local, or national level.

Fourteen: Ban Politicians from "Retiring" into Jobs They Funded

One of the favorite retirement plans for state and national politicians is to shower a local university with taxpayer cash and then, upon retirement, recoup those dollars by becoming the university president or well-paid professor. If a congressman or governor believes a university or hospital or museum deserves tax dollars, he is free to vote for such expenditures. He should, however, then be forbidden from ever retiring into a job he has prepaid in the very institution he funded using taxpayer blood, sweat, and tears. Politicians who vote to build a prison should not later become the high-paid warden. It would not violate anyone's sense of propriety, however, if the politician does spend his retirement in that prison in a deserved lesser capacity: inmate.

CHAPTER 9

The Best Cure: Strong Economic Growth

If your personal fitness goal is to reduce your body fat index, you can either eat less fat or you can exercise more and build more muscle. Either or both work to the same end.

If our goal as Americans is to maximize individual liberty and reduce the cost and intrusiveness of government, we want to reduce the percentage of our income that is spent by government. There are two dials to manipulate: Spending less is one; creating economic growth that increases national income is the second.

A federal budget of $100 billion crushes liberty and individual freedom in a national economy of $200 billion. It means 50 percent of everything the people create is taken by force by the government. Lords in the Middle Ages took 20 to 25 percent from the peasants.

A federal budget of $100 billion with a national economy of $1 trillion is a lighter load, only 10 percent of the national income. The same size government—$100 billion—can be either large or small depending on the size of the economy. Stronger horses can pull heavier carts.

Economic growth is also a powerful way to increase federal revenues *without* raising taxes. How powerful?

One rule of thumb was given to us by the CBO in 2012. If the American economy grows an additional 1 percent a year for one decade, say at 3 percent rather than 2 percent, for ten years in a row, the federal government brings in an additional $2.8 trillion in tax dollars.[1]

If the United States were to grow at 4 percent a year for the next decade rather than the Obama rate of about 2 percent, the federal government would raise—without any tax hike—$5.6 trillion over those ten years.

To completely wipe out the $14 trillion debt, we need only grow at 4 percent for twenty-five years. Or if we grew at the rate China has been growing at, say 8 percent for one decade, and use all the additional revenue from growth to pay down debt, we would pay off the national debt in less than ten years.

Economic growth is a powerful way to reduce taxes and spending as a percentage of the economy. Small changes in growth over time make big changes—in the good or bad direction.

The best way to increase federal tax revenue is to have greater economic growth. Politicians who say they "need" more money for government programs should support pro-growth economic policies. Not raise taxes.

What economic policies have proven to increase economic growth?

One: Reduce Marginal Tax Rates on Individuals and Businesses

During World War I the top marginal income tax rate reached 77 percent. By 1925 President Calvin Coolidge and Treasury Secretary Mellon brought the top marginal income tax rate down to 25 percent. The economy grew by 4.2 percent a year between 1920 and 1929. (Herbert Hoover stopped further reduction of the income tax rates and dramatically increased the taxes on imported goods with the Smoot-Hawley Tariff Act. This was unhelpful.)

In the 1960s, after the Kennedy tax cuts reduced all rates by 22 percent and brought the top rate from 91 percent to 70 percent, the economy grew by 26 percent between 1964 and 1969.

In the 1980s Reagan's tax cuts took effect January 1, 1983, and the economy grew 29 percent over the next seven years.

In addition to reducing the tax burden, how else might we increase economic growth?

Two: Reform Tort Law So the Trial Lawyers Do Less Damage

All those lawsuits where billionaire trial lawyers get rich working on 30 percent commission as they sue companies because their client spilled coffee on themselves or tried to trim the hedges with a lawn mower are expensive. Lawsuits against the drug industry make all new drugs more expensive. Suing doctors forces hospitals to spend billions on "defensive medicine" and drives up the cost of our doctor's bills as doctors must pay hundreds of thousands in malpractice insurance.

The Manhattan Institute calculated the cost of such litigation in America in 2009 to be over $250 billion, or more than 2 percent of the entire economy.[2] Three times what it costs the people of Japan or France or Britain.

Reforming tort laws to reduce junk lawsuits would help the economy in two ways: First, it drops the costs of inventing, creating, and producing in America. Second, it cuts off the flow of billions of dollars to left-wing trial lawyers, who are the major funding source of the modern Democrat Party after the labor union bosses. Trial lawyers know that any party or candidate dedicated to economic growth will soon push them away from the trough.

Three: Spend Less

Richard Rahn, the former chief economist of the US Chamber of Commerce, has discovered the "Rahn Curve," which shows historically that once-basic government functions such as national defense, rule of law, defense of property rights, and a neutral judiciary have been funded, the less the government spends the faster the economy grows. The Rahn Curve does for spending and growth what the "Laffer Curve" did for tax rates and economic growth: Spend less, grow more.

Four: Regulate Less

The Competitive Enterprise Institute estimates that regulations cost the American economy $1.863 trillion in 2013, or 11 percent of the national economy.[3] The National Association of Manufacturers puts the 2012 number at more than $2 trillion in 2014 dollars, or 12 percent of the total economy. Regulations consume 11 percent to 12 percent of the economy, meaning they cost half as much as federal spending and just a bit less than all state and local spending combined.[4]

Regulations have been flowing out of Washington at the rate of more than 3,500 "final rules" each year. Since 1992, we have had 87,282 regulatory rules piled on the American economy. Every product and service in America costs more because companies are forced to hire lawyers rather than engineers and factory workers.

Today, even before a business begins to produce goods—and has to follow Uncle Sam's regulations—it first must jump through a series of bureaucratic hoops to get the government's permission to produce.

The US Chamber of Commerce did a study in 2011 that if the projects then stuck in the permitting process were allowed to proceed, it would create 1.9 million jobs and add $1.1 trillion to the economy.[5] This is a massive hidden cost to our economy that could be easily fixed—with the political power and will to tackle the regulators.

Why does Washington damage the economy through overregulation? Too often the best way for a politician to hide his "spending problem" is to pass a regulation making you or a business spend money rather than take the money in taxes and spend it through the government. Easier. Not as visible. Tougher to hold politicians responsible as they pass a law and allow a nonelected person who is unionized and therefore protected from voter wrath to actually write and impose the regulation months, even years, after the politician voted for the relevant law.

CEI points out that the regulatory burden placed on the United States is larger than the total economy of Canada or Australia.[6]

Imagine if the bureaucrats focused and reformed regulations to reduce their cost by only 20 percent—that would save $360 billion a year, roughly the size of Denmark's GDP.

Five: Maintain a Dollar as Good as Gold

Inflation and the fear of future inflation slows economic growth by misdirecting investment and by allowing the government to steal your money in the bank by printing more dollars and reducing the value of all existing dollars. The ancient Romans had the honesty to clip the coins to reduce the amount of silver or gold in each coin. The Fed doesn't need such a hands-on approach to reduce the value of your life savings.

Six: Have Congress Stay Home

There is an actual investment fund called the Congressional Effect Fund, created by Eric T. Singer. His research showed that over the past twenty-six years the stock market rose, on an annual basis, 17 percent when Congress was out of session and 1.7 percent when Congress was in session. The fear that Congress might do something destructive to the economy is so serious that it holds down the stock market.

By going home and not meeting, Congress can actually create wealth in a more highly valued stock market.

CHAPTER 10

Don't Raise Taxes—
Sell Stuff

There are ways for government to get money other than raising taxes.

The government could buy or steal a factory and use the "profits," after wages and investment costs, to finance the government. But government tends to do poorly as a wealth creator, even when they grant themselves a monopoly and ban competitors. Pre–Margaret Thatcher Britain specialized in "Lemmon Socialism." The very businesses producing steel, coal, or railroads that once made men wealthy, after being nationalized by Labor governments, tended to lose money for taxpayers rather than create profits to fund the government.

You can run an economy this way. Cuba did. Largely still does. This became clear when Fidel Castro's Cuba announced in 2014 that it was going to impose its first tax in sixty years. No taxes in a socialist economy? Did that work? Well, Castro's government had been living off the rent of owning everything in the nation. Kind of like kings used to do. However, Cuba has not been viewed as an overly successful model these last several decades.

Governments are pretty good at blowing things up and spending other people's money. Governments are not so good at creating wealth: Government-run lotteries are a worse deal for participants than the mob's numbers racket. Amtrak loses money while the railroad barons of the 1800s got rich building and running railroads. And the one really bad idea dating back to the US Constitution— the government-run postal service, now a monopoly—-one is reminded, bleeds cash.

Modernity frowns on what was once considered the model for state actors: invading and conquering your neighbor, looting his cities, and then taxing the folks you forgot to kill or enslave.

But there is one thing the government, even incompetent governments, can do to raise funds without raising taxes. And this actually makes all concerned better off—citizens, the government, and the overall economy.

Sell stuff.

And thanks to the greed and acquisitiveness of federal, state, and local governments over the years, our governments in America own a great deal of such stuff: land, buildings, the telecommunications spectrum, toll roads, airports, rail lines, and mineral rights in the fifty states and under the water up to two hundred miles out, in internationally recognized American territory.

This is not a particularly new idea. In America's early years a significant source of federal-government revenue came from selling land owned by the federal government.

From 1800 to 1860, the federal government sold off millions of acres of land. In 1810, total federal revenue was $9,385,000. Land sales were $697,000, or 7.4 percent of federal revenues. In 1820, federal revenues were $17,881,000 and land sales were $1,636,000, or 9 percent. In 1830, federal revenues were $24,844,000—you can see how the federal government is growing—and land sales were $2,339,000, just under 10 percent. Total revenues from the sale of federal lands from 1830 to 1860 were 11.94 percent of federal revenues. Later, from 1860 to 1900, land sales were less than 1 percent (0.89 percent) of total revenues.

This financed a good chunk of the federal budget. Government revenues were raised without taxing Americans. Pretty cool. In fact, land moving from federal control to individual use became economically useful, and real jobs and real wealth were created in the real economy.

Could we do this today? Let's check. The federal government owns as much of the land in America as Henry VIII of England owned after he nationalized the monasteries. More specifically: the federal government owns almost 640 million acres of land, or 28 percent of the total land base of 2.27 billion acres. We are not talking about Yosemite and the Grand Canyon here. Only 12.45 percent of federal land in 397 different parks is owned by the park service.

Let's pretend for a moment that the federal government is a competent manager of parks. . . . I know. . . . But for this exercise, let's set aside the national parks and assume that they are creditably and better run by Uncle Sam than they would be by a private conservation group or by Disney. And no snotty comments about forest fires on government-"protected" land . . . So let's just look at the rest of the government's holdings.

That leaves 540 million acres, or about 85 percent of land, owned by the federal government of the United States free to be sold to Americans to develop for farming, timber, hunting and recreation, housing, private conservation, mining, and energy production.[1] One notes that the federal government owns almost no land east of the Mississippi because early states were promised all federal land would transfer to state ownership when they became states. States could then sell or give that land to settlers. Despite a promise that all new states would come into the union with the same rule and rights, western states were not all granted this equal status. (This can and should be fixed. Fair is fair.)

This is how 69 percent of Alaska ended up being owned by the federal government, 45 percent of California, 84 percent of Nevada, 48 percent of Arizona, 41 percent of New Mexico, 53 percent of Oregon, and 50 percent of Idaho, but only 2.7 percent of North Dakota, 1.4 percent of Nebraska, 1.9 percent of Texas, and 0.8 percent of New York, where all the "Greens" live who believe that government

Who Owns the West?
Federal Land as Percentage of Total State Land Area

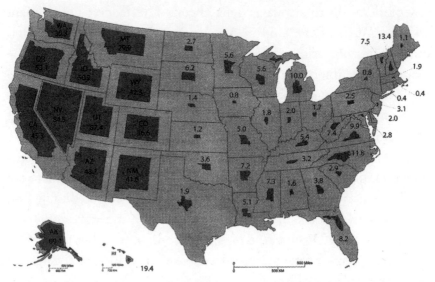

Data source: U.S. General Services Administrataion, *Federal Real Property Profile 2004*, excludes trust properties.

Graphic from http://endfedaddiction.org/

ownership is good for the soul, if not particularly useful in preventing forest fires.[2] The Obama administration in 2012 estimated the value of all federal lands at $408 billion.[3] As you might suspect, the government understates the value of the land it sits on, possibly, just possibly, to reduce the pressure to sell it off for productive use.

Let's look at how some present government spending could be paid for by selling or leasing federal land rather than raising taxes. Or perhaps we could use the cash to begin to pay down the national debt. Keep in mind that when "federal" land becomes productive private land, the resulting economic activity creates incomes that in turn pay federal income taxes and the new owners of the land pay local property taxes.

Here are six ways to raise revenue without raising taxes:

One: Legalize Drilling for Oil Offshore

The United States has legal ownership/control of the land under the water in the Atlantic Ocean to our east and the Pacific to our West and in the Gulf of Mexico to our south as far out as two hundred miles. The old rule was that nations owned the waters out as far as a cannon ball would fly. Now we have more impressive cannons and in 1982 international treaties agreed that every nation would have an exclusive economic zone up to two hundred miles off their shore. This is a very big deal if we take advantage of it.

The American Energy Alliance calculates that opening up all that area for leasing would raise $400 billion in direct-leasing payments to the federal and state governments and an additional $2.2 trillion in taxes from the economic activity of actually going and getting the oil, natural gas, and minerals under the sea.[4]

This estimate is quite conservative. It understates the likely benefits. It only deals with the known value of underwater oil, gas, and minerals. Just a decade ago, we did not know that North Dakota was actually Qatar and Western Pennsylvania was Kuwait, because fracking had not yet changed the world to make it easier to get to and exploit underground deposits of oil and gas.

Now, the politicians may only care about how much loot the government gets from leasing and drilling offshore, but Americans would be happy to learn this would create an estimated 1.2 million jobs and increase total national income by more than $8 trillion.[5] (And since the feds scrape off 20 percent of GDP in federal taxes, think $2 trillion in revenues there. We could buy Canada, or fund the defense budget for four years.)

For starters, anytime some politician tells us that he "has" to have an extra $400 billion, we can say, "Fine, go sell off or lease the offshore oil rights. Do not use this as an excuse for higher taxes." There is not an argument for any tax increase by the federal government until they have taken off the table the cash available by selling stuff.

Two: Free Up ANWR in Alaska

The politicians in Congress passed a law limiting oil exploration in the very northern part of Alaska. I have been up there. It looks like a frozen parking lot. The pictures of mountains and caribou the Greens put in TV ads are taken many miles away. In the 1990s, Congress voted to allow drilling on just 3 percent of what Congress called the Arctic National Wildlife Refuge (ANWR). Bill Clinton vetoed this. Should that decision on just that one small area be reversed, opening less than 3 percent of ANWR would ensure the Trans-Alaska Pipeline stays open and thus create up to 130,000 jobs and nearly $300 billion in tax revenue.[6] Every day there are families with no breadwinner because some politicians could not care less.

Three: Open Up Federal Lands

Back in the "Lower 48," on dry land, the federal government owns hundreds of millions of acres.

We have recently seen a job boom on private land in North Dakota, Pennsylvania, Texas, and Ohio. But oil and natural gas production during the Obama years has actually fallen in the areas under the federal government's control. The Democrats could slow exploration on "federal" land. And they did. They couldn't (yet) kill those jobs on private or state land. Thus, from 2009 to 2015, under the Obama administration, oil and natural gas production on federal lands has declined, while it has soared on state and private lands. If the Obama administration were to simply get out of the way, development of America's oil and natural gas resources on federal lands would create over 200,000 jobs and $26.5 billion in annual gross regional product.[7] And—this is what the politicians need to hear—an additional $5 billion in leasing and tax revenue would be generated each and every year.[8]

If a politician tells you he or she wants more money for some "very important" project, tell them to go sell off, or at least lease, the oil rights to federal land, and get the money from selling stuff, not raising taxes.

Heck, You can sell stuff you cannot see.

Four: Sell Off Spectrum

Another federal asset that can be sold to raise significant revenue for the US Treasury is the spectrum used by radio, television, and telecommunications. Hard to believe, but in the days before the wireless industry took off, the federal government actually gave away spectrum via lotteries and "comparative hearings" (or, as they were also colloquially known, "beauty pageants"). In the 1990s someone noticed that this "stuff" was worth real money and could be auctioned off to raise money for the government rather than given away to the politically connected.

Just as the Bureau of Land Management "manages" much federal land, the Federal Communications Commission "manages," and, with Congress's OK, can sell off, spectrum that TV, radio, and our wireless phones use.

The FCC's first large-scale spectrum auction—Auction 4—ended in March 1995, netted $7 billion for two 15 MHz blocks known as Blocks A and B.[9] A year later, in Auction 5, the agency would net $10 billion for the 30 MHz C-Block in the same band.[10] This auction would have raised $13.4 billion, but the FCC actually subsidized "preferred bidders" to rig the game, allowing the government to pick winners and losers in an auction. This reduced the revenue by $3.3 billion. When some pol tells you he needs $3 billion, tell him to go get it from his friends he "preferred" in this bid. Future auctions should not allow such bid rigging. It is corrupt and costs taxpayers real money.

Since those early auctions in the 1990s, which demonstrated the value of such sales, the FCC has held nearly one hundred auctions that have generated billions for the federal government. Examples are Auction 71, which netted $13.7 billion in 2006; Auction 73, which brought in $19 billion; Auction 96, which raised $1.56 billion; and Auction 95, which netted $1.7 billion.[11]

There is other spectrum that is not "unused" but is inefficiently used: spectrum used by government agencies. Surprise. If only one-quarter of government spectrum could be reclaimed through restructuring it to be used more effectively and then sold off, the government could plausibly raise between $100 billion and $200 billion. Not chicken feed.

Five: Selling Roads to Pay for Highway Construction

More good news. We don't have to raise gasoline taxes to pay for roads.

In 2006, the state of Indiana was able to solve much of its highway-funding woes by leasing the 157-mile Indiana toll road (Interstate 90) to Australia-based Macquarie Group and Spain-based Cintra. In exchange for a seventy-five-year lease granting the right to toll, these two firms paid the state of Indiana an up-front lump sum of $3.8 billion. The sale of the toll road allowed Indiana to spend $3.1 billion of that lump sum payment to add 375 miles of new roads, improve pavement on 5,000 miles of roads, and rehabilitate over seven hundred bridges. Then $200 million of the $3.8 billion was used to retire outstanding toll-road bonds, $500 million was used to establish a charitable trust to generate interest and distribute it every five years to the Major Moves Construction Fund, which planned to build 104 new roadways with 1,600 lane miles by 2015.[12]

There was strong opposition to "leasing" the state's toll road. Why was it being leased to a foreign company? Worse, two foreign companies—one from Australia, where the water runs down the drain the wrong direction, and the other in Spain, where they speak Mexican. Worse yet, might these foreign-type people move the Indiana toll road to Spain or Australia? The fears were unfounded, silly and now laughable. But Indiana did the nation a great service by taking them on and refuting them by going ahead with it. Now other states can move forward as well, and when "populists" or "xenophobes" or "state-owned-pavement cultists" predict disaster, we can send them to look at Indiana and its perfectly well run turnpike and the new roads they built with the cash. What if the company buying the Indiana highway were to go bankrupt? Well, it did. It had to reorganize and its investors were annoyed, but it didn't affect the benefits to Indiana, Indiana taxpayers, and highway users. The bottom line is that private firms can run a toll road so much more effectively than a government agency that it greatly increases the value of the road. To everyone. And this should surprise who?

Then the state of Pennsylvania tried to follow Indiana's success. In June 2008, Governor Ed Rendell accepted a $12.8 billion bid to lease, repair, and operate the Pennsylvania Turnpike for seventy-five years. The lease would be held jointly by the Spanish firm Abertis Infraestructuras and Citi Infrastructure Investors. Abertis would be allowed to increase tolls by 25 percent in the first year, but only by 2.5 percent or the rate of inflation each following year. Unfortunately, in the final days of session, the legislators turned on the governor. They wanted to defend the toll-collector patronage system that made the government-run turnpike less desirable to investors. If they could not keep their relatives on the payroll, they didn't want the $12.8 billion to build new roads. They had their priorities. Lousy priorities, but theirs. The legislature let the plan to lease the Turnpike die without a vote.

So what did happen? No money was available from leasing off the Turnpike and yet all the spending interests that wanted contracts to build and fix Pennsylvania roads kept yapping at the governor until Rendell's successor, Governor Tom Corbett, who had been elected having promised to oppose any and all new tax increases, broke his promise and signed two separate tax increases on energy producers (also known as hidden taxes on Pennsylvania's workers and consumers).

Pennsylvania could have had $12.8 billion in road-building

resources—enough to pay for eight full years of the state's road budget or enough for 6.5 years and the later Corbett road-building program for which he raised taxes. This better deal was available without a tax hike. Now the government of Pennsylvania doesn't have the $12.8 billion and the roads that money would buy; they do have a tax hike, they have fewer and less-safe roads, and the governor has lost his reelection bid because he raised taxes. Cluster screwup. Some states serve as bad examples. Some governors take it on the chin for the sins of their self-interested legislators.

Six: Local Governments Can Sell Stuff Too

We laugh at European nations that have government-run steel mills, coal mines, or railroads. They are poorly run and lose money. But in the United States, the home of the free market and brave entrepreneurs, a generation after the fall of the Berlin Wall, 11.1 percent of US power plants are still municipally owned. City socialism does not work well. They are often cesspools of patronage and unwarranted sources of profitable contracts to politicians' friends. City power plants can be sold off for millions. Two examples: In 2013, Vero Beach, Florida, population 340,000, sold its electric system for $179 million,[13] and Hercules, California, with only 694 customers, sold its utility for $12.7 million.[14] Both sales took place in 2013.

Water and sewer systems can be sold to private firms that provide the services a municipal system does without the corruption and government-union problems government ownership creates. To get a sense of how much cash a city can gain by selling through such privatization, Indianapolis, Indiana, sold its waste and sewer utilities in 2010 for $1.9 billion in cash and the assumption of $1.5 billion in debt. If your city owns its waterworks and whines that it needs higher taxes, ask them to sell off government assets before they even think about a tax hike.

Towns and cities also own a great deal of land they should be told to sell off. Why does the city/town need to own certain land? When roads are built by cities and states, they often buy much adjoining land they do not really need. Then they forget about it. That can be sold off easily.

King John of England and the Sheriff of Nottingham wanted to defend the king's land and the king's deer. The aristocracy liked to own land so they could keep the peasants, aka the taxpayers, out. But land should be privately owned unless there is a direct government use for it, and even then, one can lease land, as with toll roads or buildings.

Before your family goes into debt, you should look to see what you can find in the basement that can be sold, or consider selling the extra car or other unused goods. Governments should be more careful with "our" assets and should sell off what is not completely required. It is good for the economy and good for taxpayers.

When a federal, state, or local politician tells you he "has to raise taxes" to gain revenue, tell him to empty his pockets and first sell off government–owned/controlled assets.

CHAPTER 11

Government Transparency: The Best Way to Reduce Waste and Corruption

The Internet is the friend of the taxpayer.

It is now possible for all government spending to be visible to all Americans—to be completely transparent. In real time. Every check the government writes, every salary, pension, contract, expense-account, and credit card expenditure can be up on the web for every taxpayer to see.

Federal, state, and local spending has always been public information. It just sat in shoeboxes in the basement of the town hall or in the files of a federal agency. If you could hire a Washington lobbyist or a detective, you might find out how much is spent where. Or if you were willing to wait for an annual budget report. If you knew how to read it, you would at least have a summary. Long after the fact.

But the Internet can post all checks and spending online now. Before the money is spent. It is available to everyone on the planet. Not just during office hours, but 24/7. Weekends and holidays. You don't have to drive down to the city hall or fly to your state capital to access its spending secrets. There need be no secrets. Who is getting state contracts and for how much money can be available not just to an intrepid reporter tipped off on what to look for but to everyone with a search engine.

The Move to Transparency in the States

Back in 2006, I was calling around to governors asking what good ideas or new projects they had that might be shared with other states. Texas's governor Rick Perry had several projects moving forward, but some were quite Texas-specific. One idea—complete transparency in government spending—was clearly a good idea that could move to other states as well as to both local and the federal governments.

Governor Perry put all his official spending online. No law required it. He just did it. If the government paid for his lunch or a magazine subscription, it went online.

Susan Combs, the Texas comptroller and a great Reagan Republican, could and did require the same of the comptroller's office and then twenty-four of the state's largest agencies. Combs put the case for transparency succinctly: "Government spending is often seen as impenetrable and unknowable. Taxpayers have the absolute right to know how their money is being spent, and it is only with transparency that government can be held accountable. We are helping citizens with an easy way to examine state expenditures in one place without needing to contact multiple agencies."

Governor Perry issued Executive Order RP 47, demanding that two-thirds of "education" spending actually be spent in the classroom rather than on bureaucratic overhead. A number of school districts complained that their accounting was so messed up that they could not meet that standard. Perry allowed schools either to prove they were directing two-thirds of education spending into actual education or to post their check registers and salaries online. Many school districts chose to open up their books to avoid having to police their own spending. Transparency then made it easier to root out corruption, such as contracts to friends, and to locate overspending on overhead.

Transparency was such an obviously good idea that it traveled quickly to other states, to local government, and even to Washington. In 2008, Collin County, Texas, became the first county government to post its check register online, with Smith County soon following suit. The Texas legislature later got into the act and codified the executive orders into state law HB 3430 so that future governors could not return to opaque government. The website, texastransparency.org, is more commonly known as "Where the Money Goes."

Kansas Representative Kasha Kelley introduced the Kansas Taxpayer Transparency Act of 2007, making the Sunflower State the first in the nation to propose codifying state-spending transparency into law. KanView, the state's portal, was launched in March 2008, allowing taxpayers to view state expenditures as well as information on revenues and state debt.

Missouri governor Matt Blunt created the Missouri Accountability Portal (MAP) by executive order in 2007. The Show-Me State hit the ground running, updating its portal daily and including data from as far back as 2000. It provided access to users in unparalleled ways, giving visitors the option to drill down on a number of data sets. The portal included state employee salaries in its spending data.

By 2008, seven states—Arkansas, Kansas, Louisiana, Oklahoma, Missouri, South Carolina, and Texas—had created spending-transparency websites. Eight states—Arizona, Georgia, Illinois, Kentucky, Michigan, Nebraska, New York, and Pennsylvania—had active state-spending websites initiated by a state constitutional officer who did not wait for the legislature or the governor to act. They put their own department's spending online.

OK, you can put all this information on the web, but does anyone really care? Well, the Missouri transparency website had 14 million hits in its first year.

All fifty states have a checkbook-level transparency portal, and forty-eight states—all except California and Vermont—are easily searchable. Forty-nine states list all government grants.[1] These websites are immediately available either through costofgovernment .org or a simple Google search.

Two states were ahead of the curve when it came to providing local data: When the Florida legislature passed its transparency law in 2009, it required state, regional, county, and municipal governments to provide financial information to the Florida chief financial officer's website. In the same year, Utah passed legislation that required local entities to disclose financial information on the state-spending portal as well.

Americans are now used to being able to see their own checking accounts in real time. We can track our UPS or FedEx packages as they travel across the nation. We can watch ourselves walk down the street using GPS on our iPhones. We can monitor our credit card statements online. Why shouldn't government be as transparent? It is "our" government.

Opposition to transparency came from several sources. First, those politicians used to handing out contracts to their friends and campaign contributors didn't want the world to be able to see if contracts went to the lowest bidder. Or not. Some opponents of transparency said it would cost a great deal of money. I put together a conference call with the leaders of the transparency movement in Missouri, Kansas, Oklahoma, Texas, and Florida, and the legislators and governor's office staff told each other how much their bureaucracies were claiming transparency would cost. Some said $15 million, one claimed hundreds of millions. Such nonsense is bureaucratic talk for "I don't want to be bothered...we have never done this before...and...I am not so sure I really want you looking at how we spent your money last year and next." In reality, transparency is surprisingly inexpensive. The Texas move to transparency cost $310,000, but was paid for with existing revenues. The Missouri executive order told the agencies to do this within existing budgets.

Transparency in Washington

The power of the transparency movement can be seen by the odd-couple cosponsors of a federal transparency act, the Federal Funding Accountability and Transparency Act (FFATA): conservative Oklahoma senator Tom Coburn and the then–little-known senator from Illinois, Barack Obama. The legislation ordered the Office of Management and Budget to create an online portal where all grants and contracts above $25,000 would be available to every American. This covered about 70 percent of the government's discretionary spending. Senator Rob Portman, who was then the director of the OMB, went beyond the law's requirements to make government spending more transparent. He tried to get Congress to put into law his higher level of transparency.

In 2008, Senators Coburn and Obama introduced the Strengthening Transparency and Accountability in Federal Spending Act. This bill would have improved data quality on USAspending.gov and increased accessibility to information. Updates included requiring contracts to be available in a searchable format, and provided details about whether an award was competitively bid, whether the amount was the product of an earmark or an assessment, and whether the terms of a contract or grant were sufficiently fulfilled.

The cynics among us note that Senator Obama had, by 2008, one legislative accomplishment—the original transparency law he coauthored with Coburn. In the middle of his presidential campaign he didn't lift a finger to actually pass his legislation through a Democrat House and Senate. Nor did Obama move his legislation once he was president and had a pliable Democrat majority in the House and Senate. The president who claimed, "My administration is committed to creating an unprecedented level of openness in government" and "This is the most transparent administration in history," did not move transparency legislation he claimed to have coauthored and supported. Still, hypocrisy is the tribute vice pays to virtue. A smart politician who moved quickly from voting present as a state legislator to a noneventful four years as a senator decided that the one issue he thought politically advantageous to identify with was transparency.

Once in office, Obama viewed transparency from the other side of the mirror. It was not about citizens being able to watch their government as it spent but rather about being able to use the government's resources to sell citizens on the government's own programs. Propaganda, not transparency.

The Stimulus spending spree, officially known as the American Recovery and Reinvestment Act of 2009, was supposed to be transparent so that taxpayers could track "every dime" of the $800 billion being spent to "create or save" jobs. The "transparency" portal to allow every American to track stimulus spending was recovery. gov. It was actually a propaganda outlet proclaiming how many jobs were being created in each congressional district. Not state. Not the nation. Not cities. By congressional district, a wholly political view. Be sure and thank your congressman for the goodies. One slight problem was that money and projects were supposedly spent in districts that did not actually exist, such as $2 million in the "99th District of North Dakota."[2]

The power of the transparency movement is that it cannot be stopped by any one politician. If the legislature will not pass a law making state spending transparent, the governor can act unilaterally to open his or her direct spending. Any constitutional officer, the secretary of state, or attorney general can make his or her department's spending visible online. An ambitious mayor can put the city's spending online. Challenger candidates can make the case that the incumbent has failed to go transparent. Why? What, a challenger might suggest to voters and the media, is being hidden?

You don't have to be elected to anything to play a key role in making government transparent. The Buckeye Institute in Ohio and the Maine Heritage Policy Center created transparency portals using information they won through Freedom of Information Act requests. They didn't wait for their state and local governments.

American Transparency, a project founded by former Illinois gubernatorial candidate Adam Andrzejewski, has archived over a billion government spending records from across the nation. How did they do this? They asked for the public information through the Freedom of Information Act and they then put it together in a usable and searchable form. Should the federal government have done this? Yes. But why wait for them? They will catch up eventually. Andrzejewski's website, OpenTheBooks.com, is expected to soon host the data on ninety cents of every dollar taxed and spent in the United States from the previous five years. Even more remarkable, this data is available through a smartphone app; users can access nearly every tax dollar spent in the country at the touch of their fingertips. The name of the app is Open the Books.

When the Veterans Affairs scandal hit and the public learned that VA staff were denying and delaying care to American veterans and hiding this with false documentation, it was Open the Books that had amassed spending data going back seven years so that every American could see that the officials at a Veterans hospital in Phoenix, Arizona, had been paid exorbitant salaries and bonuses. The online data from Open the Books showed that the hospital had been spending hundreds of thousands of dollars on interior decorators and public relations professionals and that only 41 percent of the Phoenix VA budget had gone to direct medical care. Open the Books exposed that forty thousand VA employees had "earned bonuses." Americans cared, and they learned directly from the facts. They did not have to wait until some commission appointed by the people who created and/or tolerated this abuse reported that nothing was really wrong or that many things were wrong but those responsible had quit or moved or died months and years earlier.

Millions of searches by nearly half a million visitors were done on the OpenTheBooks website in the six weeks following the release of its VA spending data. Americans wanted to know. They had the ability to get to the truth—not because their government was making it easy but because Adam Andrzejewski and his group openthebooks

.com decided the public had the right to know in a timely and useful manner—online.

Read the Bills

A transparency portal listing all present spending is a powerful protection against waste, corruption, and mismanagement. But like an autopsy, the information you wanted arrives a tad late.

One proactive approach is to require that all legislation stand online for a full week before it is voted on by either the House or the Senate. Nancy Pelosi said she would do this for all legislation before the House. But the first test of this was the Stimulus spending bill, which was written in the basement of the capitol with only lobbyists and Democrat congressmen able to see the legislation. Then it was rushed to passage. What was in it? Well, as Speaker Pelosi famously said about Obamacare, "We have to pass the bill so that you can find out what is in it." Within days of passage, when the details of the bill leaked out, it was clear this was simply a collection of earmarks stapled together, such as $47.6 million for a streetcar project in Atlanta, and $90,000 for dog park improvement in Washington, D.C.[3] Had the Stimulus bill been online for seven full days, individual Americans, members of the media, and competing spending interests would have torn it to shreds and exposed it as a collection of wasteful earmarks that had not passed the laugh test over the past ten years. Any spending idea that had to wait for the Stimulus spending bill had been passed over before many times and been repeatedly judged unworthy of taxpayer dollars.

Obamacare would never have passed the House and Senate if the 3,000 pages had been online for a week. Not everyone would read 3,000 pages. Maybe no one person would real all 3,000 pages—OK, Congressman Justin Amash would read all 3,000 pages—but with search engines those people damaged by each part of the legislation would be able to look at what was going to happen to their health care or health insurance or job. Obama and two Democrat majorities in the House and Senate might well have passed legislation—it just would not have had that many errors and costly regulations. Even without a law requiring a waiting period, we created one in 1994, when Republicans were concerned that any day the Clinton administration might announce they had reached a "deal" and plop down a 2,000- or 3,000-page Hillarycare takeover of health care and demand a vote that day. Americans for Tax Reform wrote up a "Probity Pledge"—helpfully reprinted on the editorial page of the *Wall Street Journal*—that simply read, "I promise not to vote for any health care reform law that I have not personally read." Should a member sign that pledge, they could reasonably demand that any vote be delayed for ten days or more, as they were required to read the measure. When Senator Robert Dole of Kansas signed the Probity Pledge in the summer of 1994, it was clear Hillarycare was dead. No Republican could fail to join Dole in requiring the time to read the thousands of pages of legislation before being asked to vote on it. This meant the Republicans could not be jammed into voting for an unread, unexamined, "bipartisan deal" to enact 70 percent of Hillarycare in year one and the rest to follow. That was fun. A law would be better.

There was a first stab at making legislation more transparent when in January 1995, newly sworn-in Speaker of the House Newt Gingrich announced the creation of the THOMAS system at the Library of Congress. Since then, all legislation would be available online for any American to see. In the past those with lobbyists in Washington who could cab up to the Capitol and photocopy new legislation had an advantage over Americans who lived outside D.C. and would not have access to the first draft of legislation for days or weeks, and in fact might not learn of its existence until it was "too late." Still, the Gingrich initiative, while a giant first step, was not enough. It is the final bill that needs to be online for seven days— and polling shows that Americans believe the final bill, after all edits and amendments, should be online for weeks——not just the first draft.

Making Tax Hikes Transparent

In Texas, Representative Van Taylor introduced and passed legislation that requires that any bill that includes a tax increase must have that highlighted in the bill summary. Too often legislation that is many pages long has tax or fee increases hidden in its nooks and crannies of mind-deadening and perhaps deliberately boring language. That good idea from Texas should also be law at the national and state levels.

Texas senator John Cornyn and Texas congressman Sam Johnson introduced the National Tax Transparency Act in 2013 in the national House and Senate, modeled after Representative Taylor's successful effort in Texas that required each bill to carry with it a clear statement on how the legislation impacts federal taxes.

Making Government Projections of Costs Transparent

The CBO Transparency Act, authored by Representative Jason Murphy, would require the Congressional Budget Office to submit to Congress all the data, models, and any information used to provide cost estimates to bills. Right now the CBO pulls their estimates out of a black box and they tell Congress how much certain laws will or will not cost. Who knows what political pressures are brought to bear in massaging those numbers and equations. Let's get those formulas, assumptions, and mathematical models out in the open and let every econometrician critique the models Washington uses to control the spending debate in Washington. The same should be done for the Joint Tax Committee.

CHAPTER 12

Dynamic Scoring: The Sine Qua Non of Tax Reform

Joseph Stalin reportedly said that it didn't really matter who voted. What mattered was who counted the votes. One bad umpire can beat a very strong team. The person who sets the rules has already won the game.

Why do so many well-meaning and serious efforts to reduce the tax burden get shot down or even grounded before they take off? The answer is that there is a bureaucracy that can make or break any tax reduction or tax reform, because they get to "score" the legislation. You write your tax cut or tax reform bill. In a back room and using assumptions and calculations that you are not allowed to see or challenge, the Joint Committee on Taxation (JCT) will announce to the world that your bill will "cost" the government x billion dollars over the next decade.

If the tax cut is considered "too large," if the JCT "calculates" or "estimates" or "guesstimates" that the tax cut will "cost" the government "too much," then official Washington goes into a panic and tries to water down the tax relief. This is exactly what happened to both President Reagan and President George W. Bush in their respective first-term tax cuts. In 1981, the Kemp-Roth tax cut was supposed to be an immediate 33 percent cut in all tax rates. It was reduced to being roughly a 25 percent cut. While the top rate fell from 70 to 50 percent in 1982, the tax rate reductions in the lower brackets were not fully phased in until 1983. Delaying implementation delayed the recovery and cost Reagan's party greatly in the 1982 election. Compare that to the 1984 Reagan landslide once the tax cuts were fully implemented. This little congressional agency changed history for the worse.

The JCT scorekeepers themselves act as a sort of nerdy priesthood, refusing to divulge their full methodology, make their work available for peer review, or be asked questions by either the media or the taxpayers who pay their salaries. Imagine a baseball umpire who cannot get fired. Bad calls cannot be challenged and they can throw a game. This year. Next year. The year after.

All tax legislation must be stamped and labeled by the Joint Committee on Taxation, or JCT. The JCT's rulings are beyond authoritative—they're considered infallible. Senate supermajority requirements and points of order hinge on what a tax analyst comes up with in his cubicle on a computer spreadsheet. (One notes that these hard-and-fast rules can be bent by the establishment Left.) But we live in a world where the JCT can kill tax cuts and tax reform, and at the same time is open to pressure from a White House pushing for higher spending. Life is not fair. Still we fight on.

Yes, the JCT technically answers to the House Ways and Means Committee and the Senate Finance Committee, but actual oversight is nearly nonexistent for fear of being accused of politicizing "nonpartisan" scoring. Like many "nonpartisan" institutions in Washington, D.C., the JCT tends to lean left in its staffing, and personnel is policy. Most of the employees are there to check a career box before cashing out to a lucrative tax law practice on K Street. They are decidedly not free-market conservatives. They inhabit the government-influence circulatory system of the Washington Beltway, and rarely pretend otherwise.

Where do their numbers come from? More than one tax lobbyist in Washington suspects that the numbers are actually mere guesstimates, and that no one can really know what will happen to federal tax revenues when this or that tax law is changed. The reality is actually much worse.

Nonetheless, the JCT is a Washington institution that has to be reckoned with by anyone serious about reform. All plans to reform the tax code must first take on the challenge of reforming or replacing the Joint Committee on Taxation.

Are Taxpayers Mindless Drones? JCT Thinks So

It's bad enough that JCT has the ability to set the playing field when it comes to tax bills and their fates in Congress. They could at least try to get their guesstimates correct. Sadly, they don't, and haven't really tried to until very recently.

Suppose you face a marginal tax rate of 80 percent. That is, if you earn an extra $1,000 this year, the government will take $800 of it, and you only get to keep $200. Picture what that does to your willingness to get up early on a Saturday morning to work to earn that $1,000.

Now, suppose your marginal tax rate is cut all the way down to 10 percent. That is, if you earn an extra $1,000 this year, the government only keeps $100, and you get to keep $900 of it.

Same amount of work, but when the tax rate is 10 percent, you take home $900 and when the rate is 80 percent you take home $200. A tax rate increase is a pay cut.

My guess is that you would much rather roll out of bed on a Saturday morning in the second example than in the first. You may not roll out of bed at all in the first example. High tax rates reduce the return to labor and lower the cost of leisure.

This is the Laffer Curve in action. All the Laffer Curve really says is that moving from very high to very low marginal income tax rates increases the incentive of taxpayers to work, save, and invest. Doing the opposite—moving from a very low to a very high marginal income tax rate—has the opposite effect.

What if I were to tell you that JCT does not take this into

account? The JCT assumes that the taxpayer in question would dutifully do the extra Saturday work (or not) no matter what his marginal tax rate was. Ten percent, 30 percent, 50 percent, 100 percent—it doesn't matter. Taxpayers are drones, and will work no matter how much the IRS steals. (It makes the calculations easier for the staff.)

A particularly comical demonstration of this happened in 1989. Dan Mitchell, now of the Cato Institute, explains:

> "Back in 1989, I worked for Senator Bob Packwood of Oregon. As the ranking Republican on the Finance Committee, he sent a letter to the JCT, asking how much tax revenue would be raised if the government confiscated every penny of income above $200,000... [T]he JCT estimated that this 100 percent tax rate would collect $104 billion in 1989, rising to $299 billion in 1993. And when Senator Packwood asked the bureaucrats whether this was realistic, they gave him the same revenue estimate, but included a footnote stating 'that these estimated taxes do not account for any behavioral response.' This is sort of like the fiscal equivalent of 'other than that, Mrs. Lincoln, how did you like the play?' "[1]

Now, in year one the government might make money confiscating all income above $200,000. But in years two and three, who goes to work after hitting $200,000? JCT thinks this will not change behavior.

JCT does not take what are called "macroeconomic" changes into account. This is a Scrabble-word way of saying that they don't think large tax changes impact the economy. Common sense tells us otherwise.

Many in Congress want to see this changed. Representative Lynn Jenkins (R-Kan.) in 2014 sponsored a bill, H.R. 1475, that would require JCT to adopt these macroeconomic changes in calculating a score, and to open up the methodology for peer review.

Representative Tom Price (R-Ga.) and Senator Rob Portman (R-Ohio) have introduced legislation (H.R. 1874, the "Pro-Growth Budgeting Act," and S. 2371, the "Accurate Budgeting Act") to require this analysis for any large fiscal bill.

Turning Over a New Leaf?

There is hope for tax reformers here. For the first time ever, JCT did what is called a "dynamic analysis" of a large tax reform bill, the tax reform plan advanced by House Ways and Means chairman Dave Camp (R-Mich.). They modeled what would happen to overall labor markets, capital investment, and consumer demand. The result was higher economic growth.

Higher economic growth, of course, results in more taxes paid to the government. Supply-siders call this the "revenue feedback effect" of pro-growth tax policy. Unlike tax increases, higher government revenues due to economic growth or the creation of new industries is a good thing. It's also a feature of truly pro-growth tax changes.

JCT said that the revenue-feedback effect from the Camp plan (which was far from ideal supply-side tax policy in several respects) could be as high as $800 billion over a decade.[2] Here JCT is admitting that its previous "models" were off, in this case by $800 billion. Even in Washington, D.C., that's real money.

If JCT started giving this type of commonsense credit to other pro-growth tax cut bills, their apparent or "static" score would shrink. Suddenly, cutting the capital gains tax, or killing the death tax, or lowering the corporate income tax rate would get much easier. It would not mean that all tax cuts would "pay for themselves" (to repeat the Left's old canard here), but it would mean that commonsense economic effects would be taken into account.

JCT dynamic analysis should be transparent. Its assumptions and calculations should all be online for everyone in the world to read and critique. It would be helpful if the work was peer reviewed.

It should be refined and improved by serious economists in open academic literature. Methodologies should be debated. The goal, after all, is to produce a more accurate estimate of the fiscal effects of tax legislation.

It is unlikely we will get substantial tax reform until the Joint Tax Committee is forced to be fully transparent and to recognize how tax changes affect the overall economy.

Is this possible? Can we reform the Joint Tax Committee? Yes. After all, Hercules was able to perform his Fifth Labor: cleaning out the Augean Stables. It is an apt analogy.

PART IV

Six Paths Leading to Abolishing the IRS: Big Steps, Little Steps

CHAPTER 13

Path One: The FairTax

A necessary first step in the struggle to abolish the IRS is to eliminate the federal personal income tax, the Social Security tax, and the corporate income tax. They are all collected by the IRS. One might accomplish that by personalizing Social Security and dramatically reforming government spending so that we no longer need the present "cash flow" from the income tax. That would take decades of hard work. To abolish the IRS immediately would require that most of the revenue raised by the personal and corporate income taxes be replaced with an alternative tax system.

A national sales tax—or FairTax, as it is popularly known—is one such alternative.

There is popular support for such a swap. There are millions of Americans who have joined the FairTax campaign and they are hardworking and active. Would that other tax-cutting efforts had this level of grassroots engagement and persistence.

It is largely due to the efforts of several brilliant business leaders who got the FairTax movement off the ground: Jack Trotter, Leo Linbeck, Jr., and Bob McNair. They started Americans for Fair Taxation in 1994.

Powerful issues propel candidates. It was the FairTax that helped put former Arkansas governor Mike Huckabee over the top in the 2008 Iowa presidential straw poll. FairTax supporters came out in force for their champion, giving Huckabee the best day he had that year on the campaign trail.

It is technically possible to abolish the personal and corporate income taxes and the Social Security tax and replace all that revenue with taxes raised though a retail sales tax, the FairTax? Should we?

What are the questions we should ask? Would the new tax be less destructive to economic growth, individual liberty, our privacy? Would it be harder or easier to raise than the present tax? Let's look at the case for the FairTax as a replacement for today's income and wage taxes.

About the FairTax

The FairTax plan would replace all federal taxes with one single retail sales tax. It is more ambitious than either Reagan's 1986 tax reform or the flat tax. It would replace the personal and corporate income tax, the Social Security tax, Medicare taxes, death taxes, and excise taxes.

This is very good. One tax is easier to keep track of than many. Unlike the progressive income tax, the single-rate sales tax would treat all Americans the same. It would follow the constitutional mandate that federal taxes be "uniform."

It would change the culture of taxation in America. There wouldn't be a tax-filing season for most Americans, there wouldn't be audits, scary-looking letters, or out-of-control IRS employees. Unless someone owns a business, they won't have a tax-filing season at all. Fifty states will collect the tax from retailers and send the cash to Washington.

The FairTax advocates promise that they would only support replacing the income tax with the sales tax after permanent repeal of the Sixteenth Amendment, which gives the Congress power to levy an income tax. This is extremely important. Unless the Sixteenth Amendment, which allowed the income tax, is repealed and an amendment specifically banning any taxes on income is enacted, there is a great danger—correction, an absolute certainty—that the FairTax would, sooner rather than later, be *in addition to* rather than *instead of* the federal income tax.

The FairTax as proposed seeks to raise the same tax revenue as current law raises. Historically, tax revenues to the federal government have averaged around 18 percent of gross domestic product. If there was a parallel effort to reduce spending or reform entitlements, then the retail sales tax could be lower than now planned.

To raise the same amount of tax revenue as the taxes it replaces, the FairTax must be a consumption tax equal to 23 percent of the value of a new good or service sold. Excluded from this tax base are used goods (including used homes), business-to-business sales, and anything else that isn't an end-consumer new good or service.

Advocates of the FairTax point to two great advantages of the Fair-Tax regime. First, Americans could take home 100 percent of their paychecks. Nothing would have to be withheld, because all current federal taxes would have been repealed. Second, embedded in the price of goods today is some measure of taxes that business owners will have to pay, and those will also be eliminated under the FairTax.

In order to maintain progressivity, the FairTax introduces the concept of a "pre-bate," a payment from the federal government to families in anticipation of their paying the FairTax. It would come monthly, and is intended to refund FairTax payments on goods and services bought by Americans under the federal poverty line. That varies based on household composition (married or single, kids or not, senior or not, etc.), so every household would have to inform the federal government in real time about its makeup. (Here we see some of the potential for the intrusiveness of the old IRS reappearing.)

Why Not Go to a FairTax? What Could Go Wrong?

The most comprehensive criticism of the FairTax can be found in a December 24, 2007, article by Bruce Bartlett in *Tax Notes* titled

"Why the FairTax Won't Work."[1] The following draws heavily from his work.

The objections of Bartlett and others can be put into four principal categories:

1. The FairTax Rate Is Commonly Discussed in Ways That Understate Its Real Cost

The FairTax is described as a 23 percent tax embedded in the cost of everything sold. If you buy something for $1.00, $0.23 of that will be the FairTax component. While that's accurately stated, most people think of sales taxes as being added onto the retail cost of a good. A 6 percent sales tax in Utah raises the price of a product from $1.00 to $1.06. To most ears a 23 percent FairTax translates into a $1.00 good costing $1.23 at the register.

If the FairTax were expressed as the tax added to the price of a good, and thus the way American state sales-tax payers are used to thinking about these things, the rate would not be 23 percent but 30 percent.

Even this 30 percent sales tax–expressed rate might be understating things. The FairTax calculation as to how much revenue it raises assumes the government pays a sales tax on its own consumption as if it were a business. This can hardly count as revenue raised. It assumes that the sales tax base will be 80 percent of GDP, when most international VAT bases (the closest comparison) are more like 50 percent of GDP. It ignores the black market that might result and lower revenues (e.g., "Either pay me a hundred dollars above the table or ninety under the table"). It assumes new homes (the only ones to face a FairTax) are dutifully built just as before. But if a new home has a 30 percent add-on tax and an old home does not—one would not be surprised to see more used homes sold and fewer new ones built.

Put all this together, and you may well need a higher rate. The Brookings Institution estimates that the sales tax–expressed rate would have to be 44 percent.[2] The Joint Committee on Taxation pegs it at 57 percent.[3] The Treasury Department thinks it's 34 percent,[4] but that's if you replace *only* the personal and corporate income taxes, leaving the Social Security and Medicare and excise taxes in place.

This is a high number compared to the highest state sales tax we experience today (California, at 7.5 percent), and the highest value-added tax rate (27 percent, in Hungary).

Could that sales tax percentage be reduced to make the FairTax more palatable? Yes. Comprehensive entitlement reform could improve all these numbers. Since Social Security and Medicare taxes account for about one-third of all federal taxes collected, a totally private retirement system would mean the government would need to collect one-third less in taxes. The tax-intrinsic rate could fall from 23 percent to 15 percent, and the tax-extrinsic rate could fall from 30 percent to 20 percent. Even the despairingly high Brookings number could fall to 30 percent, the depressing JCT number could drop to 38 percent, and the bad Treasury number to 23 percent. Privatizing Social Security and reforming Medicare to make it a defined-contribution 401(k)–style savings program would take those "programs" off budget and dramatically drop the cost of total government and the sales tax rate needed to fund government. Those promoting the FairTax could profitably spend half their time reforming/privatizing entitlements in order to minimize the sales tax percentage demanded and increase its attractiveness.

2. It's Double Taxation on Seniors and Other Savers

If you are twenty years old, there is no meaningful difference between a future with a flat tax on consumed income and a sales tax on consumption. Same base. Single rate. Either choice is a big improvement over the present mess.

But if you are sixty-five years old, the flat tax and sales tax have drastically different costs to your future.

Why?

Say you are sixty-five. You have worked all your life and paid income taxes. Now you are retired and living off savings and pensions. You now face little in the way of income taxes. You have spent a lifetime saving after-tax income and you are now expecting to draw down those savings and not have to pay taxes again. But if the nation switches today to a sales tax, you would find yourself paying 30 percent sales tax on everything you buy with that already-taxed and saved income. You once paid income taxes on everything you earned. Now you pay sales taxes on all your consumption. Tough on someone near or over sixty-five.

Considering the fact that seniors are among the biggest FairTax proponents across the nation, this concern is a serious one that needs to be addressed. It's also a key political reality that simply has to be acknowledged: Sixty-five-year-olds regularly remember to vote. Twenty-year-olds do not.

3. The Prebate May Not Work As Advertised

Under the FairTax, each household gets a monthly payment from the government, which is based on the poverty level for a household of that composition. Because this applies to everyone, even very wealthy people will get a payment every month from the government. It will require constant registration with the government by every American. It is open to fraud.

One concern with the FairTax is that Congress will not be able to leave well enough alone. There will be tremendous political pressure to adjust the prebate to make it more progressive, to make it regionally variable, to give an incentive to families with children, to exempt certain purchases from the FairTax, etc. Congress changes tax laws all the time today, and that may not change under a new type of tax regime.

The willingness for politicians to play the envy card and appeal to class warfare will not disappear when the income tax does. It will migrate over to the implementation of the FairTax.

4. Meet the New IRS, Just Like the Old IRS?

On the day we sell off the IRS building to make it into a charter school and the last IRS agent graduates from the University of Phoenix with a useful life skill, some new entity will arise to collect the national retail sales tax from the state governments that are to collect it from retail stores.

There will be tax collectors in each state watching over every retail outlet and the parking lots outside said establishments to ensure that all sales are registered, stamped, and taxed. This agency, or another one just like it, will be responsible for auditing businesses who have to remit the FairTax, in conjunction with state tax agencies. This agency, or its sister, will also administer the prebate-registration program, which itself will have to have oversight and audits to prevent fraud.

No doubt, this agency won't be called "the IRS," but how important is that? The Soviet Union is gone. The KGB is gone. Now we have Putin's Russia and the Federal Security Service. Americans won't have to file 1040s every spring anymore (that is a very big deal), but there's no painless, unobtrusive way to collect several trillion dollars in annual tax revenue from a populace that would rather keep their earnings for their families. The headache of facing the authorities will be borne by millions of business owners rather than hundreds of millions of individual citizens.

So...is the FairTax a good idea?

The FairTax has many good points. It taxes consumed income. Not savings and investments. Its advocates are committed to killing the death tax and the corporate income tax as part of the program. That is big. And the FairTax advocates have made it crystal clear they recognize the dangers of ending up with both the income tax and a national sales tax. That would make us look a lot like Europe, with a VAT as well as corporate and individual income taxes. Therefore the FairTaxers are the strongest advocates of a constitutional amendment prohibiting the return of an income tax. To do that, we must win two-thirds of the House and Senate and three-quarters of the state legislatures with limited-government statesmen. That would be a radical change returning us to a glorious part of our past.

When we create a governing class that is committed to liberty, we can then decide either to move forward with a FairTax swap for the elimination of the income tax or we can take that energy and press for increasingly lower income tax rates and less spending overall. This is not a decision we have to make next month.

CHAPTER 14

Path Two: The Flat Tax

M oving to a flat-rate income tax would be a great step forward. From the very start the federal income tax has been graduated, or "progressive," meaning that people are treated differently by the IRS depending on their income. This is not how other taxes are imposed. It is specifically forbidden by the constitutional requirement that all federal taxes be "uniform."

Everyone pays the same sales tax rate in New York. When the Kennedy kids in Massachusetts buy a pair of shoes they pay the state's 4 percent sales tax. So would you and I. Our sales taxes and property taxes are fixed, flat percentages. Not graduated. Not progressive.

If you commit a crime, there is not a ten-year sentence for a doctor and only a five-year sentence for a bricklayer and simple probation for an unemployed person. If you get a speeding ticket, it is not two hundred dollars if you are driving a Mercedes but only fifty dollars if you speed in a Focus.

The graduated or progressive income tax violates equality before the law, and taxes different incomes at different rates. In a nation proud of its tradition of equality before the law, the income tax explicitly treats people differently simply because of their income. Those different rates can be manipulated by the politicians to give and take and punish and reward...and divide and control.

The idea of a single tax rate for all Americans keeps faith with the

Constitution's requirement that taxes be "uniform." The income tax was made constitutional with the passage of the Sixteenth Amendment, which reads quite simply:

"The Congress shall have power to lay and collect taxes on incomes, from whatever source derived, without apportionment among the several States, and without regard to any census or enumeration."

The Sixteenth Amendment did repeal the requirement that "No Capitation, or other direct, Tax shall be laid, unless in Proportion to the Census or Enumeration herein before directed to be taken." It did not change the original constitutional requirement that all "Duties, Imposts and Excises shall be uniform throughout the United States."

There is a good constitutional argument that any income tax must be uniform—a single tax rate on all income. This was one of the arguments used against the first income tax imposed during the Civil War and eventually struck down in 1895 in the case of *Pollock v. Farmers' Loan & Trust Co.*[1]

But the political struggle to reform the present graduated/progressive income tax will first be won in the court of public opinion, and years from now the Supreme Court will rediscover Section 8 of Article I and recognize that the Constitution limits the government's power to tax by requiring a "uniform" or flat rate that does not discriminate between Americans.

There is a precedent for this rediscovery of the plain text of the Constitution. The Second Amendment, guaranteeing the rights of Americans to keep and bear arms, was largely ignored by the Supreme Court as federal, state, and local governments passed a series of restrictions and even bans on keeping and bearing arms.

The *Heller* case, which recognized that the Second Amendment was a right of the people deserving respect from the court and not a passing comment speaking only to government-run militias, was won by a five-to-four vote but only after 100 million American gun owners, 20 million hunters, 11.1 million Concealed Carry Permit holders, and the largest and oldest civil rights organization in the United States, the National Rifle Association, had consistently elected congressmen, senators, and state legislators demanding that Second Amendment rights be recognized and protected.

Maggie Thatcher said that first you win the debate, then you win the election. In America, first you win the debate, then you win the elections, then you win the Supreme Court. (And no, it was not supposed to work this way, but whining will not win us back our freedoms. Hard work will.)

So, in a free society is a flat tax preferable to a multitiered income tax with higher rates on some than on others. It certainly is.

There is a strong moral argument that a single-rate tax is best because it treats all Americans the same. If you earn $20,000, the government will take 10 percent, and if you earn $20 million, the government will take 10 percent. It is not a head tax, where each person pays $100, but it does take the same percentage of income from each American. It is in sync with people's general understanding of "uniformity."

Fairness, however, is a limited argument. Taxation is about taking money from people who earned it and—too often at present— giving it to people who have not earned it. Fairness is not really a concept in play here. We can argue that taking 10 percent from everyone equalizes the pain. So would cutting off everyone's little finger. Equality would be maintained, but fairness is not front and center in this debate.

Treating people equally is a central value in a just society where all are to be equal before the government.

To me, over the long haul, the most important argument for a flat tax is that it is difficult to increase. That flows directly from its uniformity. Everyone pays the same tax, so everyone is watching when politicians chat about new ways to spend our money.

Bill Clinton ran for president in 1992 both attacking George H. W. Bush's tax increase of 1990[2] and promising that he would never raise taxes on 98 percent of Americans.[3]

The top 2 percent of earners would pay for all his new spending ideas. He invited everyone else to tune out of the discussion and step outside while he would work over the top 2 percent.

The forcible extraction from the 2 percent might be unpleasant and unsightly, but you didn't need to watch or care. It was happening to someone else. So be glad you are not under the knife and you need not pay any attention.

This is the Richard Speck theory of raising taxes. If you do not feel powerful enough to take on everyone in the room at the same time...you take them out of the room one at a time. Divide and conquer. Eventually everyone's time will come. But if the American people can be divided into different groups, different classes, they can be mugged one at a time and the political class need never take on the entire populace at once.

Increasing a single-rate tax requires a president or governor to say out loud, "I have a really good idea. And you are ALL going to pay for it." At that point we are ALL listening. It had better be a really good idea.

It makes sense that a flat tax would be more difficult to increase and easier to reduce. Everyone suffers when the single-rate tax is hiked. Everyone benefits when it is reduced.

Theory is fine. What about real life?

Forty-one of the fifty states have state income taxes. Nine states have a flat rate of zero. That is pretty flat. Eight states have nonzero single-rate flat income taxes. Thirty-three states have graduated or progressive income tax structures.

The highest state top income tax rates are California at 13.3 percent and Oregon at 9.9 percent.

What about liberal, Democrat, blue states, such as Massachusetts and Illinois?

Massachusetts, by state constitution, has a flat rate. It has to tax everyone at the same rate. Today, both the top and bottom rate, the only tax rate, is 5.25 percent.

Five times the political forces desiring bigger and more expensive government have placed a measure on the Massachusetts ballot to change the state constitution to allow a graduated income tax. Five different times Massachusetts, the home state of the Kennedy clan, the sole state to vote for George McGovern in 1972, a deep-blue state, voted down a graduated tax—in 1962, 1968, 1972, 1978, and 1994.

Illinois's flat-rate income tax is 5.0 percent. Deep-blue Illinois's income tax rate is below that of many of the states that surround it: Wisconsin at 7.65; Iowa, 8.98; Missouri, 6.0; and Kentucky, 6.0.

Every effort to change the Illinois constitution to allow a graduated income tax has been defeated, including in 2014, when the party of Obama had supermajorities in the state House and Senate.

The average top tax rate for the eight states with a single-rate income tax is 4.54 percent. The average top rate for progressive income tax states is 7.15 percent.

The flat-rate states have an average total tax burden as a percentage of state personal income of 4.6 percent. The progressive income tax states take 6.8 percent of their state's personal income.

Flat-rate income taxes are harder to increase.

One also notes that many nations have moved to a flat-rate income tax.

Today there are twenty-six nations with flat taxes (many of the them occupied by the former Soviet Union), and they include places as diverse as Lithuania, Russia, Mongolia, Nepal, Estonia, Kyrgyzstan, Bulgaria, Hong Kong, and Iraq. Starting off from scratch—and trying to rebuild after fifty years of Soviet occupation qualifies—those nations have decided to move not to the progressive income tax endorsed by Karl Marx in The *Communist Manifesto* but to Steve Forbes's and economists Hall and Rabushka's single-rate flat income tax.

CHAPTER 15

Path Three: The Golden Triangle of Pro-growth Tax Reform

This is a partial reform. Not as revolutionary as repealing the income tax and replacing it with a FairTax and not as dramatic as a full flat tax.

But because life often moves in baby steps rather than giant strides, it is important for those of us working for radical change to take advantage of every opportunity to move forward to a tax system that taxes consumed income one time at one rate.

And one likely opportunity would be a smaller step forward, such as Reagan's 1986 reform. Reagan reduced the number of rates from eleven to two. Not to one. But two is smaller than eleven. Progress. Two is actually rather close to one. Not bad for a first stab. Reagan also reduced the top rate from 50 percent to 28 percent. This increases the return to work or investing from fifty cents on the dollar earned to seventy-two cents on the dollar earned. A 41 percent raise. That will change incentives. And the reform was revenue neutral. Not bad work given that the Tip O'Neill antediluvian Democrats held the House.

The Prime Directive (for those of you science fiction fans) is: No net tax hike. No hidden tax increases, no trap doors or openings where inflation over time hikes the tax burden.

Then there are three sides to the Golden Triangle of pro-growth tax reform. Reagan was only able to move forward on the first.

One, fewer and lower tax rates on corporate and individual income, moving toward one single rate. The target following Obama's damage would likely be to cut the individual rate to 25 percent and the top corporate rate to 20 percent, which, when you add the average state corporate tax of 4.8 percent (say 5 percent) yield a corporate income tax rate of 25 percent, the European average. Having a tax rate as competitive as the average European nation is not as ambitious or challenging as winning the World Series or going to the moon, but it is a heck of a lot better place than we are right now.

Two, full expensing for business investment. Right now we have many pages of the tax code to help us decide how many years each piece of equipment is depreciated over. If you pay $1 million for a machine that is determined by the IRS to have an economic lifespan of ten years, then each year you can depreciate, or expense, one-tenth of the equipment, or $100,000. But a dollar of depreciation in ten years, given inflation and the time value of money, is not worth as much as immediate expensing.

All business investment should be immediately expensed just as all labor costs are immediately expensed. This greatly simplifies the code. Why should the IRS pretend to know how long your computer or laptop or chair will be valuable?

Third, the United States should move to a territorial tax system. Most nations have long done this. Great Britain adopted it in 2009 with success. Most nations in the world tax business activity and income within their borders. If a French company or a French person earns money in France, then France taxes it. If that French company or Frenchman earns money in the United States, the United States taxes that activity and France is delighted should you bring that money back to Paris. They do not add any taxes.

The United States, at present, taxes all activity by Americans and American companies here in the United States. Makes sense.

Just like everyone else. But the IRS follows you to France, and after you or your company earns money and pays taxes in France, the United States adds personal taxes immediately, as well as corporate income taxes should you bring those profits back to America. We should have a welcome sign out for money being brought back to the United States to invest and spend—not tax it. Why chase away lovely money coming stateside? Why double-tax Americans living abroad who are already subject to foreign taxes?

Move to one lower rate. Expense all business investment immediately and move to a territorial tax system. Three sides to the Golden Triangle. As long as the tax reform is not a tax hike and all three sides of the triangle move forward as fast as politics allows, this is progress.

An Alternative Take on Incremental Reform: "Reform Conservatism"

There is a group of young conservatives who argue that in moving step-by-step on tax reform we should avoid the Reagan route of focusing on reducing marginal tax rates. They don't argue against the economic importance of doing so, but rather believe that there is a coalition to be constructed by combining "pro-family" tax credits with dramatic "pro-growth" tax relief through reducing the corporate income tax rate and moving to full expensing. The pro-growth part of their suggestions are sound. As long as the Democrats are powerful enough to veto any individual rate reduction, this is an intriguing idea. Democrats have in the past supported child tax credits, a lower corporate income tax, and even expensing of new business investment.

Everything that moves us toward taxing consumed income one time at one rate is progress.

CHAPTER 16

Path Four: The First Step toward Flat or Fair: Kill the Death Tax

Abolishing the death tax is the great unifier. Whether you view the flat tax, the FairTax, or no tax as your goal, step one is to end the death tax. The death tax,—or "estate tax," as its supporters prefer to call it, because it sounds like it only hits the landed gentry, who spend weekends hunting foxes in their oversized backyards—is another level of taxation on income that has already been taxed at least once.

It is a tax directly on your lifetime savings. If one of the goals of a pro-growth tax reform/reduction effort is to reduce the number of times savings and investment is taxed and retaxed, then the first tax to end is the death tax.

All efforts to reduce and eliminate the death tax are a direct attack on the ugly politics of envy and greed. The death tax was sold and is defended as a tax on "them." You, know, people who save a great deal during their lives and love their children enough to want to pass their life's work to them and their favorite charities. People who consume more in life than they produce never face the death tax. It is the perfect tax for discouraging savings, thrift, and strong families.

Death taxes trace their origin to a British version of the stamp tax, dating to 1796. The courts imposed a stamp tax on estate documents that had to go through probate. These were later replaced by "death duties" around the turn of the twentieth century. In the United States the death tax first showed up during the Civil War, imposed by both the governments of the North and South. The South's death tax died at Appomattox. The Union's death tax did not die until 1870.[1] Another example of taxes lasting longer than the wars that spawned them.

The modern death tax we have come to know today is nearing its one hundredth anniversary. In 1916, it was imposed to help pay for preparations for what became World War I. The tax came early and stayed late. It never went away. The top death tax rate went up and down over the years. The amount of the exemption moved up and down over the years with changes in legislation and inflation.

After the Republicans captured the House and Senate in 1994, they twice passed the abolition of the death tax. And Bill Clinton twice vetoed it. There was every reason to expect George W. Bush to put this tax on the chopping block when he won the November 2000 presidential election. And he did. Sort of.

In order to make the numbers work inside reconciliation, and using static analysis, the death tax was not eliminated immediately. It was phased out over ten years, bit by bit, and it disappeared only in the tenth year. Then, in year eleven, it bounced back to its Clinton levels of 55 percent tax on savings over $1 million. One of the victories over Obama and Harry Reid came in December 2012 when Congress voted—and Obama agreed—to continue the Bush tax cuts for all Americans earning less than $450,000 a year and to expand the amount of your life savings that is exempt from the death tax from $1 million to $10 million and to set the tax rates at 40 percent, not the previous 55 percent. The law now is that when a husband dies, his entire life savings can pass to his wife without any death tax and his $5 million exemption is added to hers. She can now pass on up to a total of $10 million to children or anyone she wishes without tax. Above $10 million the government takes 40 percent. Have a life savings totaling $20 million and the federal government takes $4 million. This is progress, but not permanent victory. Leaving any piece of the death tax in place allows it to wait for an opportunity to explode back in its previous higher-rate/lower-exemption glory.

Ending the death tax is politically popular. Jim Martin, the founding president of the seniors group 60 Plus, is the founding father of the movement to repeal the death tax. He argues we should "kill the death tax, not wound it" and that "there should never be taxation without respiration." Martin points out that "nearly 70 percent of voters consistently support complete repeal of the death tax when polled." This is a very healthy sign for the American society, because since the 1980s fewer than 5 percent of Americans have had to worry about planning for the death tax, and even fewer end up paying it. Strong and consistent support for abolition shows that Americans respect hard work and thrift and do not lust after punishing those who have been successful in life. It shows that a basic sense of fairness is stronger for most of our fellow countrymen than the pure, cold envy and selfishness that Harry Reid believes moves his supporters.

Another way to see the power of the movement to end the death tax is to note how many states have chosen to abolish the death tax. Of our fifty states, only seventeen of them have a death tax, as of January 1, 2015. That is a lot of state legislators and governors deciding their voters want the death tax gone.[2]

Death Tax Repeal Is Tax Reform

Paying the death tax requires knowing—and telling the IRS about—everything you own at the moment of death. All your bank accounts and investments. Your home. The value of your business. The stuff in the basement. The gold in your teeth. No death tax: no need to have Uncle Sam following you around in your later years watching you.

Ending the death tax would reduce the number of pages in the tax code by two hundred.

In self-defense, the death tax has given rise to an army of accountants, attorneys, actuaries, and charitable planners to "help" successful business owners get around a death tax liability. The life insurance industry, in particular, is the biggest beneficiary of estate-planning requirements (they also coincidentally are one of the biggest supporters in Washington of keeping the death tax in place). What does life insurance have to do with the death tax? Simple: Life insurance proceeds are exempt from taxation, so investing your prospective life savings in life insurance products is a tried-and-true way to escape the death tax man at the IRS. It's good business for insurance brokers, too. A similar story can be told with respect to people who run trusts, charities, and other favored death tax–avoidance schemes.

As a result of all these planning opportunities, the truly megarich don't have to worry about paying the death tax. Paris Hilton, the Left's poster child for death tax relief, is actually a bad example of a death tax–repeal beneficiary. Her family has lawyers who go back generations planning their clients' way out of any death tax liabilities. You never hear about a Kennedy or a Rockefeller paying the death tax, either. So who does?

The death tax is an avoidable tax, so the only families who pay it are those who didn't plan ahead. That generally means first- and second-generation-wealth families, with a business that took off in the founder's lifetime, or in that of his children. They were so busy opening storefronts, hiring managers and employees, and keeping up with the bills every month that they never made time to meet with lawyers or actuaries.

Upon the triggering of a death tax liability, the grieving family struggling to keep the business afloat has a choice: They can borrow the money to pay the tax, putting the company in perilous debt; or they can liquidate storefronts and fire employees to reduce costs and pay the tax. Either way, an absurd cost is shifted to a healthy business for no good reason.

Killing the Death Tax

How much would it "cost" to abolish the death tax?

Surely repealing the death tax would "cost the government" bunches of money, right? Actually, Uncle Sam wouldn't notice the difference. If all the taxes the federal government collected in one year were represented as $100, the death tax would make up less than $0.50 of that pot. The death tax collects little tax revenue, and the budget would hardly notice. The goal was social engineering and to foster envy, not raise money.

And that's using a Washington math "static score," which pretends that tax law changes are not responded to in the real world. A more realistic score, which takes into account behavior changes, tells a different story. In an October 2011 study, Reagan economist Steve Entin (now at the Tax Foundation) estimated that full death tax repeal would increase economic output nationwide by nearly $1 trillion over the following decade. This extra economic growth would increase net federal tax revenues by nearly $150 billion, even after accounting for the lost death tax revenue.[3]

In politics sometimes we take half a loaf if the other team has the votes to limit our progress. On the road to full repeal we have already compromised by cutting the rate from 55 percent to 40 percent and by increasing the amount of life savings exempt from the death tax from $1 million to $10 million for a married couple, $5 million for an individual.

Our next step might be to reduce the death tax rate to the capital gains tax rate of 23.8 percent. The goal is always "lower," and winning is a rate of zero. The "standard deduction" can be increased from $10 million.

Another option has been put forward by Maryland entrepreneur Jack Fitzgerald. His plan, known as the ASSET Plan, would allow for any American to get out of having to pay the death tax in exchange for paying a very small tax while they are alive on any income above a certain level (say, $1 million). Upon death, heirs would be able to match up these payments with capital gains on inherited property. This would smooth out the revenue loss for the federal government, cut the death tax–planning industry out of the picture, and make it easier to ultimately repeal the tax entirely.

There is one good thing to say about the death tax. Only one. It highlights the hypocrisy of rich liberals. The liberal elite tell us every day that the government spends our money better than we do. That is what taxation is all about. Taxation only improves the world if the government will spend your hard-earned money "better" and "more wisely" than you would. But when it is the liberals' turn to die, do they cheerfully pay the death tax, or send the government their life savings? No. They set up foundations, because they can spend their money—through their well-heeled friends and neighbors and their children, who run their charitable foundation—better than the government.

So, the government can spend your money better than you can, but the liberals believe they can spend their money better than the government can. They are better/smarter than the government, and the government is better/smarter than you. Note that this implies that they are better/smarter than you. When liberals speak highly of the efficiency and competence and farsightedness of government, they mean—relative to you, not them and theirs. It is nice to know that they really have this level of contempt for their fellow Americans. They don't have a high opinion of government (they did not get rich by being stupid); rather, they have a low opinion of us.

Abolishing the death tax is a blow against the politics of envy and greed. It reduces the power and intrusiveness of the IRS. It would increase total savings. It would increase the national economy, save existing jobs, and create new jobs. It is politically popular. It is a good start in dismantling the structure of the IRS. What is not to like?

CHAPTER 17

Path Five: Do the Easy Stuff First

Eliminating the entire federal income tax and the IRS will take time. Elections must be won. Voters must understand the benefits of reform. This will take longer than it should and certainly longer than we would like. There is no shortage of large, sweeping tax reform plans that have been proposed.

If you cannot eat the whole cow at once, start with small bites.

Small victories can pave the way to greater progress. They encourage and embolden taxpayers. Here are eight ideas for small reforms we can get moving on right now. In politics the door opens from time to time, allowing good ideas to become law. We must be prepared for those unpredictable moments of opportunity. For most of these ideas there is already legislation "on the shelf" that can be brought to the fore of the political agenda when possible. If even a few of these got enacted, we would be much closer to a reformed system, and the fundamental reform we all want would be less of a leap than it is now.

1. Get the IRS on a Leash

Lois Lerner has convinced even the skeptics that the IRS is completely out of control, and that it has been for a long time. The arrogance of the IRS is a natural function of its nearly limitless powers to take property from Americans.

Congress has begun to write laws to fix this mess.

Congressman Peter Roskam (R-Ill.) introduced a series of bills that, combined, would serve to restore true taxpayer and congressional oversight of the IRS:

The "SIGMA Act of 2014" would create a cross-agency inspector general for Obamacare, including IRS implementation and information gathering

The "Stop Playing on Citizens' Cash Act" would prevent the IRS from using taxpayer dollars for IRS-employee retreats or conferences until the agency can certify that money won't be wasted on things like *Star Trek* videos.

The "Taxpayer Transparency and Efficient Audit Act" would effectively cap all IRS audits to one year, and would require greater IRS disclosure to taxpayers of what information about them has been shared.

The "Protecting Taxpayers from Intrusive IRS Requests Act" would prevent the IRS from asking any taxpayer about his religious, political, or social beliefs.

The "IRS Act of 2013" would streamline the nonprofit application process that was used to harass Tea Party groups applying for nonprofit tax status.

The "Free File Act" would prevent the IRS from getting into the tax preparation business, and thus stop the IRS from determining your tax liability and sending you a bill based on their calculations.

2. Fix Retirement Savings for the Middle Class

Depending on how you count them, there are about fifteen different tax-advantaged savings accounts—mostly for retirement but also for health care and education. They come in the form of a confusing alphabet soup of acronyms, such as IRAs, SEPs, 401(k)s, 529s, and the like. Many Americans have simply thrown up their hands and, afraid of making a mistake, haven't saved at all in these accounts and are not prepared for retirement.

One of the easiest things we could do would be to streamline and consolidate many of these accounts. The Treasury Department actually drafted these three laws to simplify tax-free savings for all Americans in 2003.

Retirement Savings Accounts (RSAs). Up to $10,000 per year could be contributed. Anyone from a child to a retiree could save in this account for retirement. The money grows tax-free, and can be used for retirement income after age fifty-eight. Nonworking spouses, minors, etc., could all have one. The RSA would replace the traditional IRA, the Roth IRA, and the nondeductible IRA.

Lifetime Savings Accounts (LSAs). These work exactly the same as an RSA, except they can be used for any purpose at any time. Yes, LSAs can be used to save for retirement. But the money saved in LSAs could also be used for health expenses, to buy a home, to start a small business, to pay for college, etc. There is no restriction on their use. These are intended to replace health savings accounts, Flexible Spending Accounts, 529 college savings plans, and Coverdell Education Savings Accounts.

Employer Retirement Savings Accounts (ERSAs). These work like "safe harbor" 401(k) plans today: Employees could defer up to $17,500, and employers could give a matching contribution at the same rate for the janitor as it does for the CEO. These replace 401(k)s, 403(b)s, 457s, SEP-IRAs, and SIMPLEs. Pension- and tax-advantaged retirement account rules take up 382 pages of the tax code. Combining the many plans into these three would make life easier and the IRS code many pages shorter.

3. Business-Entity Simplification

Like retirement savings, Congress never really thought about how businesses would organize themselves, and we're left with an after-the-fact mess.

Businesses fall into two basic categories—corporations and flow-through firms.

A corporation—which is how most of our larger businesses are structured-—is a separate taxpayer. It calculates profits by subtracting expenses from revenue, and pays corporate income tax according to that rate structure. U.S. corporations face the highest tax rate in the developed world, 35 percent at the federal level plus an average of 5 percent more at the state level. This is much higher than the European average of 25 percent.

The other way to structure a business is as a "flow-through firm." These noncorporations take many forms. A single-owner business is known as a "sole proprietorship." Multiple owners create a "partnership," which itself has a few varieties. Some businesses are "Subchapter-S corporations," which despite the name act a lot like partnerships. All of these may operate inside the context of so-called "disregarded tax entities" like limited liability companies (LLCs).

Flow-throughs don't pay taxes themselves. Rather, the profits of the business "flow through" to the owner, and that person pays taxes on the profits on his or her own 1040 tax form.

In short, it's a mess. The choice a business owner makes has drastically different tax, legal, and employment consequences. It's confusing, and even expert accountants and attorneys have trouble keeping up with it.

Congressman Dave Camp (R-Mich.) introduced a discussion draft that would allow for an optional consolidation of the various forms of flow-throughs into one entity composed of the best rules from each one today. However it's done, simplifying business-entity choice should be an easy lift that will make it easier for start-ups to compete. Today's rules for taxing flow-through businesses occupy eighty-five pages of the tax code. Fewer pages would be good.

4. Repatriation

International tax reform is probably the most difficult single aspect of doing comprehensive reform. It's extraordinarily complicated, to the point that only a small slice of tax experts even begin to understand it themselves. Industries are pitted against each other depending on the complicated form the international structure takes, and the most likely result is gridlock.

Making this situation very damaging for job creation here in the United States is the fact that we have a "worldwide" tax system. That means that in addition to taxing money a company earns here in the United States the IRS demands its pound of flesh, its vig, its tax payment on income earned in France by companies that have—you guessed it—already paid taxes in France. Or any other nation.

America is used to being unique. Usually this is good. Not this time. The rest of the world has a territorial tax system. They tax money earned in their country but welcome the return—tax-free—of money earned abroad. We have a uniquely stupid system. Like our tort laws. Dumb. Destructive. And we are almost alone in this self-inflicted wound.

There is a small step toward fixing this. It is called "repatriation." It was done in 2005 with very good results. We can and should do it again. ASAP.

In 2005, American companies were allowed to bring after-tax corporate profits earned overseas (and which had already faced taxation abroad) back to the United States. In so doing, they had to pay an entry rate of 5.25 percent to the IRS—less than the worldwide double tax the IRS normally would impose, which is closer to 15 percent, depending on which country the money is coming from

The result was that more than $300 billion in cash returned to the United States in that one year alone—money that almost certainly would have continued to remain overseas absent the "repatriation holiday." Today, American companies hold roughly $2 trillion overseas. That money could return to the United States to create jobs, reduce debt, fund pension plans, and increase wages. Only our stupid "worldwide tax system" stops that.

Passing repatriation would create a real stimulus program—up to $2 trillion in real wealth returning to America. Not to fund politically driven temporary jobs or increase government spending, as Obama's "Stimulus" did. But a real boost to the economy.

5. Full Expensing for Business Investment

One of the most important pieces of pro-growth tax reform—second only to rate reduction, and potentially even more important—is full-cost recovery for business purchases. It's a basic principle of tax reform that the tax base should reflect the actual cash flow of a business.

Under current tax law, business purchases for things like plant and equipment cannot be deducted in the year of purchase. Rather, these costs must be slowly deducted over several to many years, using a complicated formula called "depreciation."

There is a simple way to get this vital tax reform implemented quickly. One "temporary" tax provision Congress has renewed again and again in recent years is called "bonus depreciation." It should really be called "partial expensing," because that's what it is. It allows a business to immediately deduct/expense some percentage of equipment purchases (over the years this has variably been 30 percent, 50 percent, or 100 percent). Any remaining cost is subject to the complex depreciation rules.

Congress should make 100 percent expensing of all investment a permanent part of tax law. And Congress would do us all a favor by accurately naming this as "full expensing." There isn't any bonus about it.

Today's existing depreciation rules take up eighty-nine pages of the tax code.

6. Health Care Tax Reform

Today Americans are treated very differently by the IRS depending on how they handle their health insurance. The IRS doesn't tax health insurance paid for by your employer. Not now. But in 2018 Obama changes that and there will be a 40 percent tax on much of your health insurance if the IRS thinks you have too nice a plan. So much for being able to keep your health insurance if you like it.

If you buy your own insurance, the IRS does not give you the tax-free treatment employees at GM get.

How about this for a reform of how we tax or do not tax health care benefits or insurance? Treat everyone the same? Sounds almost American.

There are many ways to do this. You could allow tax-free Health Savings Account dollars to pay for health insurance premiums. You could create a "standard deduction" for the purchase of insurance. You could create a tax credit for the purchase of health insurance. There could be some combination of all these. Various ideas have been introduced by conservative members of Congress and senators such as Congressman Phil Roe (R-Tenn.), Congressman Tom Price (R-Ga.), Congressman Michael Burgess, M.D. (R-Texas), Senator Orrin Hatch (R-Utah), Senator Tom Coburn (R-Okla.), and others.

And rule number one for equalizing the tax treatment of health insurance: Lower the tax on those now taxed more heavily. Obama is already thinking of ways to increase the taxes on those the IRS abuses less than others. Let us instead equalize "downward" in order to lower taxes and have less IRS interference in our health care decisions.

7. Consolidate Child Tax Provisions and Fix Refundable Credits

It's a bitter irony of the current tax code that the population least able to handle its complexity—low- and moderate-income families with children—bear some of the worst aspects of that complexity.

Take children. There's a personal exemption for a dependent child, which has one set of rules. There's a child tax credit, with another set of rules. There's a child care credit with a whole other set of rules. This makes the folks at the IRS happy. Not you.

If a family's income is low enough that the various tax credits zero out their tax liability, they often get yet more money from the IRS in the form of "outlay effects" from refundable credits. For example, suppose you have an income tax liability (before credits) of $500. However, if you are eligible for $1,200 in refundable tax credits, you not only get to zero out your $500 income tax liability but you also get the $700 difference as a check from the IRS.

These various refundable credits are confusing to everyone involved, and are open to being abused and subject to fraud. Even the IRS's inspector general admits that the original "refundable credit," the Earned Income Tax Credit (EITC), has a 25 percent "improper payment rate."

A very simple reform would be to replace all these child provisions with a unified, refundable child credit. If there was one credit, with one set of rules and with one refundable aspect to police, it would help a lot. Taxpayers would be able to comply more easily, fraud could be reduced, and the IRS would be out of the business of trying to design your family structure.

8. Make the Best Part of the "Extenders" Permanent and Set a Pro-Taxpayer Revenue Baseline to Facilitate Fundamental Tax Reform

Over the past forty or so years, the IRS has extracted a remarkably consistent amount of revenue from the American people: about 18 percent of gross domestic product, or GDP. During boom times, this number has been higher as Americans flush with cash faced bigger tax bills. During not-so-good times, this number has been lower. But it's always reverted to this mean.

But there's a huge "*x* factor" in future tax projections. Every year or two, like clockwork, Congress reauthorizes about fifty-five tax provisions that are about to expire or have recently expired. Most of the money associated with this "tax-extenders package" is represented by a few provisions: a research-and-development tax credit, a couple of provisions to prevent international double taxation, and accelerated cost recovery in lieu of depreciation. At least these tax provisions should be made permanent. The rest of the fifty-five extenders Congress can decide to let expire for good, or make them permanent law.

Making much of this extenders package permanent would give a much greater degree of certainty to taxpayers, especially job creators. Separately, it would give policy makers a much more fixed idea of what the tax revenue baseline will be. Having that revenue baseline be fixed (and low) makes it far easier to do pro-growth tax reform.

CHAPTER 18

Path Six: Do-It-Yourself Tax Reform: Twelve Ways to Cut Your Own Taxes

Getting the IRS off your back and out of your wallet need not wait for the political world to embrace comprehensive tax reform. You don't even have to wait for baby steps, the small, incremental changes to our tax system that would improve your life. Those changes require an act of Congress. That could take weeks. Several hundred weeks.

The good news is that there are some simple, commonsense ways you can reduce the IRS bite out of your paycheck today. You don't have to wait for Congress to pass a new law. None of these items solve all the world's problems. You won't be quitting your day job anytime soon. But they are smart, lower-tax opportunities that the current tax system allows, and that are likely to survive no matter what changes happen to tax law—good or bad.

You can start now to defund the IRS, from the comfort of your home.

1. Don't Give the IRS Free Money

One of the simplest ways to avoid paying extra money to the IRS is to not give them extra money. That sounds simple enough, but millions of Americans end up paying more than their tax liability to the IRS because of interest and penalties every year.

The IRS, contrary to popular belief, does not want you to pay them on April 15. By then, it's already been three and one-half months since you stopped earning money for the year. They want to get paid in something close to real time, as you earn the money.

Ideally, that's done through payroll and other third-party withholding—ideal for the IRS, that is. But for people who don't have a withholding option, the IRS has four quarterly payment windows in April, June, September, and the following January.

What happens if you don't pay the IRS enough money, quickly enough? You may be liable for an underpayment penalty and interest (which is charged at a rate higher than what you can get at the bank). If you don't file your tax return on time, you have to pay a "failure to file" penalty. If you don't pay all your taxes by April 15, you have to pay a "failure to pay" penalty (on top of the regular penalties and interest).

All of this can really add up. If the clock keeps ticking long enough on these penalties and interest, a tax liability could easily double in size. That's all free money to the IRS, and you don't get to deduct it anywhere.

They are going to get the cash anyway, so pay what you owe, on time, and you've automatically kept money in your pocket and not given it to the IRS.

2. Don't Give the IRS an Interest-Free Loan

You can give the IRS too much money by paying too little or too late. You can also give the IRS an interest-free loan if you pay too much too early. The IRS reports that about three in four tax returns—more than 100 million taxpayers—are due a refund every filing season. The average refund is now approaching almost $3,000. About $300 billion is effectively loaned to the IRS every year (mostly paycheck by paycheck), only to be returned to taxpayers as a lump sum every springtime.

If you're reading this, there's a good chance that you are one of those taxpayers. When you get a refund, you might think of it as found money, or a windfall. It's not. It's simply your money that you paid too much of to the IRS over the course of the year. You could have had that money to earn interest at the bank, pay down debt, fund a retirement plan, save for your kids' college education, or even take a nice vacation with your family. Instead, you gave it—for free—to the IRS for a whole year or more.

Try to pay what you owe to the IRS. They don't deserve more than that, and you are not the IRS's bank.

3. Know Your Rights as a Taxpayer

Believe it or not, there's a list of taxpayer rights maintained by the IRS. Most taxpayers don't know about them, but they might come in handy in the event of an audit or other IRS action against you or your family. It's contained in IRS Publication 1.[1]

The list of rights is as follows:

The right to be informed about tax law, IRS publications,
    and IRS decisions
The right to quality service. I'll leave the jokes to you, the
    reader.
The right to pay no more than the correct amount of tax.
The right to challenge the IRS's position and be heard.
The right to appeal an IRS decision in an independent
    forum.
The right to finality in all audits and other IRS investigations.
The right to privacy. Presumably, this even applies to Tea
    Party leaders.
The right to confidentiality. Someone needs to tell Lois
    Lerner about this one.
The right to retain representation in any IRS audit or
    procedure.
The right to a fair and just tax system.

Now, some of those might have elicited a well-deserved har-rumph or guffaw from you, especially if you've ever been through an audit. But what's important is that these are rights you have as articulated by the IRS itself. If you feel that your rights are being violated, this is the first resource to consult.

4. Participate in Your 401(k) Plan at Work

The biggest tax benefit in the entire tax code is one that you prob-ably have access to, or if not you, a spouse or a child. It's nothing that you have to get a law school degree to understand, either.

Would you believe it's the simple act of signing up for your work-place retirement plan, which is often a 401(k)?

Most 401(k) plans are structured with a match on contributions. Under the most common form of these, you need to defer 5 percent of your wages in order for your employer to contribute the equiva-lent of 4 percent of your wages toward your 401(k) account.

Right off the bat, you're getting a fantastic rate of return there. In fact, it's the equivalent of getting an 80 percent rate of return before taking any other action (4 percent on top of 5 percent). Where else can you get a tax-free 80 percent rate of return on anything?

The money your employer contributes to your 401(k) is not tax-able to you. It will grow and build in your 401(k) (or an IRA, if you roll it over someday) until retirement. Only then will you pay tax on your nest egg. So not only is the original employer contribution tax-free—it is free of taxes for decades and decades of growth.

What about the 5 percent you yourself have to put in to get this free money? It also has a tax advantage. Most employers now offer an option between a traditional pretax elective deferral (where your taxes are cut merely by contributing, but you pay taxes in retire-ment) and a "Roth-style" after-tax deferral (where you don't get any tax benefit for contributing but the money grows tax-free forever, into your retirement and beyond).

Whichever method you use to contribute, getting that free

money from your employer is an absolute no-brainer. It's also the best tax advantage out there that is available to almost anyone in the working world.

5. Open a Roth IRA

The good news is that most Americans are already eligible to save in an account very much resembling the Retirement Savings Account mentioned earlier. A "Roth IRA" is an account where you get no immediate tax advantage for making contributions. However, the money grows and builds over time tax-free, and withdrawals after retirement are tax-free. Contributions can be withdrawn on a tax-free basis, usually at any time.

The contribution limit to a Roth IRA is $5,500 in 2014, and those over age fifty are allowed to make a $1,000 "catch-up" contribution. You have to have earned income (wages and salary and self-employment income) at least equal to your contribution amount.

Roth IRA eligibility is limited by income, but those limits are very high. The limit is over $100,000 for single taxpayers, and nearly $200,000 for married couples. That means that Roth IRAs are available to over 90 percent of workers today. There are also no income limits on converting a traditional IRA to a Roth IRA.

Can't wait for Congress to reform tax-free savings accounts or create a yield-exempt savings system? Make your own—use a Roth IRA.

6. Save for College Tax-Free

Just as a Roth IRA is a pretty good rough substitute for a Retirement Savings Account, there are ways to construct something like a Lifetime Savings Account for yourself, too. One of the main reasons you might choose to use an LSA in a reformed system is to save for college. You might also want to save for precollege education expenses, such as for parochial school or homeschooling costs.

The "529 plan" (named after its section in the tax code) is a tax-free account for college savings. As with a Roth IRA, you get no tax benefit for making contributions. However, the money grows completely tax-free, and distributions are tax-free if they are used to pay for college costs. Unlike a Roth IRA, there is no income limit on contributions—anyone can give. Also unlike a Roth IRA, the contribution limits are very high—most states merely have an account accumulation limit, and the only contribution limits you need to worry about involve potential interactions with the federal gift tax.

Do you need to save for both college and precollege expenses? Then you should look at a Coverdell Education Savings Account, or Coverdell ESA. These work like Roth IRAs (after-tax contributions, etc.) The contribution cap is $2,000 per year, and there are very high income limits. Coverdell ESAs certainly can be used for college savings, but they can also be used for precollege costs such as tuition and homeschooling expenses.

7. Open a Health Savings Account (HSA)

The other way to use your LSA is to save for future health care needs. There is an existing tax benefit that can do this. It's known as a "Health Savings Account," or HSA.

An HSA is a tax-free savings account on "both ends." That is, contributions to HSAs are tax-deductible (or they are tax-free if received from your employer). Money invested inside an HSA grows tax-free. Withdrawals from HSAs for health expenses are also tax-free.

That's quite a benefit. In fact, it's unlike any other benefit in the tax code, with the possible exception of the tax breaks given to employer-provided health insurance. What do you have to do to qualify for it?

There's the catch. Not just anyone can fund an HSA. You have to have a consumer-directed health insurance plan that is HSA-eligible. In order for one of these plans to be HSA-eligible, it must have (among other things) a deductible of (in 2014) $1,250 for singles and $2,500 for adults. These amounts are indexed for inflation.

A deductible, just as with car or home insurance, is the cost you must pay before insurance coverage "kicks in." As you save money in the years you do not spend your entire HSA contribution, it builds and is available to cover costs in a year when you have higher-than-expected health costs. That allows you to have a larger deductible, and that reduces your overall HSA insurance cost.

Plans with people paying for their own routine medical expenses result in health insurance policies that are less expensive than traditional, first-dollar coverage. According to AHIP, the trade association for health insurance plans, the cost savings from moving from a traditional plan to an HSA-qualified consumer-directed plan is about 33 percent.[2]

The typical family plan today is over $15,000, also according to the Kaiser Family Foundation.[3] So a 33 percent savings from there is an annual savings of $5,000. This number will only grow larger over time. Someone with an HSA could deposit these savings each and every year into their account. It would not take too long before a high deductible is not only not scary but not relevant. The maximum amount that can be annually saved in an HSA is nearly $7,000 for families, and nearly $3,500 for singles, so the opportunity to accumulate more is certainly there.

What happens to money you save in the account but did not need to use for medical expenses? Unlike other health accounts, such as Flexible Spending Accounts you might have had at work, HSAs have no "use it or lose it" rule. Whatever you don't use simply rolls over to the next year. Over time, HSA balances can become quite large, even into the five- and six-figure range. Most people with HSAs will find that they have more than enough money to pay for routine medical expenses, and they always have the health insurance plan as a backstop in the case of a very high-cost year (remember that you never owe more than your deductible and any coinsurance costs).

HSA dollars that are carried into retirement can be used to offset

Medicare premiums and pay for any other expenses that Medicare does not cover. Even better, starting at age sixty-five, HSA owners can take withdrawals for nonmedical purposes while avoiding any early-withdrawal penalties (they simply must pay income tax on what they withdraw).

HSAs also help keep the cost of health care down for all Americans. If more people were paying their routine medical expenses with their own money (leaving insurance for the unusual year when they have unusual health challenges or have a baby), they would care what things cost at the doctor's office and at the pharmacy. When consumers pay directly, they shop around. One notes that LASIK surgery and plastic surgery declined in cost when *not* covered by insurance. Ideally, the major government health expenditure programs (Obamacare, Medicare, Medicaid, S-CHIP, and Veterans) would be encouraged to become consumer focused. (Not as the Veterans Affairs system sadly turned out to be: bureaucracy centered.)

Senator Orrin Hatch (R-Utah) has legislation he introduces every Congress to expand HSAs, the "Family and Health Retirement Investment Act." These and other efforts to grow HSAs are an important part of incremental tax reform.

8. Start a Small Business

There's an old adage that "no man ever got rich working for someone else." It's true that most wealthy Americans didn't inherit their money—they built it by starting businesses. The tax code has all sorts of things that small business owners can do to prevent as much of that start-up money as possible from going to the IRS.

Business owners get to deduct all "ordinary and necessary" expenses of running their firm. This includes things like travel, rent, supplies, home offices, etc. In addition, they can expense in the first year up to $250,000 of business-asset purchases (as opposed to subjecting them to slow depreciation tables). Health insurance expenses can be deducted.

If you're an employee, you probably can't deduct those things, even if they are business related. The IRS makes that very difficult. But if you're self-employed, the deductions tend to be much more straightforward. Think about becoming your own boss and your own employee.

There are special retirement savings accounts for small businesses. The most popular is the SEP-IRA, in which 20 percent of business profits can be deposited—tax deductible—for retirement. That's one of the most powerful tax benefits in the entire tax code.

As with everything in taxes, there's a catch. Self-employed people are subject to the income tax, and they are also subject to both the employer and employee halves of the Social Security and Medicare payroll tax. The combined FICA rate is 15.3 percent. That means that small business owners face some of the highest marginal income tax rates of anyone in our tax system.

9. Take Classes to Increase Your Marketable Skills, and Talk to Your Employer about Paying for It

If you take classes in order to acquire a new skill or to become self-employed, that's obviously going to be a good thing for your long-term wealth accumulation prospects. But it's also a pretty good way to prevent money from going to the IRS.

There are three separate tax preferences for taking higher education classes—the Tuition and Fees Deduction, the Lifetime Learning Credit, and the American Opportunity Credit. They all have different rules, levels, phase-out rates, etc. But they are available to you if you know how to use them.

You can also receive a limited amount of tuition benefits ($5,250 per year) as a tax-free fringe benefit from your employer. This money is deductible to them and tax-free to you, so it's a great way to shield even more money from the IRS. In fact, there are a whole host of tax-advantaged benefits you can get from your employer. Talking to your employer about what's in your benefits package is a good idea in any event. Common things it can include (and should if it doesn't) are:

- A 401(k) or other retirement plan
- Pretax employee contributions to health insurance premiums or HSAs
- A Flexible Spending Account (FSA)
- A special type of FSA for dependent care
- Employee parking or public transportation benefits

10. Don't die

Sadly, the death tax, while pruned back during the Bush years, still exists.

The federal death tax now stands at 40 percent above $10 million for a couple. But watch out because fourteen states have lower exemption levels from their own death taxes. If you cannot follow my sound advice to avoid dying, you might wish to move to one of the thirty-three states with no death tax.[4]

Death Tax States with Top Rates

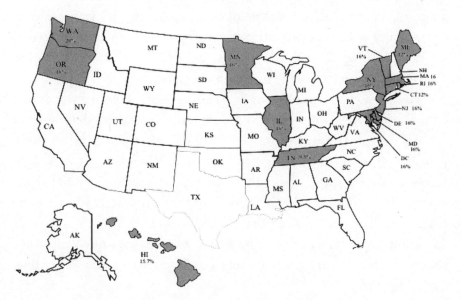

In order to avoid paying the death tax, there are some common-sense things you can do. For this, you should consult a financial planner and perhaps an attorney.

Another thing to avoid is tripping up against the "gift tax," which is intended to prevent estate transfers before death. Yes, the government limits how much you can give your kids and grandkids as a gift each year.

If you're smart about it, you can prevent your family from having to face both the undertaker and the IRS on the same day.

11. Move to a Low-Tax State

Between 1995 and 2010, 2,461,687 Americans moved from the ten highest-income-tax states, while the ten lowest-income-tax states have gained 3,838,694 Americans.[5]

12. Keep Taxes in Mind When Investing

If you're investing in a taxable brokerage account (say, using mutual funds or just buying stocks), it's easy just to focus on the headline rate of return on the investment in the past. But it's important to remember that this investing is not happening in the context of a tax-advantaged account, such as an IRA. Any taxable income thrown off will be taxable to you in the here and now.

For stocks and mutual funds, there are two taxes to watch for. First, dividends, the payments companies make to shareholders when they distribute profits. Shareholders must pay taxes on these profits, at a rate that can go as high as 23.8 percent. The average dividend yield (that is, the dividend payment divided by the share price) in the stock market is about 2 percent per year. If you are buying a stock or mutual fund that returns cash to you in excess of this amount, know that you're going to pay taxes on it. Some companies, such as utilities and financial services firms, pay a very high dividend by design.

The other principal tax is capital gains. Capital gains taxes take two forms in this context: First, you have the capital gain that is a result of the share price of your investment rising. You buy a stock for $1 per share, and it grows in price to $10 per share. You have a $9 capital gain. This is not due to the IRS until you sell the shares (capital gains face the same taxation as dividends).

The other type of capital gains is those that are realized inside of a mutual fund you might own shares in. A mutual fund is just a bucket that itself contains stocks. You own a piece of the bucket. Any stock sales that happen within that bucket are passed along to you, the mutual fund shareholder. Some mutual funds have a lot of "churn," meaning there's lots of buying and selling going on within the fund. Generally, these types of mutual funds will throw off a large annual tax bill, even if you haven't sold any mutual fund shares.

It's important to be conscious of taxes, fees, and the total return on an investment before deciding to hold it outside of a tax-advantaged account.

PART V

Defeating the IRS's Brezhnev Doctrine: The Strategy for Victory over the IRS

CHAPTER 19

Make Governments Compete: It Works in the Real World

W hy does Apple create great products? Why has the cost of a computer fallen by 77 percent in the last thirty years?[1] Why do we spend 11 percent of our budget on food in 2014 when it was 46 percent in 1900?[2] Why are only 2 percent of Americans working on the farm when it was 30 percent in 1920 and 64 percent in 1850?[3]

Why are we greeted more cheerfully at Walmart or Whole Foods than we are at the Department of Motor Vehicles?

Competition. Choice.

Success replaces failure. Creative destruction. The new displaces the old. "New and improved" at "lower cost" takes over from "always done it this way."

Competition drives improvements in a free market. That is the genius of capitalism. But can this approach work with governments? Maybe governments, like other monopolies, are immune to competition?

Government is first and foremost the legal monopoly of power. Government alone claims to itself the right to initiate force. Try to compete with that.

And yet governments do compete, if not as cheerfully and constructively as Hertz and Avis.

The history of the ancient world is one of constant competition between city-states, tribes, and nations—one nation would conquer another. They didn't compete on price and quality of service, but on the one-dimensional "capacity of their respective armies." The success of Attila the Hun and the Mongols suggests that being the most competent general is not the same as being the best king or governor. There was, however, a Darwinian competition between empires, city-states, and nations. More "successful" nations expanded, and less successful ones receded. The Roman legions won more often than they lost. By the law of large numbers, their empire grew over the centuries.

This is why, even today, the army is the one part of government that works best in "less successful" nations. Think of the modern Egyptian army or the Turkish army over the years. This was the one part of the government that had to work, because it competed with that of other nations. When your army was less effective, your borders began to shrink, and over time the nation would disappear.

But even in neighborhoods in our present world where governments do not "compete" for territory using armies, governments can still be forced to compete for citizens. They compete to provide the best government at the lowest cost. People and their personal human capital (their experience, education, and skills) can move. Even before individuals leave their home country, they often move their money by investing overseas.

There have been efforts to restrict such competition. East Germany built a wall that was proof to the world that they knew perfectly well they had failed to create a workers' paradise where any worker—given the option—would choose to live. They had no intention of competing for the affections and loyalty of "their" citizens. They built the Berlin Wall.

Two jokes highlight this failure to compete. The last dictator of East Germany, Erich Honecker, was talking with his wife near the end of the Soviet Empire, when she suggested he open the checkpoints along the Berlin Wall. The dictator was taken aback, because he knew his wife to be a committed Communist, but then smiled and kissed her, saying, "How romantic, you wish to be alone with me."

Second, two East German border guards stood in their watch tower and one said to the other, "What do you think about the relative virtues of East and West Germany? Is it better on the other side—the West?" The second guard was careful and replied, "Why I think just as you do."

"Well, then," snapped the first guard, "I shall have to arrest you for treason."

Some states live in the delusion that their citizens are, or should be, happy or that they have no alternatives.

Yet we have watched the Beatles all depart Liverpool and move to America when the taxman was taking "nineteen for me and one for you." Somehow the Swedish tennis pros end up living in Monaco.

In 1948 forty thousand people left Ireland and British occupation, high taxes, and a famine to move to the United States. The Pilgrims voted with their feet twice: First they left England and then they left Holland for Plymouth Rock, Massachusetts.

Faced with a lousy government, one might work to either reform that government or overthrow it. If you live in a monarchy, there are limits to what you can do to choose the next king. How would you like to spend your life and your children's lives trying to reform a corrupt monarchy or dictatorship? Best to leave. Many do, which sends a signal to the nation you move to that it is doing something right and to the nation you flee that it sucks.

We have some test cases. North and South Korea are both filled with Koreans. At the end of the World War II, the North was the more industrialized and richer "nation." North Korea embarked on a path of socialist development, while South Korea, particularly after 1965, had a more open society and a freer economy—more open to private property and free trade with the world. East and

West Germany were peopled by the same ethnic group with originally the same culture. And then for fifty years there was a controlled experiment contrasting socialism and a more free-market economy. The market beat the commissar.

On the Korean peninsula 25,000 North Koreans fled south.[4] Four million East Germans fled to free Berlin and West Germany.[5] Eventually the Communists had to build the Berlin Wall and man it with armed guards to reduce the flow. Tragically, 916 Germans were murdered trying to leave the blessings of socialism.[6] East Germany began its final collapse when Hungary allowed nearly 8,000 East Germans to cross into the fellow Warsaw Pact nation, and then slip out across the border to Austria and West Germany.[7]

What size of government do people want? How much of their lives are they willing to have taken in taxes? Do they like the benefits promised by government programs or would they rather spend their own money?

The Statue of Liberty is a monument to people "voting with their feet" choosing "exit" as the way to let the world know what they think and what they value.

Once one has crossed the Atlantic or Pacific to get to the United States, one has other choices to make. Which state? Which city?

The fifty U.S. states are a great example of how states can be forced to compete to provide more competent, consistent government at the lowest cost. When one asks why we can't amend the Constitution to limit government, the first response is that the Constitution already gives us our first and most powerful tool to limit government: competition between the states, where the American Constitution guarantees that any citizen can leave or enter any other state unimpeded. No Berlin Wall. No exit fees or tariffs. Leave a high-tax state and head out west, or south, or north to a lower tax state. The Constitution says, "The Citizens of each State shall be entitled to all Privileges and Immunities of Citizens in the several States." You can bring your wife, your car, and your bank account with you.

The Articles of Confederation, even before the Constitution came into effect, promised all Americans that "the people of each state shall have free ingress and regress to and from any other State."

We were peopled, and still are, by men and women who chose to come here, not for the climate but for limited government and unlimited liberty.

The most extreme example of interstate competition was the ability to flee from total slavery. In the United States before the Civil War, many slaves fled from slave states to free states. How many? Enough that the defenders of slavery felt they needed to pass the "Fugitive Slave Acts" to require Northern states to return men and women fleeing states where they were enslaved. To their credit, many states and localities refused to enforce that law restricting freedom of movement across the United States. Before the Civil War, some abolitionists in the North thought the best approach would be for the North to secede and bring an end to slavery by allowing slaves to flee to the North.

Returning to today's politics, politicians like to tell Americans what would be good for them. But movement of people across state lines tells us, and should inform the politicians, what people really want. The good news for Americans who wish to maximize liberty and limit the power of the government is that Americans demonstrate year after year, every day that they move from big-government/high-tax states to live in limited-government/low-tax states.

From 2002 to 2012, economic growth in the nine states with no personal income tax outperformed the national average by 25.6 percent and outperformed by 39.2 percent economic growth in the nine states with the highest income taxes. The more hospitable tax climates of no-income-tax states also draw jobs and people from high-income-tax states. Population growth over the past decade was 148.6 percent higher in no-income-tax states than in the afore-mentioned high-income-tax states.[8]

Now, it is a great deal of work to move your family dozens or hundreds or even thousands of miles to another state. The difference between two states must be significant for someone to make that decision.

The federal government keeps track of how many Americans move from one state to another and, through the IRS, how much money they earn. So we actually have data on how many Americans and how much annual income is moving from one state to another. (Sometimes it is useful to have this information to understand how the world works. It is also scary to know that the government has this information for its own reasons.)

Between 1995 and 2000, two million Americans moved across state lines.[9] How might the relative tax burdens have driven those decisions? Do Americans move to higher-taxed states that have promised more government services, or do they tend to move to lower tax states that have smaller state and local budgets?

Where do people leave? Where do they go?

The top ten states with net outmigration during that period were New York, California, Illinois, New Jersey, Ohio, Michigan, Massachusetts, Pennsylvania, Maryland, and Connecticut.[10]

During the same period, the top ten states with in-migration are Florida, Arizona, Texas, North Carolina, Nevada, South Carolina, Georgia, Colorado, Washington and Tennessee.[11]

Let's take a quick look at the ten states with the highest income tax rates. Between 1995 and 2010 the highest-income-tax states lost 4.2 million citizens, who took $131.5 billion in annual income with them.[12]

From 1995 to 2010, the nine states with no income tax gained 3.54 million citizens who brought $162.47 billion in annual income with them, including New Hampshire, which gained 57,778 people and $3.64 billion, and Tennessee, which gained 345,462 people and $9 billion.[13]

When people leave California, they take their families and income with them. One notes that California takes 12 percent of its citizens' income from them in taxes and fees each year. Had people stayed behind in California, their $37 billion in income would have paid property and sales and income taxes averaging more than 12 percent. So the tax hikes that drive folks out of California cost the state over $4 billion in revenue each year.[14] (And of course, the politicians' answer to this lost revenue is to raise taxes on those "left behind," and the destructive cycle continues.)

Migration means that the state and local governments in Florida get $8.9 billion in additional revenue because 1.45 million people with $96 billion in income have moved into Florida, which extracts an average of 9.3 percent of its citizens' income each year. Florida has low taxes and has gained $1.2 billion in annual state and local income from New York and Illinois, not from raising taxes but by being a low-tax state that attracts immigrants from California and New York.[15]

OK, so Americans move from high-tax states and into lower-tax states. That makes sense. But don't Americans "demand" more government services?

No. Americans tend to move away from big government and toward smaller government. Every day, year after year.

The ten states that have the largest governments as a percentage of state income lost a total of 2.5 million population, and the total income lost was $198 billion.[16]

The ten states that are being mean to their citizens by not lavishing as much on spending for government "services" gained 3.8 million in population, and they brought $2.25 trillion in income with them.[17]

The difference in fiscal policy has real-world consequences.

In 2013 alone, the Texas economy grew 85 percent faster than California's, up 3.7 percent compared to California's 2.0 percent growth, according to the Bureau of Labor Statistics. From 2000 to 2012, census data revealed that California's population grew 11.9 percent, and Texas grew by 24.3 percent.[18]

Travis H. Brown is a great taxpayer advocate living in Missouri and leading the charge there to abolish its state income tax. He has taken the IRS and census data and written a wonderful book, *How Money Walks*, about how people and their income move between the various states over time, and has the world's most interesting website—to taxpayers—also named howmoneywalks.com which will provide you with hours of fun looking at how many people with how much money have moved from one state to another over different decades. The Tax Foundation has a similar website tracking how taxpayers move between the states: interactive.taxfoundation .org/migration/.

This message is getting through, albeit slowly, in some blue/ high-tax states.

The idea of "millionaire's" taxes on those who earn more than a million dollars in one year has soured as Maryland passed a millionaire tax in 2008 and found that the next year they had a third fewer millionaires, and that a thousand fewer millionaires filed taxes in Maryland. Did they move, or move their income, or simply retire? One way or the other, all that lovely money is lost to the Maryland government.

If tradition is the democracy of the dead, reluctance to excessively loot the peasantry is the revenge of, or perhaps the lesson taught by, those who fled the last tax hike. If you live in New York, you can best help your friends and neighbors still in the state by leaving for a low-tax state. This is the only way some governments learn. And even the worst do learn: The Illinois state legislature refused to support the Democrat governor's drive to change from their flat-rate income tax to a graduated or progressive income tax. Massachusetts has voted down efforts five times to amend their state income tax to allow a graduated or progressive income tax. In New York, the quite liberal governor, Andrew Cuomo, vetoed the continuation of their "millionaire" tax. New Jersey's governor Chris Christie did the same.

After the plague in Europe in the 1400s, the lords had to be much nicer to the peasants, as there was a labor shortage and the once-despised peasantry was now appreciated by other lords. If you want to be an aristocrat, you need peasants to loot. Tax too much and, mixing metaphors, you have a shortage of sheep to shear.

After World War II, Hong Kong, Korea, and Taiwan were very poor. They were also anti-Communist, and American liberals did not like them. They didn't want to help them. So they pushed to cut them off from getting foreign aid. As a result, those nations denied foreign aid developed more open and free-market economies and became Asian Tigers. Was it coincidental they began to get rich after we were "mean" to them by reducing foreign aid?

Because America and European nations tried to "help" others by shipping money to poor nations, the leaders in those countries could have nice palaces, Swiss bank accounts, and Mercedes-Benzes, all courtesy of foreign aid. There was no need to create the conditions for economic development, small businesses, a middle class, or foreign investment. For many political leaders those are all attractive prospects, because they are needed as a source of tax revenue. If the revenue shows up in foreign aid, there is no reason to notice whether people are educated, employed, or happy. There is an army to deal with whining.

Federal funds flowing to poorly governed states also mask the failure of some politicians. Reducing federal funding to states, and particularly cities, would force those governments to govern well and to compete for the affections and loyalty of citizens. Detroit's government stood like the soldiers at the battlements in *Beau Geste*, even as the taxpayers slipped away. Detroit's population fell from 1,670,144 in 1960 to 713,862 in 2010. But its city budget, flush with cash from state and federal taxpayers, increased spending per capita from $2,973 per resident in 1975 to $4,077 per resident in 2014—an increase in spending per person of more than $1,200 a year (in 2014 dollars).[19]

The threat of golden geese fleeing high-tax states grows as some governors have followed Obama's advice to go to war against high-income earners—the "one percent."

But those high-earners are an increasingly important source of taxes to state and local governments.

In 2012, 50.6 percent of California's income tax revenue flowed from the top 1 percent of income taxpayers.

In New York, 57.5 percent of the state's income tax revenue came from 5.6 percent of taxpayers.[20]

The novel *Atlas Shrugged* asks what would happen if all the producers—the investors and inventors and business leaders—went on strike and quit working. In the novel, they all head out to a hidden valley in Colorado, and the United States economy has some slight problems.

People and their money can move. They don't tell you. They just do it.

Competition is a powerful tool in limiting any government's ability to tax and push around its citizens. America's federal structure makes it easier to leave bad governments and flee to less expensive and annoying ones. Those founding fathers were smart.

CHAPTER 20

Capturing Washington by First Seizing the Countryside: Fifty in 2050

Can we abolish the federal income tax?

Well, America thrived for 138 years, from 1776 to 1913, without the federal income tax and has only lived under the income tax for a hundred years. Washington and Jefferson didn't want or need one.

OK, that was a while ago. What about now? We have fifty states, and some have income taxes and some do not. Clearly income taxes are not a requirement. Seven states have no personal income tax: Texas, Florida, Nevada, Wyoming, Alaska, South Dakota, and Washington. Tennessee and New Hampshire have no income taxes on wages—but do levy taxes on income from dividends and interest. How do the states with no income tax survive and function? Could America do likewise?

The other forty-one states have state income taxes, with top rates ranging from a low of the 3.07 percent flat tax in Pennsylvania to a high of 13.3 percent in California. What if many or even all of these forty-one states wanted to abolish their income taxes? Could they make ends meet by reforming government to cost less?

Americans for Tax Reform has started a "Fifty in 2050" campaign to repeal the income tax in all fifty states by the year 2050. At a minimum, success will help us end the little state versions of the IRS that each state must now maintain in order to collect a state income tax. And as each additional state phases out its income tax, we begin to make the case that perhaps the federal government could also get along without a national income tax run by the IRS.

The spending interests in each state will whine and moan and explain that they cannot possibly live without access to your paycheck and mine. They do have to explain how seven states manage quite well without an income tax. And those seven states are quite diverse. Texas and Florida have populations of 26.4 million and 19.5 million respectively. South Dakota and Washington State are smaller and do not have oil. Or sun-drenched beaches. There is no "trick" to the no-income tax states. They do more with less. Maybe all fifty states could.

As we move forward, every state that kills its income tax dead strengthens the case that states do not "have to" have an income tax. The argument now heard in New York and Massachusetts that "we cannot live without an income tax" will ring increasingly hollow. Think of it as a taxpayers march through the state capitols toward Washington. A constructive version of Sherman's "March to the Sea," this time spreading jobs, growth, and prosperity in its wake.

Term limits moved onto the national political agenda this way. State by state the term-limits movement marched across America.

The president of the United States was limited to two terms by tradition and then by the Twenty-Second Amendment to the Constitution in response to Franklin Delano Roosevelt violating that tradition. Then twenty-three states limited their state legislators' terms to six, eight, or twelve years, and in 1995, the incoming Republican majorities in the House and Senate limited their powerful committee chairmen to six years' tenure as the head of a committee.

Because of the real-life experience of the states with term limits, the arguments against term limits—the staff will run everything, the lobbyists will run everything—fell apart. Staff only has power because the long-serving legislator they work for wields real power. Lobbyists hated term limits—they could no longer build a career off knowing one key legislative leader. And worse, term limits dumped dozens of ex-state legislators into the lobbyist job market, driving down the price/pay of lobbyists. It would be like doubling and tripling the number of cab medallions in New York City...the cost of getting a cab would drop.

Sometimes the best way to kill a bad argument is to surround it with counterexamples. The cheerleaders for keeping the income tax have survived the existence of seven states with no income tax. How will they argue against the experience of ten, or twenty, thirty, or forty? Or fifty?

This march on Washington is under way.

Kansas

In Kansas, Governor Sam Brownback had a vision when he was elected in 2010: He wanted to make Kansas the low-tax state in the midwestern Plains states. As he entered the governor's mansion, the top personal income tax rate in Kansas was 6.45 percent. In nearby Missouri, it was 6 percent. In Nebraska, to the north, it was 6.84 percent and Oklahoma was at 5.25 percent.

Sam Brownback had returned after fifteen years as congressman and then senator in Washington, D.C., to make Kansas the strongest economy in the region.

Brownback knew that lowering taxes was both good policy and good politics. Some state legislators understood the argument for phasing out the Kansas income tax. Others could be convinced by looking at the success of the other states with no income tax. But some politicians, who had sold their souls to the spending interests years ago, would never change their minds. The only way the movement for lower taxes could succeed was if they were replaced.

The Kansas House of Representatives had a Reagan Republican

majority. But while the Senate had a Republican majority of thirty-one out of a total of forty seats in the Senate, many of those Republicans were "Lincoln Republicans"—meaning that the reason they were Republicans was that Abraham Lincoln had been a Republican in 1861 and Kansas was a Northern/Union state at that time. So while you could be fairly certain those congenital Republicans, those Lincoln Republicans, were for maintaining the Union and opposed to the extension of slavery above the 36°30′ parallel, it was not at all clear that they had fixed positions on labor union abuses, high taxes, and corrupt spending. They were the flip side of Yellow Dog Democrats in the South, whose partisan affiliation was fixed in 1861 and had not been rethought since.

Governor Sam Brownback and the Kansas Chamber of Commerce, led by free-market hero Mike O'Neal, decided to find primary challengers to thirteen of the Senate Republicans, who were nominal Republicans but not Reagan Republicans. (Would your Chamber of Commerce be this gutsy?)

Thirteen Reagan Republicans willing to run serious and competent campaigns in the primary and general elections were found. Two of the thirteen targets found discretion the better part of valor and announced they would retire to a convent somewhere and not run for reelection. Of the eleven challenged incumbents, nine were defeated—including the president of the state senate, Stephen Morris, who was defeated and replaced by challenger Larry Powell. Thus eleven nominal Republicans were replaced with Reagan Republicans who could be counted on to support tax cuts as well as the continued maintenance of the Union.

But before the August 2012 primary elections that defeated or drove out the eleven non-Reagan Republicans, there was a little drama that helped speed the path to zero income tax in Kansas.

On March 21, 2012, the anti-Reaganite Senate Republican leadership decided to play a trick on Governor Brownback: They would pass the income tax cut Brownback had prepared but remove the sales tax extension that was meant to "pay for" some of the income tax cuts. So instead of a significant tax cut that dropped rates and began the move to zero income tax, the Senate Republicans passed a "massive" income tax cut without any "offsetting" tax increases. They were sure they had checkmated the governor. They had passed a big tax cut. No one could now suggest they were not tax cutters. And the tax cut was so large that surely the Republican House would never pass it and Brownback would not sign it. They were wrong. The House Republicans decided to take the "too large to pass" Senate tax-cut legislation and pass it themselves. And so the race was on. Democrats in the House—allowed only one minute to speak before they each cast their vote—walked very, very slowly to the podium, taking up to five minutes per vote, as they tried to delay House passage of the Senate's amended bill in order to give the pro-tax Senate time to repeal its own already passed legislation. On the Senate side, the quisling Republicans and the Democrats raced to repeal the large tax cut they only weeks earlier passed. Reagan Republicans were able to give long speeches to slow down the repeal. Not dueling banjos but dueling "filibusters."

The House Republicans got there "Firstest with the Mostest," and the "massive" tax cut was passed.

I was sitting in the audience in Topeka, Kansas, when the governor of Kansas announced at his State of the State Address on January 15, 2013, that the goal was to phase out completely the personal and corporate Kansas state income tax. The next day, the governor of Nebraska said it was also his goal to end the state's income tax. Nebraska sits just north of Kansas.

Next-door Missouri has watched Kansas cut its income taxes. Job creation and employment have swelled on the Kansas side of the border—Kansas City stands astride the Missouri-Kansas border.

According to the U.S. Bureau of Labor Statistics, since the first round of tax cuts were passed in 2012, Kansas City, Kansas, has outpaced Kansas City, Missouri, every month. While Kansas City, Missouri, has posted negative job numbers three times since the 2012 tax reform, Kansas City, Kansas, has not once posted negative job growth. In 2014, responding to Kansas's successful tax cuts, Missouri Speaker of the House Tim Jones and Senate leader Tom Dempsey passed the first income tax cut in one hundred years over the veto of Governor Jay Nixon. Competition works.

Kansas has now passed two pieces of tax legislation that together will phase out the state income tax. The initial state tax rates were 6.45 percent, 6.25 percent, and 3.5 percent before his two tax cuts, and now stand to be phased down to 3.9 percent and 2.3 percent in 2018. And here is the key innovation passed by Brownback and his legislative allies: After 2018, every year that state revenues increase by more than 2 percent—which is expected with ordinary growth— the income tax rate will be ratcheted down by the amount tax revenue increases beyond 2 percent growth, each and every year, until it reaches zero for individuals, and once the personal income tax is gone, the corporate rate will ratchet down from its present rate of 7 percent to zero, and then the bank tax will be dropped from rates of 4.50 percent and 4.375 percent in 2015 to zero.

Kansas does not need any more heroics or dueling filibusters. Those income taxes on individuals, businesses, and banks phase out to zero with normal economic growth and time. In the past in Kansas and other states, whenever more money flowed into the state coffers from simple economic growth, the additional cash flow was gobbled up by the spending interests. There was no vote to raise taxes, but higher incomes hitting the same old tax rates and more people being hit by the same old tax rates brought in additional cash to the state treasury. From now on all that 'extra" money caused by growth will flow back to taxpayers in lower income tax rates until the personal income tax, then the corporate income tax, and then the bank tax are brought to zero. Gone. Kaput. Finished.

This is the model for all other states.

In November 2014 Governor Brownback and the Kansas Reagan Republicans were targeted because they were a double threat.

First, yes, they are the model for how best to phase out the state income tax. But that would not have happened without his second "sin" in the eyes of the Left.

And that "second unforgiveable sin" was that Kansas provided the model for how a governor, business community, and conservative movement must sometimes replace sitting legislators rather than accept the limited vision of politicians elected years and decades ago. A number of states have Republican majorities where the Republicans fail to reform taxes, labor law, and tort law because they have cozy relationships with spending interests, labor unions, or trial lawyers. Progress towards limited government can only move forward with new and improved state legislators.

Too many Republican governors balk at "fratricide" or a "civil war." There are real dangers and costs to running primary campaigns against politicians who have built up political machines and webs of friends and dependents. In 2011 Governor Bob McDonnell of Virginia found his Republican senate would not support his effort to sell off the state-owned-and-operated liquor stores and use the money for roads. He took their "no" for an answer and under pressure from the road building contractors ended up agreeing to tax increases. He did have a war—with taxpayers and the Reagan Republicans in his legislature. His tax hike cost Republicans the following governor's race. Had he run primary campaigns against those who stood against taxpayers and for Bulgaria 1956–style government-run liquor stores, he could have won the issue and avoided the tax hike, which cost him all credibility with the Reagan Republicans in the legislature and the electorate. The exact same tragedy played out for Republican governor Corbett, elected in 2010 and defeated in 2014 for the same failure. He did not primary those Republicans committed—for a variety of despicable reasons—to state-owned liquor stores. He raised taxes. He lost in 2014.

After Brownback defeated and replaced eleven old-school "Republicans" with eleven Reagan Republicans, the press would selectively quote the defeated candidates and their allies as if Brownback and his tax cut policies were unpopular with Republicans.

So how did Brownback's aggressive "legislative improvement strategy" work out? Despite attacks from the establishment Left at the national level, Brownback was elected by a margin of 49.8 percent to 46.1 percent, and Republicans gained five seats in the House, increasing their majority from 93–32 to 98–27. The law will phase out the income tax over time. Will there be delays, or compromises as things move forward? Probably. Is the victory inevitable? Yes.

North Carolina

In North Carolina, Senate Finance Chairman Bob Rucho (R) designed a phase-out of the state income tax. His measure would immediately cut the top rate from 7.75 to 5.25 percent in 2014, to 4.75 percent in 2015, and to 4.5 percent in 2016, and set the stage for final abolition by directing the Revenue Laws Study Committee to study and propose how best to eliminate the income tax.

He was strongly supported by Senate Leader Berger and House Speaker Thom Tillis. This was no fantasy. Berger and Tillis were battle-hardened Republican leaders with a plan to make North Carolina a job-creating machine. They regularly challenged then Democratic governor, Beverly Perdue, passing eleven bills over her veto, including the state budget, which did not include tax increases demanded by the governor.

When former Charlotte mayor Pat McCrory, a Republican, was elected governor in November 2012, Tillis and Berger sent the incoming governor a flurry of pro-market, conservative reforms, such as an education voucher program, regulatory reform, and arguably the most significant state tax reform in two decades.

The original legislation to begin the march toward abolishing the income tax phased out the income tax and "paid for it" by reducing some spending and by decreasing the sales tax from 6.75 percent to 6.5 percent but extending it to over 130 services not yet taxed like prescription drugs. Many service industry workers and business owners worried about the extension of the sales tax to goods and services that have previously been exempt. Trying to abolish the income tax too soon forced this effort to "pay for" the phase-out of the income tax with a broader sales tax. Taxpayers understandably focused on the immediate certainty of the sales tax hikes on services and less on the promised income tax phase-out. This is exactly the problem avoided by Kansas as they use future revenues to "pay for" the phase-out of the income tax.

Tillis and Berger made it clear that they were determined to end the North Carolina income tax but were flexible on timing. Goals are based on principle. Timing is a matter of strategy and tactics. On the goal of no income tax: no compromise. On the tactical question of how we get there: Sooner is better than later and later is better than never. The first installment of the phase-out was passed on July 17, 2013, and signed by the governor on July 23, 2013. It dropped the personal income tax rates from 7.75 percent maximum and 6 percent minimum to 5.8 percent in 2014 and 5.75 percent in 2015. The corporate tax rate was reduced from 6.9 percent to 6 percent in 2014 and to 5 percent in 2015. When the governor worried about putting further rate reduction into the legislation—what if there was another economic slowdown under Obama?—the legislative leaders made the further reduction of the corporate income tax rate to 3 percent to move forward as it was "paid for" by increasing revenues from economic growth. The continued reduction of the tax rate to 3 percent was virtually certain. How long that took would be determined by how the North Carolina economy grew and revenues came in. The corporate rate would move to 3 percent.

The next step will be to pass legislation requiring that all new revenues past a certain growth rate flow to phasing out both corporate and personal income tax to zero. And how did North Carolina voters react to the Republican legislature's drive to zero income tax? First, they maintained Republican supermajority control of the legislature: in 2015, the Republicans control the House 74 to 46 and the Senate by 34 to 16. And second, North Carolina elected House leader Thom Tillis to the United States Senate, defeating the incumbent Democrat who burned through $65 million of local and national Democrat and union money trying to hold on to her job.

North Carolina is on the way to ending its state income tax.

Tennessee

Tennessee has long been in limbo. There is no income tax on wages and salaries. That is good. But in 1929 state senator Frank S. Hall passed a complicated tax hike that put income taxes on dividends and interest income. Some of that money went to the state and some to the local government. It isn't a big deal for the state of Tennessee— it is just 0.9 percent of Tennessee's state and local revenue—but for some towns it is a large percentage of their local budget.

It was time, Tennessee conservatives decided, to finally kill the income tax. When one is trying to bring new citizens and job-creating businesses to the state, it is problematic to have to explain the asterisk on Tennessee's otherwise honest claim to be one of the "no-income-tax states." A small targeted income tax theoretically limited to dividends and interest can always be expanded to all income. Only a few years earlier Republican governor Don Sundquist had led the charge to do just that. The effort to create a full-fledged tax on all income was defeated by massive rallies at the state capitol and by the leadership of radio talk show hosts such as Phil Valentine and Steve Gill, who kept the focus on the income tax grab. The people of Tennessee know how close they came to seeing a full-blown income tax arrive in the Volunteer State.

Tennessee remains dedicated to keeping the state income tax free. On November 4, 2014, the state voted 66.2 percent to 33.8 percent to enact a constitutional amendment banning the imposition of an income tax in the state. Before that an income tax could be passed by a simple law. Now it would take a constitutional amendment.

That year, Georgia applied a similar prophylactic, passing a constitutional amendment freezing their income tax rates. They cannot be raised without amending the constitution.

Dr. Mark Green, a Tennessee state senator and a rising star in Republican politics, joined forces with House Ways and Means Committee Chairman Charles Sargent to write a Hall tax repeal bill that would first phase out the state's portion of the tax and, having given local governments time to prepare, then eliminate the portion going to local governments. The final plan, designed to meet Governor Bill Haslam's fears of "losing too much revenue," was to phase out the Hall tax over six years as revenue met certain targets that, barring a recession, would be hit within eight years. The Hall tax would go. Only the timing was a question. Hall tax repeal legislation will be introduced again in 2015. The Hall tax is a dead man walking and it's only a matter of time before Tennessee removes the asterisk next to its name and becomes a true no-income-tax state.

Louisiana

In March 2013, Louisiana governor Bobby Jindal unveiled a complete overhaul of his state's tax code that would eliminate all state personal and corporate income taxes, as well as the state franchise tax on capital stock. The elimination of these taxes was to be replaced with an increase in the state sales tax rate to 5.88 percent, up from 4 percent. The sales tax would also apply to a broader base of goods as well as a number of services previously untaxed.

Louisiana ranked thirty-second on the nonpartisan Tax Foundation's 2013 State Business Tax Climate Index.[1] Enactment of Jindal's tax plan would cause the state to jump to number 4 on that index. While Jindal's tax plan failed to pass in 2013, ten bills were filed by state legislators that would do the same thing as Jindal's plan: eliminate the state income tax. So the legislature is on board with the ultimate goal and the Speaker of the Louisiana House has commissioned a tax study to make recommendations for improving the state's tax code, with a report to be released in early 2015.

Oklahoma

The governor of Oklahoma called for ending the state income tax in 2012. The House and Senate have fought over the particulars, but the desire to take Oklahoma to zero income taxes—as it has a 540-mile border with zero-income-tax Texas—remains strong. In 2001, Oklahoma enacted a Right to Work Law making membership in a labor union voluntary, largely because Texas has one and they were tired of losing businesses that chose to move to Texas rather than to Oklahoma. The income tax competition is driving a similar path of Oklahoma playing "catch-up."

When one, two, three, and then fifty states in 2050 follow the Kansas and North Carolina model of phasing out the personal income tax and corporate income tax to zero, the pressure will grow on other states. Already, states with income taxes stand mute and embarrassed when businesses looking to relocate are looking for no-income-tax states. Soon every state will be within a few hundred miles of a no-income-tax state. The competition will drive more and more states toward zero income tax. And when we reach fifty states by 2050—do you really think New York can maintain a top rate of 8.82 percent and California can keep its top rate of 13.3 percent as more states move to zero?—the question will present itself. "You said we could never run this state without an income tax. Now we do. So why is the federal income tax—only newly arrived 100 years ago in a nation 237 years old—considered inevitable?" The federal income tax will then be on the block. And the IRS will be on the run.

CHAPTER 21

Making a U-turn on the Present Road to Serfdom: The Paul Ryan and Rand Paul Plans

In 2015, federal spending is roughly 20.5 percent of the economy. If nothing is done, if no new laws or spending programs are enacted by Congress, spending will drift up to 40 percent of the economy. Why the dramatic increase? Federal spending as a percentage of the economy has been at 20 percent, with minor blips up and down in the modern era.

The culprit is entitlement spending on Medicaid, Medicare, Food Stamps, and Social Security. Americans are living longer, causing these programs to become more expensive, in conjunction with the fact that Americans are having fewer children, resulting in fewer workers and fewer taxpayers per beneficiary.

When Social Security was enacted in 1935, there were 42 Americans in the workforce for every retiree of an age to get Social Security. That ratio dropped to 5.04 workers per retiree in 1980 and 4.65 workers per retiree in 2000, and by 2050 there will be 2.65 workers per retiree.[1] And retirees will be living longer.

People living longer is a good thing. The number of children people have is their business. To "fix" this entitlement challenge over the next several decades, we need either to double taxation on working Americans or to reform these entitlement programs.

This problem has been coming at us with the certainty of the changing of the seasons. But Congress after Congress has failed to reform entitlement programs that will bankrupt the nation and its taxpayers.

So why haven't "they" done anything?

The good news is that there is a solution. It is called the Ryan budget. Congressman Paul Ryan modestly calls it "The Path to Prosperity."

In various reform proposals, Congressman Ryan has advocated for dozens of means-tested welfare programs to be block-granted to the states—things such as Food Stamps, jobs programs, public housing, and Medicaid. In the 1990s, the Republican Congress passed this very reform for Aid to Families with Dependent Children (AFDC), commonly known as "Welfare." Congress block-granted AFDC to the fifty states, and total federal and state spending dropped 31 percent over the next ten years, while states had more flexibility to manage their own budgets.[2, 3] The number of Americans on welfare declined by more than 50 percent over the first five years.[4] Bill Clinton actually signed the legislation—after vetoing it twice.

The Ryan plan does not have a specific proposal to reform Social Security, and for good reason: One needs an absolute minimum of sixty votes in the Senate to commit to Social Security reform. We do know, however, that the obvious reform—the only reform that would make Social Security solvent and protect younger workers and taxpayers—is to allow all younger workers to shift from the present "pay as you go" system (aka Ponzi scheme) to a fully funded individual account like an IRA or a 401(k).

The Ryan budget calls for Medicare beneficiaries to have a choice of Medicare plan options available to them, including traditional Medicare. Seniors would be given a subsidy ("premium support") to purchase insurance coverage inside of Medicare. Older, sicker, and poorer seniors would receive a bigger subsidy than younger, healthier, and wealthier seniors. This is not a new idea. A version of "premium support" was recommended by the bipartisan Breaux-Thomas Medicare Reform proposal in 2000 and is still supported by former senator John Breaux (D-La.). Congressman Ryan developed the latest version of this plan with chief Senate Finance Committee Democrat Ron Wyden (D-Ore.). He developed an earlier version with Democrat and former CBO and Clinton OMB director Alice Rivlin.

In sum, the Ryan budget reduces federal spending by more than $5 trillion over the next decade. It bends down the cost curve of government entitlement spending through block grants and reforms. Without Ryan, federal spending increases to 35 percent in 2040 and 39.3 percent in 2050. If the Ryan plan were passed in 2017, federal spending would decline to 20 percent of GDP by 2040. The federal debt would decline from today's 73 percent of GDP to 38 percent of GDP by 2040 as spending on other programs reduced and more revenue flowed in from growth.

On the tax front, the Ryan budget provides a framework for tax reform that is simple and powerful: a top tax rate on individuals and companies of 25 percent, robust territoriality so we do not double-tax American firms that compete internationally, and moving toward full expensing of new business investment. This would strongly increase economic growth and make government a smaller percentage of a larger economy in the future.

Looking forward prospectively past the Ryan plan's implementation, we can begin to consider Senator Rand Paul's (R-Ky.) "A Clear Vision to Revitalize America" budget plan.[5] It's a real budget—it goes agency by agency making cuts and reforms, it has all the summary tables and appendices any budget wonk could ever ask for, and it's serious.

Federal spending under Paul's plan would decline from about 21 percent of the economy today to under 17 percent of GDP a decade from now. Social Security personal accounts would become available to younger workers who want them. Four cabinet agencies would be eliminated. Medicare would transition to a better system similar to that offered to federal government retirees. Obamacare is repealed. There's a balanced-budget amendment that rules out tax increases. The personal and corporate income tax would be replaced by the Hall-Rabushka flat tax. If the Ryan plan is the equivalent of going to the Super Bowl, the Rand plan is the equivalent of winning it in a rout.

So why do we hear the laments that "no one" has a plan for entitlement reform?

The establishment press is aware that these plans reform major entitlements and means-tested welfare programs so that they do not collapse under their own weight and/or tank the US economy. They ignore them because they do all these things…without raising taxes. The establishment tax-and-spenders hope to hold entitlement reform hostage to a massive tax hike. Most likely the imposition of a Value-Added Tax alongside income tax increases measured in trillions.

That's right. Their objection is that these plans do not include any tax hikes. The establishment has long hoped that the approaching collapse of the American federal budget and economy would be yet another "emergency" that would drive bipartisan agreement on massive tax hikes.

Here was the Democrats' plan before Paul Ryan wrecked everything by coming up with something sane.

If nothing changes, federal spending increases over fifty years to 40 percent of GDP. This even the establishment Left understands is not, to use one of their favorite buzzwords, "sustainable." But we could have a "compromise." Taxes could increase from just under 20 percent to 30 percent of GDP, and spending could be reined in at 30 percent of GDP and prevented from increasing all the way up to 40 percent.

See. A compromise. Taxes are raised and spending is cut. Actually taxes are raised 50 percent and total spending increases 50 percent, but not 100 percent, so it is a "cut" in Washington-speak.

Who loses? Taxpayers. Freedom. The idea of limited government. America would have been reabsorbed into the European model. Not kings, but the modern welfare state, where the aristocracy are government managers who manage not the government but you and me. Because they are better than we are. The kings thought this too.

The establishment ignores the Ryan plan—when was the last time you read about it in the *New York Times* or heard about it on CBS—because they want to use the created crisis to push for higher taxes. A solution that doesn't include a permanent higher tax burden will have wasted this entire crisis. Worse, by reforming government it will avoid a series of future crises that might have made the case for more and higher taxes in decades to come.

"But the Ryan plan cannot be passed into law," whines the establishment. "Not while Obama is president." Quite true. Time will fix that. Next objection?

The Ryan plan has been passed by the House of Representatives four times. Twice before and twice after the 2010 election. A majority of the House has voted for the Ryan plan and been reelected. Twice.

The number of Republicans who voted no on the Ryan plan was four in 2011, three in 2012, ten in 2013, and twelve in 2014. And many of those later "no" votes were conservatives who were showboating to let everyone know they were demanding even deeper spending cuts. The great Republican Macho Flash.

How deep is the GOP commitment to the Ryan reforms? In the spring of 2014, I called Congressman Ryan and wanted him to meet with the right's don of property rights, Peruvian economist Hernando De Soto, who happened to be in Washington. Ryan was delighted and let me know that he had read De Soto's works and would love to meet with him...in two and a half months. "Two and half months?" It would only be a thirty-minute meeting. Ryan explained that for the next two and a half months he was employing all his "free" time meeting for half an hour at a time with Republican congressmen about the changes that year in the Ryan plan. Ryan would not let Republicans cosponsor his initial legislation until he was convinced they understood the legislation. Every year he sits down with all the Republican congressmen and updates them on the budget.

This means that every Republican who has voted four times for the Ryan plan has now spent two hours being schooled on the entire reform. There is not a piece of legislation or budget that is more thoroughly understood by congressmen.

And every one of these Republican congressmen has been reelected once or twice after voting for the budget. They can make the case to their constituents about a rather significant, yes, radical, reform that can and will save America. Congress does work. Just not the way the *New York Times* editorial page would like.

The Republicans in the Senate have also had the opportunity to vote for the Ryan plan in 2011. Only five Republican senators voted "no": Snowe of Maine, who retired; Collins of Maine; Brown of Massachusetts, who lost; Murkowski of Alaska, who votes oddly when her vote is not required; and Rand Paul, who wanted to make the case he wanted more quickly.

When there is a Republican president, a Republican majority in the House, and at least fifty-one Republican senators, then we can and will pass the Ryan budget and turn the nation around on spending—and pass the attached pro-growth tax reform. This can and will happen in either 2017 or 2021 following the presidential elections of 2016 or 2020. Two golden opportunities to turn us back from the brink. Maybe the last two.

The preceding paragraph is filled with justified hope that we can begin to restore limited government in the United States. There is a path. The politics simply requires a GOP win in the presidency in 2016 or 2020. And yet, all the years of drifting and sometimes lurching in the wrong direction have convinced many Americans that only temporary victories, delaying tactics, and Parthian shots while retreating are possible. Win it all back at one blow?

I am reminded of a wonderful *Far Side* cartoon where one American cavalryman in a fort besieged by Indians asks his fellow solider, "The Indians are lighting their arrows on fire. Can they do that?"

Yes. The trajectory of America can be dramatically altered with one political strike. It has before. In fact, fully half of all federal spending flows from two brief periods of Democrat Party dominance that were used to create government programs that were designed to grow dramatically and now consume fully half of the federal budget. When FDR was elected in 1932, he carried forty-two states and won the popular vote 58 percent to 40 percent. Republicans lost 101 seats in the House and 12 in the Senate. Republicans lost again in 1934, shedding another 14 house seats and 12 Senate seats. Between 1934 and 1936, FDR passed Social Security and Unemployment Insurance, and the Child Welfare Services program that today respectively make up 4.8, 0.25, and 0.18 percent of the national economy. Laws passed in the two years between the 1934 and 1936 elections together consume 5.25 percent of our national income in 2014 and one-quarter of the federal budget. Another explosion of federal spending was created in the two years following the Lyndon Johnson landslide of 1964. Medicare and Medicaid were created, which today consume 2.93 and 1.77 percent, respectively, of the economy for a total of 4.7 percent of our nation's output.

Thus in two two-year short bursts, the Democrats expanded the federal budget from what would be 10 percent of the economy to today's 20 percent of the national income spent by the government.

The forces of freedom can and will reform government to cost less and make a full U-turn away from our present road to serfdom.

PART VI

Changing the Correlation of Forces

CHAPTER 22

Strengthening the "Leave Us Alone" Coalition for Liberty

The Leave Us Alone Coalition v. the Takings Coalition

There are a number of steps forward—some large, some small—in our long march to limit or end the Internal Revenue Service and the federal income tax it defines and enforces. We know the direction in which we wish to move.

Options. We got options. There is Reagan 1986–style tax reform. A flat tax. The FairTax. Taking aim at specific taxes one at a time. Killing the death tax. Expanding IRAs and 401(k) accounts. Ending state income taxes one state at a time. Spending restraint that makes tax reform and reduction much easier. Selling off government land, buildings, military bases, and spectrum. Enacting the Ryan budget plan and/or the Rand Paul budget. Creating an Anti-appropriations Committee in Congress. Term limits for the Appropriations Committee. Passing a constitutional amendment to require a balanced budget, a two-thirds vote to raise taxes or borrow money, and a limitation on total spending.

There is no shortage of partial solutions and first steps that can be taken on the longer road to fundamental reform. So what are we waiting for?

Each of these strategies requires more congressmen, senators, state legislators, governors—and at the national level—at least one more president supportive of lower taxes than we have right now. The means: winning elections. And winning reelection. Again and again. It is not enough to win once. A governing movement must hold power year after year, because reforming government takes longer that we might wish. Government did not grow because the statists won one election. The Democrats held control of the House of Representatives from 1954 to 1994 without interruption.

So how do those of us committed to expanding liberty and reducing the government tax burden win more elections? And reelections?

To change America's future, we have to build a stronger coalition committed to liberty. The Tea Party sprang into being in April 2009, focused on reducing spending, government debt, and taxation. But if the Tea Party movement alone was a permanent functioning majority, we would not be in the mess we are in now. Not everyone is focused today on the tax burden or on spending and debt. Heck, the millions of Americans who joined the Tea Party in 2009 were living in America as our problems grew. They were not focused on the growing threat. They were not engaged. Now they are. But for how long? We are still not enough—yet—to win enough elections enough times in a row to reverse-engineer the destruction caused by years of government growth and accumulated barnacles.

We must search out, identify, and ally with millions of other Americans who may vote for candidates based on their positions on different issues but whose goals are consistent with—and well served by—limited government and increased liberty. Who are our potential allies? Who could make our political movement for liberty larger, stronger, smarter, and more consistently focused in the American political world?

There is today a growing coalition supporting liberty, which includes Americans committed to reducing the tax-and-spending burden. The members of that coalition give various answers when asked, "What is the most important issue to you?" But they all have one big thing in common. They all want the same thing from the federal government: They Want to Be Left Alone. Full Stop. They don't want the government stealing other people's money or running other people's lives. They don't want anything from the government. They want the government to stay within the bounds of the Constitution. They wish to be left alone.

Let's focus on that: They simply wish to be left alone.

People who wish to be left alone by the government on a particular issue are potential allies for a movement looking to expand liberty generally and limiting the power of the state across-the-board.

Who are the "Leave Us Alone" coalition today? Who on their central "vote-moving issue" simply wishes to be left alone?

Taxpayers

Taxpayers who wish the government would take less of their money each year are an important part of the Leave Us Alone coalition, going back to our nation's founding. At different times in history the "taxpayers movement" has focused on different taxes: the stamp tax in 1765, the excise taxes that sparked the Whiskey Rebellion, the high tariffs in the Tariff of Abomination of 1828. And later, the income tax. In the 1970s, the increasing property tax assessments and property taxes driven by inflation created a nationwide tax revolt, seen first in California's Proposition 13. Inflation also pushed more Americans into higher income tax brackets, and taxpayers responded with the Kemp-Roth income tax cut, the Steiger halving of the capital gains tax, and the election of Ronald Reagan. The important role played by taxpayers in the "leave us alone" coalition is that they want lower taxes on everyone. They are not pushing for higher taxes on their neighbors or on "the other." They are the friend of every man's liberty and the enemy of no one's freedom.

Here one must note that some tax revolts rise up in response to a new tax, perhaps a soda tax or a hike in the property tax. But then the threat is beaten back. Perhaps politicians with fully functioning political survival instincts choose to "withdraw" the offending tax hikes (for the moment). Or maybe a new mayor is elected, a new city council majority created. The tax rebels believe the issue is won. They go home. They form no permanent citizens' watchdog group. The energy of the "tax revolt" dissipates. Later the tax increasers will return with smaller, better-hidden taxes to gain what they were earlier denied.

Tax revolts change the world when they create, activate, and maintain taxpayer organizations. Think of the Sons of Liberty, following the imposition of the Stamp Act of 1765. Even when the Stamp Act was withdrawn, the Sons of Liberty remained and were ready for the next effort by Britain to increase taxes and control over the colonies. When California taxpayers rebelled against rising property taxes, they created the Howard Jarvis Taxpayers Association, "dedicated to protecting Proposition 13 and promoting taxpayers' rights"—and it is dedicated to fighting tax hikes to this day. Citizens for Limited Taxation in Massachusetts rose up against a progressive income tax in 1978, and stands today at the ramparts against tax hikers in the Bay State. The National Taxpayers Union was the first national taxpayer organizing in the modern era and first fought for the balanced-budget amendment through the path outlined in Article V of the Constitution—an amendment proposed and ratified by the states alone. That movement fell short. But the NTU continues to this day, rating congressmen on how much they spend and leading the fight for a balanced-budget amendment that also restrains taxes. Citizens Against Government Waste, run by Tom Schatz, was created to promote the spending-reform ideas put forward in the Grace Commission, organized at President Reagan's request and run by W. R. Grace. The Grace Commission proposed spending reforms worth $424 billion in taxpayer savings over three years[1] and was promptly ignored by Congress. Without CAGW working over the years to push spending/tax restraint, many of the reforms would have evaporated. Americans for Tax Reform was created in 1985 to enact Reagan's tax reform, and continued year after year to fight all tax hikes and to defend the lower rates won in 1986. Americans for Prosperity and FreedomWorks were created in 2004 and have grown into national structures fighting for liberty in all fifty states.

Active and informed taxpayers have long been the base of the Leave Us Alone coalition.

Property Owners

Property owners who would like the government to protect, rather than attack, their property rights are an important part of the Leave Us Alone coalition. Their demand that their homes, farms, and places of business be protected from overtaxation, regulation, and even confiscation builds the liberty movement in cities, suburbs, and the West. It was seen throughout American history, and most recently in the Sagebrush Rebellion of the 1970s and '80s. The Institute for Justice fights for limited government on many fronts and has won significant victories for property rights at all levels of government.

Small Businessmen and Businesswomen: The Self-employed

Small businessmen and businesswomen, professionals, the self-employed simply wish to be left alone to run their business and professional lives without harassment, regulations, abusive litigation, and overtaxation. In protecting their businesses and professional lives they act in concert with all lovers of liberty. They fight taxes, regulations, and government controls at the national, state, and local levels. Are there businessmen who like big government? Yes, sadly. Some like subsidies and regulations that kneecap their competitors or stop them from ever coming into existence. (Watch the taxi companies fight Uber.) Those "businessmen" are simply an extension of the state, and they bat for the other team. They are a funding source for statism. The Competitive Enterprise Institute has long stood for free enterprise and against protectionism and crony corruption. Businessmen and businesswomen, professionals, and the self-employed who wish to earn their living and place in society are unalloyed allies of the Leave Us Alone coalition. They are not asking for small business stamps. Or higher taxes. They pay taxes.

Gun Owners, Hunters, and Concealed Carry Permit Holders

Not all fights for freedom are about money and property or one's job. Some Americans vote to protect their gun rights. Some focus on their right to homeschool or send their children to private or parochial schools. Some vote to protect their religious liberty, their ability to practice their faith and share it with their families. Each wants to be left alone by the government.

Some Americans care so deeply about their Second Amendment rights to keep and bear arms that they will vote for or against a candidate on that issue alone. They are not asking the government to give them guns. They are not demanding that every fourth grader in a public school be required to read a book titled *Heather Has Two Hunters*. They do not knock on your door on Saturday and tell you to become a gun owner. They don't care if you hunt or own a gun. They simply wish to be left alone.

I serve on the board of directors of the National Rifle Association (NRA). Polls have shown that 20 percent of Americans will tell you they are a member of the NRA. Fifty-four percent say they generally agree with the positions of the NRA.[2] Half of American households own guns.

Many groups have millions of members, but they don't have

the power of the NRA. Why? Because the Second Amendment is a "vote-moving issue," not simply an issue to whine about with radio talk show hosts. The NRA's power comes from the fact that for millions of Americans the Second Amendment is their primary vote-moving issue.

In the 1990s polls told us that a majority of voters supported more restrictive gun control laws. Bill Clinton and many congressmen and senators thought they were winning new friends by passing the assault weapons ban and law requiring a waiting period to buy guns. But polls measure opinions and not intensity. The pollsters forgot to ask, "And do you vote on that issue?" When the dust settled, on November 8, 1994, the Democrats lost fifty-four seats in the House of Representatives and eight seats in the Senate. Bill Clinton, using twenty-twenty hindsight, said he believed twenty-six of those House losses were due to voters who both opposed the gun control legislation and cast their vote based on the gun issue.

After they lost the 1994 elections over their grab for gun control, many leading Democrats said, "OK, let's shut up about taking people's guns." But once Obama was in office, he began a campaign against gun ownership through the "Fast and Furious" scheme. Then following Rahm Emanuel's axiom: "You never want a serious crisis to go to waste."[3] Obama tried to exploit the murders in Connecticut to push for gun control. The NRA membership swelled to five million in response. The NRA's budget increased from $196 million in 2009 to $250 million in 2014[4] in response to Obama's unleashed gun control agenda.

Beginning in 1987 Florida passed a law instructing local governments that they "shall" issue a Concealed Carry Permit to any Floridian of the right age who was not a criminal or insane. Not "*may* issue" but "*shall* issue." Today, 1.3 million Floridians have active Concealed Carry Permits.[5] The total number of Concealed Carry Permits in the United States was 11.1 million.[6]

This is the base of the gun rights movement in the future. In 2007 the number of Concealed Carry Permits was 4.6 million.[7] It has doubled in seven years. Ten states have more than 8 percent of their adult population with these permits.[8] The longer a state has "shall issue" Concealed Carry laws, the greater the number of Carry Permits.

A person who has decided to take control of his or her own life and the protection of their family is a different human being that the one who says, "Well, the government hires nice first responders who, should something happen, will helpfully draw a white line around my body."

Homeschoolers

Some Americans vote to protect their right to homeschool.

The homeschool movement was illegal thirty years ago. People went to jail for educating their own children at home outside of the public school system. They were "truants." Thanks to the leadership of Michael Farris, who organized the Home School Legal Defense Association, it is now legal to homeschool one's own children in all fifty states. Today, in 2015, there are about two million students being educated at home. There are ten million young people who have been homeschooled for some period of their education between kindergarten and high school.

The homeschoolers not only win all the spelling bees but studies show they are more engaged in the community, more active in volunteering in election campaigns. Generation Joshua organizes homeschool students into volunteer brigades that are deployed in House, Senate, and state legislative campaigns.[9]

The parents who homeschool—or hope to in the future—hold this freedom very dear. They are making a tremendous sacrifice in time and energy and are taking a pass on the government's kind offer to educate or at least babysit their children for twelve years. They tend to vote on this issue because it is such a large part of their lives. They know that the party owned and controlled by the teachers union would crush them in a moment if they had the political power to do so. Homeschoolers once fighting to win their freedom to homeschool now fight to protect it. They did not retire from the field. They are wiser, more committed, and more consistent than some groups that see a threat, beat it back, and then ignore politics until the statists are once again at their throat.

Religious Liberty: School Choice

Americans whose highest value is to practice their religious faith and transmit it to their children are part of the Leave Us Alone coalition. They're not asking the government to subsidize their churches, synagogues, mosques, or temples. They simply wish to be left alone to practice their faith. They are not asking for Baptist stamps. Obamacare was designed to have the government force Americans to pay for types of insurance that violate the consciences of millions of Americans. That was not a mistake by the Obama administration. It was on purpose: to break down dissenting views that flow from deeply held religious beliefs. Diversity is, in the government's view, about skin color or ethnicity. Not belief or faith.

Parents who want school choice for their children so they can attend religious schools or private or public schools outside their assigned area also wish less government control and must fight the teachers union and bureaucracy to win this. About 10 percent of Americans send their children to private schools—often parochial schools, Jewish day schools, or Christian schools.

The school choice movement has created new opportunities for Americans to control their own children's education. Some states allow tax dollars to follow the child to a public, private, or religious school. Some states have created scholarship funds—which pay for school tuition—that citizens can fund with tax-free contributions. Some have legalized charter schools that are half-public/half-private. As 2014 ended, more than 300,000 parents used school choice scholarships to send their children outside the government school system, according to the Friedman Foundation.[10]

In Arizona in 2009, the state legislature updated and expanded laws allowing individuals and businesses to contribute up to five hundred dollars a year (and receive a dollar-for-dollar tax credit for the contribution) to private-tuition charities that give scholarships to students in K–12. This got around the Blaine Amendment, which exists in thirty-seven states and prevents tax dollars from flowing directly to private or religious schools. The various state Blaine Amendments were passed around 1870 as part of a national movement that was explicitly anti-Catholic. Politicians such as Maine's congressman James Blaine did not want Catholics to be able to attend parochial schools using the tax funds that follow students to any school outside the public school system. Now, long after anti-Catholic bias has receded from polite company and politics, those amendments are used by the teachers unions to hobble efforts to give parents the ability to direct funding to follow their child to a private school, religious or secular.

Several states have passed laws allowing many—usually lower-income students—to take a good percentage of the state funding that would normally flow to their local government school and have it go instead to the private school of their choice.

Louisiana passed a school choice law in 2012 that makes 380,000 scholarships, worth $5,000 each, available to Louisiana students.

Indiana passed a school choice bill in 2011 providing for up to 500,000 scholarships worth $5,000 each. Arizona created Education Savings Accounts (ESAs) in 2011 (expanded in 2012 and 2013) that will admit 200,000 children. Who is allowed an ESA? The children of American servicemen and women assigned to bases in Arizona, as well as students with special needs, students in public schools receiving a D or lower on the State Accountability Report Card, students adopted from the state's foster care system or placed with family and have a case plan of adoption, and incoming kindergarten students who meet any of these criteria. They can take the state's $5,000 contribution to each student's education to any school, public or private, they wish.

For more than twenty years now, since the spring of 1993, representatives and leaders of the Leave Us Alone coalition have met at the office of Americans for Tax Reform every Wednesday. Rain or shine. The original goal was to stop Hillary Clinton's drive to have the government take over control of America's health care. We started with twenty attendees. The first meeting had the chief of staff for Dick Armey's office, Ralph Reed, and his Christian Coalition, taxpayer groups, Citizens Against Government Waste's Tom Schatz, GOPAC, the Heritage Foundation, US Term Limits, the National Federation of Independent Business, and others. In a few months we knew this was no longer solely about stopping Hillarycare. If we hoped to stop Hillarycare—the nationalization of 15 percent of the American economy; doctors, hospital, health insurance—we needed to slow down the entire Clinton political agenda of higher spending, higher taxes, gun control, energy taxes, and regulations.

A policy working group became a self-conscious coalition meeting that focused on the entire battlefield.

By the summer of 1994 the Wednesday meeting had forty participants, and Don Fierce, the key deputy to Republican National Committee chairman Haley Barbour, attended each week. The focus was then putting the final stake in the heart of Hillarycare and winning the 1994 elections.

By 1996, the Wednesday meeting grew to sixty participants each week. Elizabeth Drew, the longtime political writer for the *New Yorker* magazine, called me and said she believed the conservative movement and much of the Republican Party was more focused on maintaining control of the House and Senate than winning the presidency for Bob Dole. I said I certainly agreed that the Leave Us Alone coalition of activists believed control of the House and Senate to be the highest priority and that while we certainly would prefer Dole to Clinton in the White House, there was little the movement could do by then for the Dole campaign. It would win or lose on its own merit. So, yes. The focus of the movement would be on the House and Senate. Elizabeth Drew joined the weekly meetings with the understanding that the meetings were "off the record," but that she could ask individuals who spoke at the meeting for permission to quote them directly. She was professional and her book, *Whatever It Takes—The Real Struggle for Political Power in America*, correctly captured the role of the Leave Us Alone coalition in that election cycle.

Useful political meetings should both keep the entire conservative/liberty movement informed about what others are doing and how they might work together, and teach them how to present their ideas to a broad audience. Too often conservatives think that shouting loudly or being the most radical person in the room demonstrates how principled one is. However, the goal is not to convince the world that you are truly a believer in freedom. The goal is to convince millions of Americans that they should move in your direction. Coming across as loud, radical, or coarse drives people away. Some true believers might not be turned off, but those are the ones who are already on your side, and talking to them for the twelfth time about how you agree about everything is of limited value. Study, learn, and practice how to speak to and convince undecided voters.

In a broad-coalition meeting, the economists learn you cannot cite the OMB and CBO and JEC without explaining what the acronyms mean. Most people leading ordinary, decent lives cannot be expected to follow jargon. The Christian Right activists learn that quoting Leviticus does not win an argument unless everyone listening first knows what Leviticus is and recognizes it as a final authority. This works in certain church groups but not in races for governor of Connecticut. Or in those of several other states for that matter.

The Wednesday meeting is by invitation only. It is off the record, and today there are 150 to 180 attendees. You are not talking to a group of people who will agree with all your positions. Rather everyone in the room agrees on a central premise: Americans should be free. Liberty is the goal. And on their personal vote-moving issue, they want only one thing from the government: They wish to be left alone.

But even 150 to 180 activists and leaders in Washington, D.C., have limited capacity to move the world. Beginning in the late 1990s, I began speaking with taxpayer leaders and others in the fifty states to recommend that they might come by the Washington Wednesday meeting and themselves consider organizing such a meeting in their state capital. As more and more state leaders came by over the years, we had a broader appreciation of how the meeting worked, and state leaders saw the need in their state.

Today there are forty-five states with similar meetings. Some states have multiple meetings: Cincinnati, Cleveland, and Columbus in Ohio; Tallahassee and Orlando in Florida; Sacramento, Los Angeles, San Diego, and Orange County in California. Interestingly the strongest meetings are not always in the "reddest" states. Chip Faulkner, of Citizens for Limited Taxation in Massachusetts, has for more than a decade led a monthly meeting of more than sixty participants just outside Boston on the 128/495 beltway. Maine's meeting, led by taxpayer and property rights leader Mary Adams, regularly has forty attendees in Augusta. Where the Republican Party is weaker, it is even more important to have a strong center-right coalition.

Some believed that the Wednesday meeting could work only in Washington, D.C., because there are so many full-time political activists in the nation's capital. In states it is certainly true that there are fewer center-right activists who make a living doing political work. Most of the state meetings are monthly meetings. In Texas, for example, the Austin meeting of ninety attendees chaired by Michael Quinn Sullivan is held weekly when the legislature is in session and monthly when the legislature is out of session—the Texas legislature meets for only a hundred days every two years. But there are taxpayer activists, business leaders, state legislators, political donors, and key staff for governors' offices in all fifty states. They should know each other. They should be in touch every month at least. And no fight should be lost or go unfought because potential allies were unaware of a threat or an opportunity.

The center-right/Leave Us Alone coalition meeting has also gone international. Year after year visitors from around the globe traveling to Washington would drop by the Wednesday meeting to get a one-stop *tour d'horizon* of American politics. The French de Tocqueville Foundation would bring fifteen conservatives by each year. Two dozen Swedish conservatives visit annually. Canadian, Australian, and British political leaders have come by regularly. We always invited our foreign guests to present on what was happening in their home countries. What could we learn from their efforts, successes, and failures? It was humbling to learn from the "socialist" Swedes that they had abolished their death tax, had no capital gains tax, and that every child in Sweden had full school choice. Every country was doing something better than we were. We could learn something from each nation's struggle to expand freedom. No country had a tort law mess or trial lawyer abuses as bad as we have in the United States.

Today, the monthly London meeting chaired by Matthew Elliott, founder of the TaxPayers' Alliance of the United Kingdom, boasts eighty-plus participants. The Australian meeting is chaired by Tim Andrews, a former staffer of ATR, and has twenty-five participants. Meetings are also held in Canada, Japan, Australia, Kyrgyzstan, Denmark, Kazakhstan, Belgium, Austria, Italy, Serbia, Sweden, the United Kingdom, Spain, Chile, Peru, and Venezuela.

Now a good idea, tactic, strategy, or legislative proposal can flood Washington, D.C., in a week and be heard in forty-five states and in the conservative nerve centers of sixteen nations in a month.

The Takings Coalition

When Hillary Clinton was running for the Senate in New York in 2000, I received a phone call from a New York reporter informing me that Ms. Clinton had just announced that what the progressives in the United States needed was a meeting similar to the regular Wednesday meeting I chaired in Washington. What, the reporter wanted to know, did I think of that?

I briefly explained how the center-right meeting worked. Yes, I chaired the meeting, but the participants themselves set the agenda each week by putting themselves on the agenda or simply bringing handouts, publications, and other material to share. Our meeting worked because no one in the meeting wanted anything at the political expense of anyone else. No one's vote-moving issue was in conflict with a vote-moving issue of anyone else. Certainly, on secondary, tertiary, quaternary (and whatever five is) issues there can be lively debate. But those are not vote moving issues for the participants. One sees that the taxpayer who votes for low taxes is not in conflict in any way with the person who votes on the gun rights issue, and neither were in conflict with the person whose most important issue was the right to practice their faith and transmit it to their children.

To highlight through simplification and exaggeration: The person who wants to make money all day can look across the table at our meeting at the fellow who wants to go to church all day and say to himself, "That is not how I spend my time." And both of them can look over at the person who wants to fondle his guns all day and note that this is not how they choose to exercise their freedom. But it is not important that everyone in the center-right/Leave Us Alone coalition agree about what they wish to do with their freedom and their lives. It is only important that they tend to vote for the same candidates, the ones who promise to leave each of them alone in the zone most important to them.

Wise candidates stand in the center of this coalition and look out at the assembled crowd and explain, "I will leave your money alone; I will leave your property alone; I will leave your guns alone; I will leave your child's education alone; I will leave your church, synagogue, mosque, temple, or reading room alone; I will leave your business or your profession alone."

What, I asked myself, would Hillary's coalition table (soon thereafter stolen by Barack Obama) look like? Around the table would sit a collection of individuals and organizations who view the proper role of government as taking things from some people ("them") and giving them to other people ("us").

Let's go around that table: Here are the trial lawyers, whose ability to pillage businesses large and small is only made possible by the corruption of tort law by lawyers and judges who believe they have the right to break open any contract (or absence of contract) and decide they can/should rewrite everyone's obligations. Did someone spill hot coffee on someone's lap? Clearly McDonald's—or more honestly other McDonald's customers—should pay millions to the clumsy guy. The fellow who picked up a lawn mower to trim his hedges and then accidentally dropped it on himself—do not do this at home—should be able to demand that all other customers of the lawn mower company pay millions in higher costs to cover his bad judgment. And of course, the burglar who slips and hurts himself inside your business after hours should be able to sue you for unsafe workplace conditions. (His workplace or yours?) Trial lawyers are among the largest campaign contributors to the modern Democrat Party. They contributed an average of 75 percent of the entire Texas Democrat Party's annual budget from 2002 to 2012.[11]

Next around the table are the labor union bosses, who earn hundreds of thousands of dollars off the mandatory union dues workers are forced to fork over to keep their jobs in twenty-eight states. According to the National Right to Work Committee, "Union officials collect some $4.5 billion annually in compulsory dues."[12]

Then there would be the unionized government workers, who extract benefits and pensions way beyond anything taxpayers in the private sector can ever expect to earn. The average compensation package in the private sector is roughly $60,000. For state and local government workers, $80,000. And for federal workers, $120,000. Much of this high compensation flows from defined-benefit pensions indexed to inflation. Try to find that in the real economy. There are 5.3 million state employees and 14 million local government employees (this includes both full-time and part-time). Roughly 35 percent are forced to pay union dues as a condition of keeping those jobs.

Further around the table would be the two wings of the dependency movement. First, there are those locked into welfare dependency. Second, there are those earning $100,000 a year and managing the dependency of others while making sure none of these dependents escape dependency, get a job, and become Republicans. A great deal of the taxpayers' money spent to fight poverty never gets past the bureaucracy.

And then there are the "coercive utopians." The folks who get government grants to run organizations dedicated to telling the rest of us how to run our lives.

There are the people who mandated that cars be too small to fit your entire family into. These are also the folks who invented the CAFE (Corporate Average Fuel Economy) standards, which force cars to be built with less metal and are therefore less safe in accidents.

And then there are the folks who insist that toilets be built so they cannot flush completely.

These are the folks who mandated the squiggle lightbulbs that put out so little light you are convinced you have glaucoma.

These are the people who force you, on the Sabbath, to separate the green glass from the brown glass from the white glass for the recycling priests.

In fact our friends concerned with our moral uplift have a set of rules and requirements and prohibitions about what we must and must not now do that is somewhat longer and more tedious than Leviticus.

At our Wednesday meeting years ago, just before his movie *An Inconvenient Truth* came out, Al Gore asked to join the Wednesday meeting to present on his views on climate change. He attended the meeting for an hour to understand our coalition and then showed parts of his not-quite-finished movie and presented his views. He spoke clearly and slowly so we might better understand his theory. Vice President Gore is a gentleman, and deeply convinced of his theories and policy prescriptions.

I asked him that day, "Mr. Vice President, I remember when the coming cataclysm was 'Global Cooling,' and the solution was a list of ten things, such as riding bikes and using less energy and having smaller cars. Then briefly it was 'Global Warming.' And today, the coming Armageddon that demands our attention and immediate action is 'Climate Change.' The solution to Climate Change is the same list of ten things focused on downsizing our energy use and riding bikes and not driving cars that was going to solve Global Cooling and Global Warming.

"Should the angels come down and sit on your shoulder and convince you that it is not man-made cooling or warming," I asked, "are there any items on that list of ten things that we should not do anyway?"

No, Gore said, we should still have the same "To Do" list—Global Cooling/Heating or not.

So at some point we wonder if the goal is to control our lives, and the reason can come later. Do this or we all freeze. Do this or we burn up. "Verdict first, trial later," said the Red Queen.

Those are the two competing coalitions in American politics. The Leave Us Alone coalition, which is held together by a desire for liberty—at least on one's own vote-moving issue—and the Takings coalition of groups and institutions who view the proper role of government as taking things from one group and giving it to another.

The Leave Us Alone coalition is a low-maintenance coalition. If the government does not tell *you* what to do, that is fine. I also want the government not to tell *me* what to do. We share a common interest in limited government. A government big enough to give you everything you want is big enough to take everything away from me.

But the Takings coalition that is the American Left is not stable. It has no equilibrium. It holds together only if the government grows endlessly, so that every interest group can get more at the expense of taxpayers.

This is where the tax issue comes into play.

As long as taxes can be raised easily, or even if taxes are raised with great difficulty but with some regularity and assurance, then the various groups on the Left in the Takings coalition can cheerfully remain friendly around their table. A happy Takings coalition assured of regular water and feeding can smile because the room resembles the scene in the bank robbery movie shortly after the successful heist and the "boss" hands each person a stack of dollars... one for you and one for you and one for you. Everyone around the table is now happy. Payday. No one's cash comes at the expense of others around the table. The "other" pays the bill, the forgotten man, the taxpayer.

But if we in the Leave Us Alone coalition do our job...

If we say, "No new taxes"... and mean it. If we stop all tax hikes... Then the pile of money in the center of the Takings coalition table begins to dwindle. There is no regularly scheduled or anticipated next feeding time. Everyone around the table now begins to look at each other like the last scene in those "lifeboat" movies. Who is going to be thrown overboard and who his going to be eaten by his seatmates?

The Left is not made up of friends and allies. The Left in America is made up of competing parasites. If they cannot dine on taxpayers, they will cheerfully gnaw on one another around the Takings coalition table.

Gypsy Voters and Legacy Voters

There are two groups who do not fit into either the Leave Us Alone coalition or the Takings coalition. The first group are those who do not vote for your candidate because you and your candidate never ask for their support—or worse, come across as hostile to that voter. I saw an exaggerated version of this while organizing with the non-Communist parties in Romania after the collapse of the Communist dictatorship. We made a list of those groups likely to support our pro-freedom candidates. These included former political prisoners, religious minorities, and the small businessmen and women emerging from the ravages of socialism. Then we made a list of those who would support the Communists: the former police, army officers, party members, waiters, and Gypsies. OK, I said, I understood most of these lists but wondered why waiters and Gypsies would be presumed to vote for the Communists. They looked at me funny and explained, slowly, for the dim-witted, that all waiters were either informants or secret police. Their job was to listen in on everyone's conversations. OK, that made a certain amount of sense. I had heard that in other former-Soviet colonies this was true of the hatcheck girls—they knew who came and went, and when. But why in the world would Gypsies want to vote for the Communists? Because, I was told, the Communists would buy them liquor before the election and get their support. Well, I explained, George Washington bought liquor for potential voters when he ran for office. We can certainly compete with the Communists in the hospitality business. This was easily fixed.

No, I was informed, that was not possible, because the Gypsies were scum and we will not talk to them. Hmm. Then you are not likely to earn their votes. Gypsy voters are those you or your movement drive away, not because they don't like you or your policies but because you, purposefully or not, make it clear you don't like them and will not reach out to them. Handing them a pamphlet about an issue where you both agree strongly will achieve nothing if you have not already reached out and shaken hands, broken bread, and listened with compassion.

The goal in politics is to have that estranged vote reduced—through hard work, outreach, inclusion, and listening—to zero.

It is not always easy to see one's own blind spots. But focus for a moment on how the modern Democrat Party and the Left insults and denigrates people of faith. Don't do that to others. Let the

Left drive away potential voters. No voter should stand outside the center-right movement—the Leave Us Alone coalition—because he or she was not asked or feels unwanted.

A second group outside both the Leave us Alone coalition and the Takings coalition are the Legacy voters, those who vote for one party or the other just because their grandparents did. Some Republicans in northern states are Republicans because their ancestors were aligned with the Union during the Civil War, and that necessarily made them Republicans. A Republican who is still voting along regional lines may be neither a Reagan Republican nor a true member of the Leave Us Alone coalition, but is rather on automatic pilot. Some Democrats in Mississippi agreed with Ronald Reagan on everything but voted for George McGovern because Sherman had been mean to Atlanta. Recently. However, this is now largely a settled issue. Most Democrats in most counties have conceded on the importance of the Union.

Different waves of immigrants picked their party affiliation by reacting negatively to those who were unpleasant to them. The Irish often became Democrats reacting to the fact that the guy who was mean to them in Boston was a Protestant Republican. The world has moved on and changed for the better, but Legacy voters are casting their votes on hundred-year-old issues.

If these Legacy voters can be approached on modern issues, they may be brought over to the Leave Us Alone coalition. They may vote Democrat, but they are not hostile to liberty. Find out what liberty issue might move them out of the political ties of the past. They just look locked in place.

The challenge before those of us committed to reducing the power, scope, and cost of the government and its business end of government, the IRS, is to increase the number and activism of Americans motivated by the desire to be left alone and to reduce the number and activism of those who see themselves as members of the Takings coalition, the Friends of Government.

In 1953, the left-of-center playwright Bertolt Brecht was

embarrassed because the Communist government of East Germany had just violently put down a workers' revolt. There were not supposed to be workers' revolts in the worker paradise recently "liberated" and occupied by the Soviet Union. It could not be a failure of the infallible Communist government. So Brecht announced that what East Germany needed was to "elect a new people."

Here in America we can "elect a new people." We can change state laws to expand liberty, giving millions more Americans a greater appreciation of their freedoms and increasing the stake they have in voting to protect it.

We hear our friends on the Left talk about the inevitability of large and smothering big government making top-down decisions for us and our children, treating us like factory workers of the 1930s: All the same, told what to do. The Left views the demographic changes they believe will cement them in power in terms of race, ethnicity, and gender.

We know that Americans come from all nations, religions, and ethnic backgrounds. The liberty coalition does not ask the color of your skin but the goals you have in life and how we can make those possible by reducing the barriers old-style government throws up. We watch city governments try to regulate or tax Uber out of existence to protect the unionized and cartelized taxi business. We see the politicians react to the Internet by first demanding that it be restricted and policed—so they can tax it.

Reducing taxes expands the freedom Americans have. A tax cut is a pay increase. Lower taxes mean more time to spend with family and friends. More focus on your own community. The more we reduce the tax burden, the greater the freedom, opportunity, and choice that Americans will have to defend.

When homeschooling was legalized thirty years ago, it allowed two million families to decide to directly control their children's education. How hard do you think they will fight to protect that right? A right they did not have thirty years ago. Expanding liberty expands the size of the Leave Us Alone coalition.

When tens of thousands of parents and then hundreds of thousands of parents were given the right to have scholarships that follow students to the schools their parents choose, that is a dramatic increase in freedom, greater choice, and real control over one's future. I want to see the politician who tries to take that away from the parents in Louisiana, Arizona, Indiana, and Florida. And as more states follow the path to greater school choice, the army of parents willing to fight to maintain that freedom—and take on the power of the teachers union—grows.

How did the nation shift from moving toward more gun control in the 1970s to expanding Second Amendment protections? State after state passed "shall issue" Concealed Carry laws, to the point where the number of Americans with Concealed Carry Permits in 2014 was more than eleven million. More freedom, more beneficiaries of freedom, more political clout behind the expansion of freedom.

As more Americans have defined-contribution pensions, such as Individual Retirement Accounts and 401(k)s, more and more Americans care about how businesses are taxed. Those taxes on "the other" are now very visible taxes on their own future, their retirement, and their ability to help their children.

As Uber, Airbnb, Lyft, and other Internet-driven technologies create jobs and opportunities and more choice for all Americans, the enemies of the future—the unions, corrupt big-city governments, and the banality of bureaucracy—stand in the way. Sometimes the enemies of freedom and the future are themselves the best recruiting agenda for the Leave Us Alone coalition.

And more freedom leads to the defunding of the Left and the Takings coalition. Now twenty-four states have right-to-work laws that stop unions from forcing you to pay $500 or $1,000 in dues. In right-to-work states you can join a union—if you want. You do not have to pay protection money to a union to keep your job.

When Wisconsin passed Act 10, allowing government workers to choose whether they wanted to join a union and pay dues, as many as 100,000 government employees chose not to pay $1,000 in dues to keep their $50,000-a-year jobs. That made many families in Wisconsin better off. One thousand dollars each and every year is not a small thing. And now the political machine of the unions are $100 million poorer. More freedom, more choices for people. Less stolen money to finance the old politics of the 1930s and '40s top-down, standardized, limited, and controlled society.

Where big cities have written rules to limit choices, state governments can step in and liberate them. Florida and Wisconsin banned tenure rules that protect incompetent or dangerous teachers at the expense of a child's education. A California court ruled that tenure is a violation of the equal rights of children. A violation of their civil rights as Americans. It is, but we cannot count on judges to save us and the future of our children. We need to elect governors and state legislatures who will lead this fight.

The path to a greater freedom is clear. Stop the runaway government spending based on yesteryear's thinking. Let us leave our children a future of opportunity and choices, not debt. Take every opportunity to reduce the tax burden and eliminate individual taxes. Expand liberty to expand the political base for more liberty. Stop the government from taking your tax dollars in order to participate in politics against you and your family. Stop the government from granting unions' letters of marque to "tax" workers though forced union dues.

We have been on a downward cycle away from the freedoms won in the American Revoluton. We can shift to a virtuous cycle away from dependency, top-down control, and the structures of a rigid past.

And here we return to the truth we learned at our nation's beginning, when we were paying 1 or 2 percent of our income in taxes and government was limited to doing a few necessary things competently:

The more freedom a people enjoy, the harder they will fight to protect and expand that freedom.

Acknowledgments

When I write a book, I begin by waking up at 4:00 a.m. and getting to the office to write from 5:00 until 8:00 a.m. Three hours a day. Beyond that I get tired, and when writing about the annoying government I become cranky and my adverbs become unkind. I note that this is more ambitious than Graham Greene, who wrote 300 words a day. Still, 300 words a day is a novel a year.

So my first acknowledgment must go to my family, who must live for a number of months with someone who is operating on Icelandic time. My wonderful wife, Samah, and delightful and faultless daughters, Grace and Giselle, are a constant source of encouragement and support.

At 8:00 in the morning I must return to life as president of Americans for Tax Reform (ATR), a national political movement dedicated to reducing the size, scope, and cost of government at the federal, state, and local levels. The government never stops pushing against our liberties, so we must never stop pushing back. Even to write a book.

This book, *End the IRS Before It Ends US*, was and is a team effort. The entire staff at ATR participated. The "community organizers" at ATR won many of the taxpayer victories I cite in the book. The book covers the history of America's struggle to keep government under control and taxes down to a dull roar. The strong staff at ATR and the network of state and local taxpayer groups we have worked with for the past thirty years were at the center of many of those battles. So the book is in part an "autobiography" of the taxpayer movement in recent years.

Christopher Butler, the chief of staff of Americans for Tax reform, John Kartch, our communications director, and state organizers Patrick Gleason, Will Upton, and Paul Blair manage, lead, and support dozens of tax battles across the national stage at any one time. This book chronicles their victories and present and future strategies.

Ryan Ellis, who focuses on federal taxation, contributed greatly to exposing the mess that is federal taxation and the intrusiveness of the IRS in our daily lives. Chapter 2 is a small subset of the invasions of our privacy he has documented and exposed.

Chris Prandoni and Mattie Duppler are policy experts on energy and regulations, and how transparency is the beginning of accountability.

Adam Andrzejewski, the head of Open the Books, has led the national fight for full transparency in government spending at the national, state, and local levels. He has not waited for politicians to act. His work at OpenTheBooks.com is a powerful source of material for all who would study, understand, and fight against government overspending. The website HowMoneyWalks.com, organized by Travis Brown and Rex Sinquefield, makes it clear to all how tax policy drives migration of jobs, work, individuals, and their incomes from high-tax states to low-tax states.

I benefited from the leadership and memory of tax fighters Barbara Anderson and Chip Faulkner of Massachusetts's Citizens for Limited Taxation, from Jon Coupal of California's Howard Jarvis Taxpayer Association, from California taxpayer leaders Jon Fleishman of the FlashReport and Ron Nerhing, most recently the GOP candidate for lieutenant governor of California, and from Chuck Muth, tireless taxpayer advocate of Nevada, the entire team at the Goldwater Institute in Arizona, Mary Adams, leader of the center-right in Maine, and Michael Quinn Sullivan and Brooke Rollins, who keep Texas Texas. The Tea Party movement has resculpted the political world, and all its state, local, and national leaders made the optimism of this book possible and realistic.

Others at ATR have helped make this book possible: Jorge Martin, Max Velthoven, Alexander Hendrie, Roger Boyd, our "computer whisperer," and Candice Boyer, who somehow seems to fit all of this onto the schedule while helping organize the Wednesday meeting.

The taxpayer movement is just that: a political movement with thousands of leaders, activists, and allies in elected offices from school boards to Congress. The State is a large and powerful monopoly. Our movement carries the collective wisdom and crowd-sourced knowledge that can topple the powerful but slow-witted Cyclops, Polyphemus.

This book is made possible by their action, leadership, consistency and patience. While all errors, omissions, and shortcomings are mine alone, the central truth of the book's thesis—that the present tax-payer movement is poised to restore our most fundamental liberties and bring the federal government and its pet vulture, the IRS, under control—is a truth created by the commitment and activism of the American people, who remain Sons and Daughters of Liberty.

Notes

Chapter 1. *Our Low-Tax Past and Our Present Tragedy*

1. Congress of the United States Congressional Budget Office, "Updated Budget Projections: 2014 to 2024," Apr. 2014, http://www.cbo.gov/sites/default/files/cbofiles/attachments/45229-UpdatedBudgetProjections_2.pdf.

2. United States Department of Commerce Bureau of Economic Analysis, "National Data: National Income and Product Accounts Tables," Sept. 29, 2014, http://bea.gov/iTable/iTable.cfm?ReqID=9&step=1#reqid=9&step=1&isuri=1.

3. White House Office of Management and Budget, "Historical Tables," 2014, http://www.whitehouse.gov/omb/budget/Historicals.

4. Internal Revenue Service's Taxpayer Advocate Service, "The Complexity of the Tax Code," 2012, http://www.taxpayeradvocate.irs.gov/userfiles/file/full-report/most-serious-problems-tax-code-complexity.pdf.

5. Andreas Madestam, Daniel Shoag, Stan Veuger, and David Yanagizawa-Drott, "Do Political Protests Matter? Evidence from the Tea Party Movement," American Enterprise Institute, Dec. 17, 2012, http://www.aei.org/files/2012/12/18/-veuger-tea-party-working-paper_095614741243.pdf.

6. Ibid.

7. Ibid.

8. Karen L. Hass, "Statistics of the Congressional Election of November 2, 2010," United States House of Representatives Clerk's Office, June 3, 2011, http://clerk.house.gov/member_info/electionInfo/2010election.pdf.

9. Staff report on Lois Lerner, United States House of Representatives Ways and Means Committee, Mar. 2, 2014.

10. Staff report from the U.S. House of Representatives Committee on Oversight and Government Reform, "Debunking the Myth That the IRS Targeted Progressives: How the IRS and Congressional Democrats Misled America about Disparate Treatment," Apr. 7, 2014, http://oversight.house.gov/wp-content/uploads/2014/04/4-7-2014-IRS-Staff-Report-w-appendix.pdf.

11. Ibid.

12. "The Internal Revenue Service's Targeting of Conservative Tax-Exempt Applicants: Report of Findings for the 113th Congress," Staff Report 113th Congress, December 23, 2014.

13. http://dailycaller.com/2013/08/23/irs-is-targeting-the-american-legion
-with-audit-new-set-of-guidelines/, accessed January 12, 2014.

14. U.S. House of Representatives Committee on Oversight and Government Reform, "The IRS Targeting Investigation: What Is the Administration Doing?" Feb. 6, 2014, http://oversight.house.gov/hearing/irs-targeting-investigation
-administration/.

15. U.S. House of Representatives Committee on Oversight and Government Reform, "Testimony of Catherine Engelbrecht from the IRS Targeting Investigation: What Is the Administration Doing?" Feb. 6, 2014, http://
oversight.house.gov/wp-content/uploads/2014/02/Engelbrecht.pdf.

Chapter 3. *The Latest Tax Outrage: The Twenty Taxes in Obamacare*

1. The Joint Committee on Taxation, "Estimated Revenue Effects of the Amendment in the Nature of a Substitute to H.R. 4872," Mar. 20, 2010, https://
www.jct.gov/publications.html?func=startdown&id=3672.

2. Ibid.

3. Ibid.

4. Ibid.

5. Ibid.

6. Ibid.

7. Ibid.

8. Congressional Budget Office, "Appendix B: Updated Estimates of the Insurance Coverage Provisions of the Affordable Care Act," *The Budget and Economic Outlook: 2014 to 2024*, Feb. 2014, http://www.cbo.gov/sites/default/
files/cbofiles/attachments/45010-breakout-AppendixB.pdf.

9. Douglas W. Elmendorf, Congressional Budget Office Letter to Majority Leader Harry Reid, Mar. 11, 2010, http://www.cbo.gov/sites/default/files/
reid_letter_hr3590.pdf.

10. Douglas W. Elmendorf, Congressional Budget Office Letter to Speaker of the House John Boehner, July 24, 2012, http://www.cbo.gov/sites/default/
files/cbofiles/attachments/43471-hr6079.pdf.

11. Congressional Budget Office, "Updated Estimates of the Effects of the Insurance Coverage Provisions of the Affordable Care Act, April 2014," Apr. 2014, http://
www.cbo.gov/sites/default/files/cbofiles/attachments/45231-ACA_Estimates.pdf.

Chapter 4. *How Taxes and Tax Revolts Shaped American History*

1. Alvin Rabushka, *Taxation in Colonial America* (Princeton, N. J.: Princeton University Press, 2008), 866.

2. Charles Adams, *Those Dirty Rotten Taxes* (New York: The Free Press, 1998), 8.

3. Ibid., 170.

4. Charles Adams, *Those Dirty Rotten Taxes* (Princeton, N. J.: Princeton University Press, 2008), 6.

5. Ibid.

6. Ibid.

7. Charles Adams, *Those Dirty Rotten Taxes* (New York: The Free Press, 1998), 54–55.

8. Thomas P. Slaughter, *The Whiskey Rebellion: Frontier Epilogue to the American Revolution* (New York: Oxford, 1986), 30.

9. Ibid.

10. Alexis de Tocqueville, *Democracy in America* (New York: Perennial, 1969), 191.

11. Ibid., 191–92.

12. Ibid., 390.

13. Ibid., 391.

14. Ibid, 392.

15. Ajay K. Mehrotra, *Making the Modern American Fiscal State: Law, Politics, and the Rise of Progressive Taxation, 1877–1929* (New York: Cambridge University Press, 2013), 72.

16. Daniel Okrent, *Last Call: The Rise and Fall of Prohibition* (New York: Scribner, 2010), 95.

17. Ibid., 331.

18. Ibid, 332.

19. GovTrack, 1964," https://www.govtrack.us/congress/votes/88-1964/s267.

Chapter 5. *How Government Grows*

1. Gary Stoller, *Rental Car Taxes Are Getting Jacked Up*, USA Today, Nov. 3, 2009, http://usatoday30.usatoday.com/travel/news/2009-11-02-rental-car-taxes-rising_n.htm.

2. Galbi Think!, "Share of U.S. Households with Telephone Service, 1920–2007," http://galbithink.org/telcos/telephones-1876-1981.xls.

3. R. J. Reynolds, "Tobacco Taxes and Payments," https://www.rjrt.com/taxpays.aspx.

4. Jonathan Bean and Donald W. Gribbon, "The State Lottery: California Hustle," *The Independent Institute*, Jan. 15, 2007, http://www.independent.org/newsroom/article.asp?id=1891.

5. Ibid.

6. Ibid.

7. Randolph Bourne (1918). "The State." Unpublished manuscript, http://fair-use.org/randolph-bourne/the-state/.

8. Stephen Moore, *Who's the Fairest of Them All: The Truth about Opportunity, Taxes, and Wealth in America* (New York: Encounter, 2012), 69.

9. Ibid.

10. Ibid., 67.

11. Ibid., 66.

12. Ibid., 49.

13. Ibid., 37.

14. Ibid., 53.

15. Ibid.

16. Scott A. Hodge, "No Country Leans on Upper-Income Households as Much as U.S.," *Tax Foundation*, Mar. 21, 2011, http://taxfoundation.org/blog/no-country-leans-upper-income-households-much-us.

17. John Kartch, "Documentation of President Obama's Middle Class Tax Pledge," Americans for Tax Reform, Dec. 12, 2012, http://www.atr.org/documentation-president-obamas-middle-class-tax-a7382.

18. Rasmussen Reports, "75% See Middle Class Tax Hikes as Likely in Debt Ceiling Deal," July 19, 2011, http://www.rasmussenreports.com/public_content/politics/general_politics/july_2011/75_see_middle_class_tax_hikes_as_likely_in_debt_ceiling_deal.

19. Americans for Tax Reform, "Obama Breaks Campaign Promise," Feb. 4, 2009, http://www.atr.org/obama-breaks-campaign-promise-a3626.

20. John Kartch, "Obama: Thank You for Not Asking about My Tax Hikes on Families Making Less than $250,000," Americans for Tax Reform, Apr. 10, 2012, http://www.atr.org/obama-thank-tax-hikes-families-making-a6834.

21. Joshua Culling, "Flashback: Buffett Rule Test Drive in Washington State," Americans for Tax Reform, Apr. 16, 2012, http://www.atr.org/flashback-buffett-rule-test-drive-washington-a6840.

22. The Joint Committee on Taxation, "Summary of Revenue Provisions of H.R. 4961 (The 'Tax Equity and Fiscal Responsibility Act of 1982') as Passed by the Senate on July 22, 1982," July 27, 1982, https://www.jct.gov/publications.html?func=startdown&id=2672.

23. Dr. Arthur B. Laffer, Stephen More, Rex A. Sinquefield, Travis H. Brown, *An Inquiry into the Nature and Causes of the Wealth of States: How Taxes, Energy, and Worker Freedom Change Everything* (Hoboken, N. J.: Wiley, 2014), 16.

24. Ibid.

25. Ibid.

26. Ibid., 18.

27. Ibid., 18–19.

28. Ibid., 19.

29. Ibid., 20.

30. Ibid.

31. Ibid.

32. Ibid., 4.

33. Ibid., 13.

34. Ibid., 4.

35. Ibid., 10.

36. Ibid., 3.

37. Ibid., 4.

38. "The Forgotten Man" (1883). In A. Galloway Keller (Ed.), *William Graham Sumner: The Forgotten Man and Other Essays* (pp. 465-495). New Haven, Conn.: Yale University Press.

39. Amity Shlaes, *The Forgotten Man: A New History of the Great Depression* (New York: Harper, 2008), 12.

40. "Letters to the Times," *New York Times*, November 24, 1938, 26.

Chapter 6. *Even Good Wars Breed Taxes*

1. Allen Schick, *The Federal Budget: Politics, Policy, Process* (Washington, D.C.: Brookings, 2007), 13.

2. Steven A. Bank, Kirk J. Stark, Joseph J. Thorndike, *War and Taxes* (Washington, D.C.: The Urban Institute, 2008), 49.

3. Ibid., 62.

4. Mitchell Yokelson, "They Answered the Call: Military Service in the United States Army during World War I, 1917–1919," *Prologue Magazine* (Fall 1998) 30:no. 3, http://www.archives.gov/publications/prologue/1998/fall/military-service-in-world-war-one.html.

5. Steven A. Bank, Kirk J. Stark, Joseph J. Thorndike, *War and Taxes* (Washington, D.C.: The Urban Institute, 2008), 62.

6. Ibid., 65.

7. Ibid., 97.

8. William Voegeli, "Why Populism Isn't Popular," *Los Angeles Times*, Nov. 29, 2010, http://articles.latimes.com/2010/nov/29/opinion/la-oe-voegeli-populism-20101129.

9. Irving Berlin, "I Paid My Income Tax Today." Oldielyrics.com. http://www.oldielyrics.com/lyrics/irving_berlin/i_paid_my_income_tax_today.html.

10. Ibid., 83.

11. Rebecca Riffkin, "More than Half of Americans Say Federal Taxes Too High," *Gallup*, Apr. 14, 2014, http://www.gallup.com/poll/168500/half-americans-say-federal-taxes-high.aspx.

12. "All Individual Income Tax Returns: Sources of Income and Tax Items, Tax Years 1913–2011," Tax Policy Center, Apr. 24, 2014, http://www.taxpolicycenter.org/taxfacts/displayafact.cfm?Docid=564.

13. "U.S. Individual Income Tax: Personal Exemptions and Lowest and Highest Tax Bracket Tax Rates and Tax Base for Regular Tax, Tax Years 1913–2015," Tax Policy Center, Sept. 18, 2014, http://www.taxpolicycenter.org/taxfacts/displayafact.cfm?Docid=543.

14. United States Office of Personnel Management, "Executive Branch Civilian Employment Service since 1940," http://www.opm.gov/policy-data-oversight/data-analysis-documentation/federal-employment-reports/historical-tables/executive-branch-civilian-employment-since-1940/.

15. White House Office of Management and Budget, "Historical Tables," http://www.whitehouse.gov/omb/budget/Historicals.

16. United States Office of Personnel Management, Executive Branch Civilian Employment Service since 1940," http://www.opm.gov/policy-data

-oversight/data-analysis-documentation/federal-employment-reports/historical
-tables/executive-branch-civilian-employment-since-1940/.

17. White House Office of Management and Budget, "Historical Tables," http://www.whitehouse.gov/omb/budget/Historicals.

18. U.S. History Pre-Columbian to the New Millennium, "Years of Escalation: 1965–68," http://www.ushistory.org/us/55b.asp.

19. Tax Policy Center, "U.S. Individual Income Tax: Personal Exemptions and Lowest and Highest Tax Bracket Tax Rates and Tax Base for Regular Tax, Tax Years 1913–2015," Sept. 18, 2014, http://www.taxpolicycenter.org/taxfacts/displayafact.cfm?Docid=543.

20. Tax Policy Center, "Alternative Minimum Tax (AMT)," http://www.taxpolicycenter.org/taxtopics/AMT.cfm.

21. Statement of Peter Orszag on "Estimated Costs of US Operations in Iraq and Afghanistan and of Other Activities Related to the War on Terrorism," U.S. House of Representatives Committee on the Budget, Oct. 24, 2007, https://www.cbo.gov/sites/default/files/cbofiles/ftpdocs/86xx/doc8690/10-24-costofwar_testimony.pdf.

22. Congressional Budget Office, "The Budget and Economic Outlook: An Update," Sept. 2008, http://www.cbo.gov/sites/default/files/cbofiles/ftpdocs/97xx/doc9706/09-08-update.pdf.

23. United States Department of Defense, "United States Department of Defense Fiscal Year 2015 Budget Request," Mar. 2014, http://comptroller.defense.gov/Portals/45/Documents/defbudget/fy2015/fy2015_Budget_Request_Overview_Book.pdf.

24. U.S. Department of Commerce Bureau of Economic Analysis, "Gross Domestic Product (GDP)," http://www.bea.gov/national/index.htm#gdp.

Chapter 7. *Stopping the Bleeding: The Taxpayer Protection Pledge*

1. U.S. Department of Labor Bureau of Labor Statistics, "Employment," http://www.bls.gov/data/#employment.

2. Ibid.

3. U.S. Department of Commerce Bureau of Economic Analysis, "Gross Domestic Product," http://www.bea.gov/national/index.htm#gdp.

4. Douglas Elmendorf, Congressional Budget Office letter to Speaker Boehner, July 24, 2012, http://www.cbo.gov/sites/default/files/cbofiles/attachments/43471-hr6079.pdf.

5. Ryan Ellis, "Senators Should Oppose Simpson-Bowles Tax Hike," Americans for Tax Reform, Dec. 2, 2010, http://www.atr.org/senators-opposebr-simpson-bowles-tax-hike-a5685.

6. Ibid.

7. Ryan Ellis, "Simpson-Bowles Plan Is a $5 Trillion Net Tax Hike in First Full Decade," Americans for Tax Reform, Oct. 5, 2012, http://www.atr.org/simpson-bowles-plan-trillion-net-tax-a7194.

8. White House Office of Management and Budget, "Historical Tables," http://www.whitehouse.gov/omb/budget/Historicals.

9. Brian Riedl, "Fiscal Commission Report: Too Much Taxes, Not Enough Spending Cuts," The Heritage Foundation, Dec. 3, 2010, http://www.heritage .org/research/reports/2010/12/fiscal-commission-report-too-much-taxes-not -enough-spending-cuts.

10. Ryan Ellis, "Simpson-Bowles Plan Is a $5 Trillion Net Tax Hike in First Full Decade," Americans for Tax Reform, Oct. 5, 2012, http://www.atr.org/ simpson-bowles-plan-trillion-net-tax-a7194.

11. Congressional Budget Office, "Historical Budget Data," Aug. 27, 2014, http://www.cbo.gov/publication/45249.

12. Ibid.

13. Speaker of the House's Office, "Speaker Boehner's Address to the Economic Club of New York on Jobs, Debt, Gas Prices," May 9, 2011, http:// www.speaker.gov/speech/full-text-speaker-boehner%E2%80%99s-address -economic-club-new-york-jobs-debt-gas-prices.

14. U.S. House of Representatives Ways and Means Committee, "Discussion Draft," Feb. 21, 2014, http://waysandmeans.house.gov/uploadedfiles/ statutory_text_tax_reform_act_of_2014_discussion_draft__022614.pdf.

15. Saxby Chambliss, Tom Coburn, Mike Crapo, Letter to Grover Norquist, Feb. 17, 2011, http://www.coburn.senate.gov/public//index.cfm?a=Files.Serve&File _id=34e3172d-d4fb-4856-bf28-7643c44e5d60.

16. Ryan Ellis, "ATR Praises Senators Chambliss, Coburn, and Crapo for Ruling Out Net Tax Hikes," Americans for Tax Reform, Feb. 22, 2011, http:// www.atr.org/atr-praises-senators-chambliss-coburn-br-a5883.

17. Brian Faler and Julie Hirschfeld Davis, "Senate's 'Gang of Six' Deficit-Cutting Talks Suffer Blow as Coburn Departs," Bloomberg News, May 18, 2011, http://www.bloomberg.com/news/2011-05-17/coburn-will-take-break-from -gang-of-six-u-s-deficit-talks-amid-impasse.html.

18. Alexander Bolton, "Reid Says Republican Lawmakers 'Being Led like Puppets' by Grover Norquist," The Hill, Nov. 1, 2011, http://thehill.com/ homenews/senate/191103-reid-says-republican-lawmakers-being-led-like -puppets-by-grover-norquist#ixzz3Bcuvnbq3.

19. Jennifer Bendery, "Harry Reid: Grover Norquist Is Thwarting Super Committee," Huffington Post, Nov. 15, 2011, http://www.huffingtonpost.com/ 2011/11/15/harry-reid-grover-norquist-super-committee_n_1095993.html.

20. The White House Office of the Press Secretary, "Remarks by the President on Economic Growth and Deficit Reduction," Sept. 19, 2011, http://www .whitehouse.gov/the-press-office/2011/09/19/remarks-president-economic -growth-and-deficit-reduction.

21. Open Secrets, "Club for Growth," http://www.opensecrets.org/orgs/ recips.php?id=D000000763&type=P&state=&sort=A&cycle=2004.

22. Tom Coburn, Newsmakers, C-SPAN, May 29, 2011.

23. Tom Coburn, *Dylan Ratigan Show*, MSNBC, June 9, 2011.

24. The White House Office of Management and Budget, "Historical Tables," http://www.whitehouse.gov/omb/budget/historicals.

25. Chris Prandoni, "What Are the Taxpayer Implications of Today's Amendments in the Senate?" Americans for Tax Reform, June 16, 2011, http://www.atr.org/taxpayer-implications-todays-amendments-senate-a6251.

26. Chris Prandoni, "Coburn: I Support Ethanol," Americans for Tax Reform, June 14, 2011, http://www.atr.org/coburn-support-ethanol-a6238.

27. Chris Prandoni, "Conservative Groups Urge Senators to Eliminate the Ethanol Mandate, Tax Credit and Tariff," Americans for Tax Reform, June 16, 2011, http://www.atr.org/conservative-groups-urge-senators-eliminate-ethanol-a6254.

28. Chris Prandoni, "ATR Applauds Passage of Sens. Feinstein/Coburn Ethanol Amendment," Americans for Tax Reform, June 16, 2011, http://www.atr.org/atr-applauds-passage-sens-feinstein-coburn-a6252.

29. Congressional Budget Office, "The Budget and Economic Outlook: 2014 to 2024," Feb. 4, 2014, http://www.cbo.gov/publication/45010.

30. Andreas Madestam, Daniel Shoag, Stan Veuger, David Yanagizawa-Drott, "Do Political Protests Matter? Evidence from the Tea Party Movement," American Enterprise Institute, Dec. 17, 2012, http://www.aei.org/files/2012/12/18/-veuger-tea-party-working-paper_095614741243.pdf.

31. Ibid.

32. Chye-Ching Huang, "Budget Deal Makes Permanent 82 Percent of President Bush's Tax Cuts," Center on Budget Policy and Priorities, Jan. 3, 2013, http://www.cbpp.org/cms/?fa=view&id=3880.

33. Liqun Liu, Andrew J. Rettenmaier, Thomas R. Saving, "How Much Does the Federal Government Owe?" National Center for Policy Analysis, June 2012, http://www.ncpa.org/pdfs/st338.pdf.

Chapter 8. *Focus: It Is the Spending, Stupid*

1. Tax Analysts, "Tax History Museum: The Civil War," http://www.taxhistory.org/www/website.nsf/Web/THM1861?OpenDocument.

2. Andreas Madestam, Daniel Shoag, Stan Veuger, and David Yanagizawa-Drott, "Do Political Protests Matter? Evidence from the Tea Party Movement," American Enterprise Institute, Dec. 17, 2012, http://www.aei.org/files/2012/12/18/-veuger-tea-party-working-paper_095614741243.pdf.

3. Office of Management and Budget, "Historical Tables," The White House Office of Management and Budget, http://www.whitehouse.gov/omb/budget/Historicals.

4. Congressional Budget Office, "Updated Budget Projections: 2014 to 2024," April 2014, http://www.cbo.gov/sites/default/files/cbofiles/attachments/45229-UpdatedBudgetProjections_2.pdf.

5. Govtrack, "S.2749—100th Congress: Defense Authorization Amendments and Base Closure and Realignment Act," https://www.govtrack.us/congress/bills/100/s2749.

6. BallotPedia, "States with Gubernatorial Term Limits," http://ballotpedia.org/States_with_gubernatorial_term_limits.

7. National Conference of State Legislatures, Feb. 11, 2013, "The Term-Limited States," http://www.ncsl.org/research/about-state-legislatures/chart-of-term-limits-states.aspx.

8. U.S. Term Limits, "State Legislative Term Limits," http://termlimits.org/term-limits/state-term-limits/state-legislative-term-limits/.

9. Congress of the United States Congressional Budget Office, "Costs of Military Pay and Benefits in Defense Budget," Nov. 2012, http://www.cbo.gov/sites/default/files/cbofiles/attachments/11-14-12-MilitaryComp_0.pdf.

10. Ida A. Brudnick, "Legislative Branch: FY2014 Appropriations," Congressional Research Service, Nov. 25, 2013, http://fas.org/sgp/crs/misc/R43151.pdf.

11. Executive Office of the President, "Fiscal Year 2013 Congressional Budget Submission," http://www.whitehouse.gov/sites/default/files/docs/2013-eop-budget1.pdf.

Chapter 9. *The Best Cure: Strong Economic Growth*

1. Congressional Budget Office, "The Budget and Economic Outlook: Fiscal Years 2012 to 2022," Table B-1, Jan. 2012, http://www.cbo.gov/sites/default/files/01-31-2012_Outlook.pdf.

2. Trial Lawyers Inc., "A Report on the Litigation Lobby 2010," 2–3, 2010.

3. Clyde Wayne Crews Jr., "Ten Thousand Commandments: An Annual Snapshot of the Federal Regulatory State," Competitive Enterprise Institute, 2014, http://cei.org/sites/default/files/Wayne%20Crews%20-%20Ten%20Thousand%20Commandments%202014.pdf.

4. Ibid.

5. "Study: Stalled Energy Projects Costing American Economy $1.1 Trillion and Nearly Two Million Jobs," U.S. Chamber of Commerce, Mar. 9, 2011, https://www.uschamber.com/press-release/study-stalled-energy-projects-costing-american-economy-11-trillion-and-nearly-two.

6. Ibid.

Chapter 10. *Don't Raise Taxes—Sell Stuff*

1. National Park Service, "Frequently Asked Questions," http://www.nps.gov/faqs.htm.

2. Coalition for Self Government in the West, "Who Owns the West?" http://endfedaddiction.org/.

3. Office of Management and Budget, "Fiscal Year 2012 Budget of the United States: Analytical Perspectives," p. 479.

4. Joseph R. Mann, "The Economic Contribution of Increased Offshore Oil Exploration and Production to Regional and National Economies," American Energy Alliance, February 2009, http://americanenergyalliance.org/docs/images/aea_offshore_updated_final.pdf.

5. Ibid.

6. Committee on Natural Resources, "ANWR: Producing American Energy and Creating American Jobs," http://naturalresources.house.gov/anwr/.

7. Coalition for Self Government in the West, "The Economic Value of Energy Resources on Federal Lands in the Rocky Mountain Region," Sept. 15, 2013, http://endfedaddiction.org/blog/2013/09/15/the-economic-value-of -energy-resources-on-federal-lands-in-the-rocky-mountain-region/.

8. Ibid.

9. "Auctions," Federal Communications Commission, http://wireless.fcc .gov/auctions/default.htm?job=auctions_home.

10. Ibid.

11. Ibid.

12. "Major Moves," Indiana Department of Transportation, http://www.in .gov/indot/2407.htm.

13. FPL, "We're Focused on the Best Solution for Our Customers and for Vero Beach," http://www.fpl.com/landing/vero_beach.shtml?cid=aliasverobeach.

14. Tom Lochner, "Hercules to Sell Money-Losing Utility to PG&E," *Contra Costa Times*, May 29, 2013, http://www.contracostatimes.com/ci_23344665/hercules-sell-money-losing-utility-pg-e.

Chapter 11. *Government Transparency: The Best Way to Reduce Waste and Corruption*

1. Benjamin Davis, Phineas Baxandall, Ryan Pierannunzi, "Following the Money 2013: How the 50 States Rate in Providing Online Access to Government Spending Data," U.S. PIRG Education Fund, March 2013, http://www.uspirgedfund.org/sites/pirg/files/reports/USP_Following_the_Money_screen_final.pdf.

2. Bill McMorris, "$6.4 Billion Stimulus Goes to Phantom Districts," Watchdog.org, Nov. 17, 2009, http://watchdog.org/1530/6-4-billion-stimulus -goes-to-phantom-districts/.

3. Senator Tom Coburn, "Wastebook: A Guide to Some of the Most Wasteful Government Spending of 2010," Dec. 2010, http://www.coburn.senate.gov/public/index.cfm?a=Files.Serve&File_id=774a6cca-18fa-4619-987b-a15eb44e7f18.

Chapter 12. *Dynamic Scoring: The Sine Qua Non of Tax Reform*

1. Center for Freedom and Prosperity, "Part III of Laffer Curve Video Series Released: CF&P Foundation Production Critiques Flawed Revenue-Estimating Model Used by the Joint Committee on Taxation," Mar. 19, 2008, http://archive.freedomandprosperity.org/press/p03-19-08/p03-19-08.shtml.

2. U.S. House of Representatives Ways and Means Committee Joint Committee of Taxation, "Macroeconomic Analysis of the Tax Reform Act of 2014," Feb. 26, 2014, http://waysandmeans.house.gov/uploadedfiles/jct_macroeconomic _analysis_jcx_22_14__022614.pdf.

Chapter 13. *Path One: The FairTax*

1. Bruce Bartlett, "Why the FairTax Won't Work," *Tax Analysts*, Dec. 24, 2007, http://taxprof.typepad.com/taxprof_blog/files/bartlett_fair_tax.pdf.
2. Ibid.
3. Ibid.
4. Ibid.

Chapter 14. *Path Two: The Flat Tax*

1. Cornell University Law School Legal Information Institute, "Pollock v. Farmers' Loan and Trust Company," http://www.law.cornell.edu/supremecourt/text/157/429.
2. Christopher Nolan, "Bill Clinton Attacks 'Read My Lips,'" Aug. 12, 2007, http://www.youtube.com/watch?v=vnUv7y4U2T0.
3. Michael Kelly, "Clinton's Economic Plan: The Campaign; Gambling That a Tax-Cut Promise Was Not Taken Seriously," *New York Times*, Feb. 18, 1993, http://www.nytimes.com/1993/02/18/us/clinton-s-economic-plan -campaign-gambling-that-tax-cut-promise-was-not-taken.html.

Chapter 16. *Path Four: The First Step toward Flat or Fair: Kill the Death Tax*

1. Gary Robbins, "Estate Taxes: An Historical Perspective," The Heritage Foundation, Jan. 16, 2004, http://www.heritage.org/research/reports/2004/01/estate-taxes-an-historical-perspective.
2. Liz Emanuel, Scott Drenkard, and Richard Borean, "State Estate and Inheritance Taxes in 2014," Tax Foundation, May 28, 2014, http://taxfoundation .org/blog/state-estate-and-inheritance-taxes-2014.
3. Grover Norquist, "Don't Forget the Death Tax," *National Review*, Feb. 28, 2013, http://www.nationalreview.com/articles/341829/don-t-forget-death-tax -grover-norquist.

Chapter 18. *Path Six: Do-It-Yourself Tax Reform: Twelve Ways to Cut Your Own Taxes*

1. Internal Revenue Service, "Your Rights as a Taxpayer," http://www.irs .gov/pub/irs-pdf/p1.pdf.
2. America's Health Insurance Plans (AHIP), "Center for Policy and Research," http://www.ahip.org/AHIPResearch/.

3. Henry J Kaiser Family Foundation, "Average Family Premium per Enrolled Employee for Employer-Based Health Insurance," http://kff.org/other/state-indicator/family-coverage/.

4. Liz Emanuel, Scott Drenkard, and Richard Borean, "State Estate and Inheritance Taxes in 2014," Tax Foundation, May 28, 2014, http://taxfoundation.org/blog/state-estate-and-inheritance-taxes-2014.

5. Travis H. Brown, "IRS Tax Migration," How Money Walks, http://www.howmoneywalks.com/irs-tax-migration/.

Chapter 19. *Make Governments Compete: It Works in the Real World*

1. "Personal computer," *Wikipedia*, http://en.wikipedia.org/wiki/Personal_computer.

2. Eva Jacobs and Stephanie Shipp, "How Family Spending Has Changed in the U.S.," *Monthly Labor Review*, March 1990, http://www.bls.gov/mlr/1990/03/art3full.pdf.

3. "Farm Population Lowest Since 1850s," *New York Times*, July 20, 1988, http://www.nytimes.com/1988/07/20/us/farm-population-lowest-since-1850-s.html.

4. Jason Strother, "North Korea Defectors Face Long Road to Integration in South," DW, July 26, 2013, http://www.dw.de/north-korea-defectors-face-long-road-to-integration-in-south/a-16973748.

5. "Escape Attempts and Victims of the Inner German Border," *Wikipedia*, http://en.wikipedia.org/wiki/Escape_attempts_and_victims_of_the_inner_German_border.

6. Ibid.

7. "This Day in History," History, http://www.history.com/this-day-in-history/hungary-allows-east-germans-refugees-to-leave.

8. Dr. Arthur B. Laffer, Stephen More, Rex A. Sinquefield, Travis H. Brown, *An Inquiry into the Nature and Causes of the Wealth of States: How Taxes, Energy, and Worker Freedom Change Everything* (Hoboken, N. J.: Wiley, 2014), 57.

9. Internal Revenue Service, "SOI Tax Stats—Migration Data," http://www.irs.gov/uac/SOI-Tax-Stats-Migration-Data.

10. Thomas H. Brown, *How Money Walks: How $2 Trillion Moved between the States, and Why It Matters* (St. Louis: Pelopidas, 2013), 58–60.

11. Ibid., 68–74.

12. Tax Foundation, "State to State Migration Data," http://interactive.taxfoundation.org/migration/.

13. Ibid.

14. Tax Foundation Tax Calculator, http://interactive.taxfoundation.org/taxcalc/#calculator.

15. Internal Revenue Service, "SOI Tax States—Migration Data—Florida," http://www.irs.gov/uac/SOI-Tax-Stats-Migration-Data-Florida.

16. Thomas H. Brown, *How Money Walks: How $2 Trillion Moved Between the States, and Why It Matters* (St. Louis: Pelopidas, 2013), 75–79.

17. Ibid., 69–74.

18. U.S. Census Bureau, "Census Explorer," generated by Will Upton, http://www.census.gov/censusexplorer/censusexplorer.html, Oct. 30, 2014.

19. Mayor Dave Bing, "2010–2011 Fiscal Year Budget-in-Brief," City of Detroit, Michigan, http://www.detroitmi.gov/Portals/0/docs/budgetdept/2010 -11_Redbook/Budget%20Overview%20and%20Summary%20Financial%20 Info/Budget-in-Brief%2010-11.pdf.

20. Dr. Arthur B. Laffer, Stephen More, Rex A. Sinquefield, Travis H. Brown, *An Inquiry into the Nature and Causes of the Wealth of States: How Taxes, Energy, and Worker Freedom Change Everything* (Hoboken, N. J.: Wiley, 2014).

Chapter 20. *Capturing Washington by First Seizing the Countryside: Fifty in 2050*

1. Scott Drenkard and Joseph Henchman, "2013 State Business Tax Climate Index," Tax Foundation, Oct. 9, 2012, http://taxfoundation.org/article/ 2013-state-business-tax-climate-index.

Chapter 21. *Making a U-turn on the Present Road to Serfdom: The Paul Ryan and Rand Paul Plans*

1. "Workers Per Retiree," Econ Data US, http://www.econdataus.com/ workers.html.

2. Peter Ferrara, "Liberating the Poor from Poverty," National Center for Policy Analysis, Apr. 17, 2014, http://www.ncpa.org/pub/ib143.

3. Peter J. Ferrara, "It's Time to Block Grant Welfare to the States," *Forbes*, Feb. 23, 2011, http://www.forbes.com/2011/02/23/welfare-poverty-economics -opinions-contributors-peter-ferrara.html.

4. NPR, "Welfare Reform's Fifth Anniversary," Aug. 22, 2001, http://www .npr.org/news/specials/welfare/010822.welfare.html.

5. Sen. Rand Paul, A Clear Vision to Revitalize America: Fiscal Year 2014 Budget of the United States Government. 22 Mar. 2013 Web. 29 Oct. 2014.

Chapter 22. *Strengthening the "Leave Us Alone" Coalition for Liberty*

1. The Library of Congress Congressional Research Service, "Grace Commission," Jan. 31, 1985, http://digital.library.unt.edu/ark:/67531/metacrs9044/ m1/1/high_res_d/IP0281G.pdf.

2. Frank Newport, "NRA Has 54% Favorable Image in US," *Gallup*, Dec. 27, 2012, http://www.gallup.com/poll/159578/nra-favorable-image.aspx.

3. Gerald F. Seib, "In Crisis, Opportunity for Obama," *Wall Street Journal*, Nov. 21, 2008, http://online.wsj.com/news/articles/SB122721278056345271.

4. GuideStar, "National Rifle Association of America," http://www.guidestar .org/organizations/53-0116130/national-rifle-association-america.aspx.

5. Fresh from Florida, "Florida Department of Agriculture and Consumer Services Division of Licensing Number of Licensees by Type as of September 30, 2014," http://www.freshfromflorida.com/content/download/7471/118627/ Number_of_Licensees_By_Type.pdf.

6. Crime Prevention Research Center, "Concealed Carry Permit Holders across the United States," July 9, 2014, http://crimepreventionresearchcenter .org/wp-content/uploads/2014/07/Concealed-Carry-Permit-Holders-Across -the-United-States.pdf.

7. Ibid.

8. Ibid.

9. "HSLDA's Generation Joshua," http://www.generationjoshua.org/dnn/.

10. Paul DiPerna, "Breaking Down 'The Chartered Course,'" Friedman Foundation for Education Choice, July 9, 2014, http://www.edchoice.org/ BreakingDownCharteredCourse.

11. W. Gardner Selby, "Sherry Sylvester Says Personal-Injury Trial Lawyers Have Accounted for Over 80 Percent of Texas Democratic Party's Contributions for Over a Decade," *Austin American-Statesman*'s PolitiFact Texas, Dec. 14, 2012, http://www.politifact.com/texas/statements/2012/dec/14/sherry -sylvester/tort-reform-spokeswoman-says-personal-injury-trial/.

12. National Right to Work Legal Defense Foundation, "Right to Work Frequently-Asked Questions," http://www.nrtw.org/b/rtw_faq.htm.

Index

About the Author

Grover Norquist is the founder and president of Americans for Tax Reform. He is the creator of the Taxpayer Protection Pledge, a signed written commitment made to the American people by candidates and elected officials publicly promising that they will oppose any and all tax hikes. Every Wednesday, Norquist chairs a "Wednesday Meeting" of more than 150 activists in the fight to expand liberty in Washington, D.C. Similar meetings are held in forty-five states and seventeen nations. He also serves on the board of directors of the National Rifle Association, the American Conservative Union, and the Parental Rights Organization. Norquist is a graduate of Harvard College and Harvard Business School. He lives in Washington, D.C., with his wife, Samah, and daughters Grace and Giselle. He enjoys performing stand-up comedy and was voted "Washington's Funniest Celebrity" in 2013.